SOCIAL EQUALITY IN INDIAN SOCIETY

About the Author

Panthapalli A. Augustine, (*b.* 1954), was born at Anicad in the Kottayam district of Kerala. After his early education he studied for ministry in the church. But soon after entering ministry, dissatisfied with its traditional forms and impelled by, a consuming interest in current affairs, he took up freelance journalism in the early 1970s. He never looked back. Barring a brief stint when he worked with a Delhi based journal, he has been freelancing ever since. His contributions have appeared in a variety of Indian periodicals. His more recent writings, which include a few monographs, are marked with a deep concern for human rights. It is this concern that led him to write *Social Equality in Indian Society: The Elusive Goal*. He has travelled widely in India anis thus well acquainted with conditions in most parts of India.

SOCIAL EQUALITY IN INDIAN SOCIETY

The Elusive Goal

P.A. AUGUSTINE

CONCEPT PUBLISHING COMPANY PVT. LTD.
NEW DELHI-110059

ISBN: 978-81-7022-303-0

Edition 2025

Published and Printed by

Concept
Since 1974

Concept Publishing Company Pvt. Ltd.
A/15-16, Commercial Block, Mohan Garden,
New Delhi-110059 (India)
T: 91-11-41101460
E: publishing@conceptpub.com, *W*: www.conceptpub.com

PREFACE

IT WAS far from my intention to write a book on social history. I would consider such a project beyond my competence. What I set out to do was to trace the high points of the millennia-long struggle for social equality. My approach to the subject has its obvious drawbacks. It is bound to leave gaps of varying widths in the narrative. Yet it has its strengths too. Hence no apology is being offered here for the gaps. And the subject has also been treated, not from a sociological, but from a human rights point of view.

The scope of the book is further delimited by the fact that it focuses on three disadvantaged groups of people, namely, the śūdras, women and the untouchables. The aborigines, an important disadvantaged segment of the population, have been left out of the purview of the study, as they fall into a separate category.

An attempt has been made to lay bare the deep roots of social inequality. A clear understanding of these roots was thought indispensable for seeing the problem of inequality in perspective. Further, a knowledge of the fate of the struggles for social equality in ages past can be very instructive.

The debate on social equality will be heard for a long time to come. It may thus become more acrimonious in the days to come. Inequality has a disconcerting way of finding new ways to legitimise itself. I hope the book has succeeded in clarifying some of the issues involved in the debate.

P.A. AUGUSTINE

ACKNOWLEDGEMENT

EXTRACTS FROM *Selections from the Sacred Writings of the Sikhs*, translated by Trilochan Singh and others, have been reproduced by kind permission of Unwin Hyman Ltd.

Grateful acknowledgement is made also to Navajivan Trust, Ahmedabad, for their permission to reproduce passages from Mahatma Gandhi's writings.

P.A. AUGUSTINE

CONTENTS

ABBREVIATIONS

BRAU	Bṛhadāraṇyaka Upaniṣad
CHAU	Chāndogya Upaniṣad
CHI	*The Cultural Heritage of India*, Vol. I-IV, edited by Haridas Bhattacharyya, Calcutta, Ramkrishna Institute, 1958 (I), 1962 (II), 1953 (III) & 1956 (IV).
CW	*The Collected Works of Mahatma Gandhi*, Vol. I-XXX, New Delhi, Govt. of India, 1958 onward.
DC	*Depressed Classes*: A Chronological Documentation, Kurseong, St. Mary's College, 1931-37.
HSL	S.N. Dasgupta (Gen. Ed.), *A History of Sanskrit Literature*, Calcutta, University of Calcutta, 1962.
OBCs	Other Backward Classes
SCs	Scheduled Castes
STs	Scheduled Tribes
SW	*The Selected Works of Mahatma Gandhi*, Vol. I-VI, edited by Shriman Narayan, Ahmedabad, Navajivan Publishing House, 1969.
SWS	*Selections from the Sacred Writings of the Sikhs*, translated by Trilochan Singh & Others, London, George Allen & Unwin, 1965.
TYB	*2500 Years of Buddhism*, edited by P.V. Bapat, New Delhi, Government of India, 1956.

PROLOGUE

IT WAS one of those rare moments in the history of a nation when a new era dawns and hopes are born anew in the hearts of its people. Creating such a moment and sharing its grandeur were 284 persons gathered on a bracing November morning in New Delhi, four decades ago. They had just given their assent to a document.

If the participants in the historic event were aware of the momentousness of the hour, they gave no indication of it. There was merely a loud applause when the motion was put to vote and carried unanimously. The President of the assembly then put his signature to the document to authenticate it. And it became law. The day was November 26, 1949. The document the assembly had adopted was the Constitution of free India. The venue was the Constitution Hall in New Delhi.

Countless men and women throughout India's long and chequered history had yearned to see this day. It was a near impossible dream come true so much so that it was difficult to believe it was actually happening.

The new Constitution had re-written history. The ancient law-givers must have writhed and squirmed in their *samādhis* (resting places). The new law rejected some of their most cherished beliefs and principles. One of the arresting features of the new Constitution was the unmistakable assertion of equality of all citizens. The ancient law-givers had never believed in it.

There was poetic justice too in the very making of the Constitution. The untouchables were traditionally thought unfit to be reckoned among humans. That a member of this community – B.R. Ambedkar – should have presided over the drafting of the Constitution, which scuttled the ancient laws, was indeed more than poetic justice. He symbolised the re-birth of a people being affected by it.

The new law made an unambiguous declaration on the equality of all citizens, regardless of sex, race, caste, descent and place of origin. One's rights were not determined by one's place in the social hierarchy. Caste was no longer held to be of value, unlike in the ancient laws. No less arresting was the stand adopted on one of the most inhuman aspects of Indian society, namely, untouchability. In the old laws, it enjoyed the status of virtually a divine ordinance. But now its practice was made a criminal offence. So definitive and complete was the break with the past. This would be a first step towards rendering justice to one most oppressed group of society. They would now be able to breathe the air of freedom, the birthright of every child of God. They could now throw off the terrible burden society had loaded them with. The Constitution went a step further when it equated the social elite with untouchables in the matter of adult franchise, and gave every adult a vote.

So began one of the boldest experiments in social democracy that the world has ever seen. The fathers of the Constitution had dared to envisage a society founded on equality, justice and fraternity.

But this precisely was the vision many saints, reformers and social activists had seen. They had striven to usher in such a society. They had dreamed of this day, but did not live to see it. They had suffered for their convictions and did so gladly. They were now vindicated. The Constitution was the greatest tribute history could pay to them.

History can be made in a day. Yet the build-up and the rehearsals could be tortuously prolonged. So it was too in the birth of this historic day. The telling of that tale is a gesture of gratitude to those who have contributed their share in its unfolding.

Here then is the tale.

1

THE ROOTS OF INDIAN SOCIETY

NOTHING WAS so characteristic of Indian society in the past as its social organisation. The model of social organisation that India followed has been the subject of great curiosity for the visitors to this land since ancient times. One simply could not speak of India without a reference to her peculiar social structure. This social structure shaped her destiny, determined her relations with the outside world and changed the course of her history. It moulded the value system of her people, their sense of right and wrong, their very world vision. Its influence was all-pervasive, affecting every sphere of life. A person who was ignorant of the written and unwritten laws that governed the life of the individuals of this society would be incapable of understanding the glory and shame, strength and weakness of the Indian people. To a student of history of the evolution of this society, the birth and growth of this social reality is of immense importance.

Psychologists attempt to trace the causes of personality problems to the very roots in a person's early childhood. The same technique of analysis could be applied in uncovering the origin of the ills of the social psyche. The present study lays no claim to being a serious attempt in this direction, but merely points to its possibilities. The roots of contemporary Indian social reality are buried deep under layers of myths and forgotten history. One might well ask if one could ever hope to uncover them. The prospects may indeed appear disheartening. That is no reason, however, why one should not ask some questions. Some answers might be found. A little gain is better than no gain.

A Society in the Making

The term '*varṇa*' assumes great importance in speaking of ancient India. It retained its currency through several millennia, though it underwent radical alterations in meaning. The story of its evolution is an index of the vast changes that occurred in ancient society. The social system that provided the framework of ancient society and of the future caste system came to be known as the *cāturvarṇya* or the four-fold division. A student of India's social history will naturally search the earliest records for clues to the institution of *cāturvarṇya.* The *Ṛgveda*, the earliest collection of religious hymns, is anything but a history book. The authors of these hymns did not intend to leave us a complete record of contemporary society. Hence the occasional reference to social conditions fails to provide sufficient ground for drawing definite conclusions. The work *varṇa* first appears to carry an ethnic connotation. There is an allusion to twin *varṇas*, that is, the *Ārya varṇa* and the *Dāsa Varṇa.*[1] Such a use of the word hardly justifies the deduction that no division or distinct groups existed in the *Ṛgvedic* society. Yet we could speak of a '*dvai-varṇya*' or a two-fold division in the *Ṛgvedic* society. But, were there no distinctions in functions or roles in society? Did not certain persons follow the calling of the priest-magicians so common in primitive societies? There must certainly have been specially trained warriors. In a community that sets out to conquer new lands, fighting cannot be confined to a select group of warriors. All able-bodied males have to lend a hand.

Hereditary functions do not appear to have come into existence as yet. However, there is mention of such functionaries as brāhmaṇas, rājanyas and viś. The śūdras do not figure in the list. Hence some scholars have concluded that the prevailing social order was a '*trāi-varṇya*'. This conclusion can be faulted on two counts. First, the term *varṇa* was not used at this time for groups within the *Ṛgvedic* people. That usage was adopted much later.[2] Second, the assumption that as the śūdras are not mentioned along with the other three groups, the group is of later creation is unwarranted. The śūdras are first mentioned as one of the four divisions of society as described in the *Puruṣa Sūkta* in the *Rgveda* (X.90) that is believed to be of later composition. Hence it is asserted that the śūdras must have come into being at a later stage of the history of the *Ṛgvedic* people. We possess some evidence from a source other than the *Ṛgveda* that seems to contradict this assertion.

Scholars are generally agreed on the common ancestry of the Zoroastrians and the *Ṛgvedic* people. Some solid proof exists to support this view. The traditions of the ancient Zoroastrians are preserved in their sacred book, the *Zend-Avesta.* The Parsis of India have inherited these traditions. The Zoroastrian people comprised three distinct groups: the *āthravan, rathaeshtār* and *vāstyosh*. There was yet another group that did not belong to the community and was known as the 'hutokhsha'.[3] In ancient India ātharvan was the word for the magician.[4] The Zoroastrian reserved the word for the priest. It is not difficult to see a common origin for the Vedic term of kṣatria and the ratheseshtār, the Vedic vaiśya and vāstyosh of the *Zend-Avesta*. The words śūdra and hutoksha appear to have had a common source. The language of the *Zend-Avesta* has substituted 'h' for 's' in several other recognisable words. Dāsa has become Daha, Asuras, Ahura etc. Hutoksha was a generic term for all subject people. If that is so, the word 'śūdra' is not of Indian origin.

Scholars maintain with good reason that a common terminology points to a period in the history of the ancestors of *Ṛgvedic* people and the Zoroastrians when they lived together in ancient Iran. But after the Indo-Iranians conquered north-west India after a grim struggle and settled there, they retained the old usage and continued to designate all subject or alien people as 'śūdra'. Hence it is quite safe to contend that the Indo-Iranians on their arrival in pre-historic India already possessed the basic elements of the *varṇa* system of the future. The use of the above terms, however, by both groups was to undergo considerable alterations in the course of long centuries when they lived apart in substantially changed conditions. For the *Ṛgvedic* people, '*asuras*' were at first good beings but gradually turned into malign spirits, while for the Zoroastrians, '*daivas*' were the evil ones and '*ahuras*' retained the older meaning of good beings.[5]

There is, of course, an alternative explanation for the similarity of the various terms employed by the Indo-Iranians. A later generation of Iranians could have borrowed these terms from the *Ṛgvedic* people. But the latter have not preserved any memory of their sojourn in Iran or of any contact with that land. A long period, lasting many centuries, seems to have elapsed between the time of departure from Iran and the composition of a major portion to the *Ṛgvedic* hymns. Else one would have expected some mention of kindred people and their country.

It has been argued that since the Āryan groups other than those who settled in India did not develop a caste system, it must, therefore, have evolved solely owing to the peculiar conditions in India.[6] As the caste system has been directly derived from the *varṇa* system which is basically an importation, the above position is wholly indefensible. All available evidence appears to contradict it.

Changing Pattern of Varṇa

The early decades and centuries of the occupation of north-west India by the Indo-Iranians must have been desperate years. There were incessant conflicts. But they had several advantages over the natives. Their forces possessed greater mobility; they had better arms. They could call upon large numbers of fighting men. The fortified cities of the new land were far from impregnable and they were not very large. In open field the native warriors, though strong-bodied, moving on foot, were no match for the mounted men who could move swiftly across the Indus plains, both in retreat and in sorties. It would seem that the opposition was stiff, prolonged and determined.[7] Finally the invaders established a toe-hold and learned to live with many aboriginal people around them who continued their own way of life and followed their tribal laws among themselves. The relationship was frequently cordial, leading even to many fruitful inter-marriages and alliances. Many brāhmaṇas even condescended to teach their religious lore to the aboriginal peoples. This was virtually the situation in the period of the great epic, the *Mahābhārata*. There Devayāni, a brāhamaṇa damsel, mixes freely with *Asura* maidens. Obviously the *Asuras* were not demons. The name 'asura', one can be quite certain, was another word like 'śūdra' that had been brought over from Iran and had its own associations. It is interesting to note that for many other peoples of the world too, their rivals, whom they had reason to fear, tended to become demons. Calling names has always been a weakling's pastime which gives a modicum of satisfaction in a state of frustration. The *asuras* were quite respectable people or otherwise *Yayāti* would not have married, though clandestinely, the *asura* maiden, Śarmistha, daughter of Asura King Vraṣparvā.

Even the fisher folk were found good enough for a marriage alliance for the great Śāntanu. True, the divine odour the maiden, Satyāvatī, exuded was a very good antidote for any lingering native odour. Satyāvatī's father turned out to be a tough customer too. He appears to have put a high price on the divine scent emanating from his daughter and was far from overawed when Śāntanu asked for his daughter's hand.

Scholar-politician C. Rajagopalachari, speaking of the epic age, maintains that one *dharma* and one culture obtained throughout the land.[8] This is somewhat a fanciful view of the period. If this had been the actual situation, there would never have been a Kurukṣetra, the scene of a fratricidal war.

Varṇa was not a bar to mixed marriages. Both types of inter-*varṇa* marriage—*anuloma* and *pratiloma*—were far from rare. In the *anuloma* type, a male married into a lower *varṇa* and in the *pratiloma*, a female married into a lower *varṇa*.

In a later Book of the *Mahābhārata* we meet women who are so modest that even the gods are denied a glimpse of them and others who would blush with shame to appear even before other women.[9] Such excessive modesty is a far cry from the free and uninhibited conduct of women in the earlier books. Yet girls married only after reaching puberty or later.[10] There is no sign here of the great alarm over a girl experiencing her first menstrual flow in her parental home as we find in the *Dharmaśāstras* of later times.

By now much had changed in the status of the śūdras. They had been reduced to subservience to the upper classes. In return for this service they were to be maintained by their masters and were to receive old umbrellas, shoes, turbans and beds.[11] In Book XIII, we are presented with a dialogue between the sage Vyāsa and a worm. The latter reveals that in his former existence he had been a wealthy śūdra who did not care for the brāhmaṇas.[12] It is difficult to believe that these sections are not interpolations.

The process of integration of indigenous groups had now been going on for quite some time; many beliefs and customs had been adopted. The assimilation of alien beliefs was so far-reaching that the religion of the Vedic people was in danger of losing its identity. Temple worship, for example, which had never been an authentic part of the cult of the Vedic people, had become an accepted practice. Image worship, quite unknown to the Vedic people was adopted. The fertility cults of the natives left their mark too. The early Vedic people had scoffed at the phallus-worshippers with the contemptuous expression, '*śiśnadevāh*'. But this very practice was to find a place in their religion. The elaborate cult of the city-dwelling natives must have cast a very great influence. A pastoral people, the Vedic communities, adopted a settled life. Fortified cities were built. They learned to construct better dwellings; agriculture became a respectable occupation. There were many other influences and borrowings. The list is endless. But who were the people that wielded such an enormous influence? As though in answer to this unarticulated question, ancient India sprang a surprise on the scholars. The unexpectedness of it took their breath away.

Ghost Cities tell a Tale

Scholars of Indian history, both Western and Indian, in the 19th and early 20th centuries thought they knew exactly how Indian society had evolved. All the different stages of its growth were neatly marked off. Only the details remained to be filled in. Then, without warning, up popped the ghost cities of the Indus and its tributaries. These cities would radically alter our understanding of ancient India and present many riddles to the historians.

The cities of the Indus valley, excavated for the first time in the 1920s of this century, revealed the existence in pre-historical times of a people who had attained heights of material civilisation unknown before. Around the time when the Indus valley cities were brought to light, the ancient Sumerian city, Ur, in Mesopotamia, was also excavated. Yet the kind of town planning employed by the builders of the Indus cities far surpassed anything witnessed in the Mesopotamian cities. The Indus civilisation remains an object of wonder even 60 years after its discovery and close study.

One of the most striking facts about the Indus cities was that the life styles they presented were in sharp contrast to those portrayed in the hymns of *Ṛgveda* regarded as the earliest records of the Indian people. These appeared to be two worlds apart. The *Ṛgvedic* people's life centred on cattle and they seemed to be at their best in open country or forest, while the Indus people were clearly city-dwellers, whose economy was sustained by agriculture. The Indus people were an ocean-going mercantile community with far-flung trade centres. They traded with Mesopotamia and possibly with the African coast. Their clay seals with their peculiar inscriptions have been found as far away as Bahrein island which is believed to be the site of ancient Dilmun of the Sumerians, where Ziasudra, the Sumerian counter-part of Biblical Noah, settled down after the Great Deluge.[13] There reed boats plied the Arabian Sea and the Persian Gulf. Pictures of reed boats engraved on clay seal have been found.

It is indeed a great irony that such a great people with marvellous achievements to their credit have not left us even their very name. Their script, which could give some clue to their identity, remains unread. New centres of this civilisation continued to be unearthed even in the 1980s, providing us a rough idea of the extent of the region where the people held sway. It is highly improbable that a far-flung civilisation which could impose uniform standards in its products and regulate urban life did not possess a code of law as many ancient peoples had. Civilisations contemporaneous with that of the Indus valley had their law codes inscribed on clay tablets. These have been unearthed in large quantities in West Asia. It is not altogether unreasonable to assume that such tablets lie buried under one of the unexcavated mounds in the Indus valley, awaiting the archaeologist's spade.

Thor Heyerdahl, a Norwegian explorer, has spent a life-time in following the trade routes of ancient mariners. He believes that ancient Sumerians sailed in their reed boats built from the reeds which grew in abundance in the marshes at the mouth of the Euphrates-Tigris. He had a reed-boat built to test his theory. Large bundles of dried reeds were lashed together. Dried reeds bobbed like cork in water.[14] A boat made of reeds could carry heavy cargoes in its hold. What was even more remarkable, it required a draught of only four to five feet and could thus anchor in very shallow harbours. Dilmum (now Bahrein) is believed to have been just such a harbour, which has been excavated on the northern side of the island in the Persian Gulf.

Heyerdahl's reed-boat was built to resemble the boat on ancient seals with high arched bow and stern. This boat *Tigris* sailed through the Persian Gulf and across the Arabian Sea to reach the site of Mohenjodaro on the Indus. Heyerdahl also demonstrated that the reed-boat was still in good condition for a return voyage by sailing to the coast of North Africa. On its onward voyage the boat had encountered a severe gale off the Makran coast and had stood the supreme test, proving thereby that the reed-boat could weather a powerful gale which would send a modern ship to the bottom of the sea.[15]

Heyerdahl has also identified Mohenjodaro with Beluha of the Sumerian records. This identification, however, must remain conjectural. Another trade post of the Sumerians, Meluhha, has been with certainty identified with Ethiopia. It is probable that Beluha lay somewhere on the African coast. Moreover nothing we know of the Indus valley people leads to conclude that they were Sumerian emigres.

It was a British archaeological team led by Professor Leonard Woolley that excavated the Sumerian city of Ur believed to be the hometown of Biblical Patriarch Abraham.[16]

What is important for us in the findings at Ur is the wide difference between the Sumerian and the Indus valley civilisations. Construction work with burned bricks began at Ur in the reign of Ur-Nammu, while the Indus valley people had built their brick-built cities nearly four centuries earlier. Town planning of the kind we observe at Mohenjodaro and Harappa was unknown at Ur. The dwellings that were uncovered at Ur differed markedly from those of Mohenjodaro and Harappa. The houses of the well-to-do people of Ur were two-storeyed and built around a central court.[17] A central court is absent in Indus valley. Here the houses were built with burned bricks. Residential buildings at Ur were, at first, hardly ever wholly of burned bricks. Sun-dried bricks were also utilised. In some respects, the Indus cities reflect a far more advanced civilisation. The language of the Indus people has little to do with the inscriptions of Sumerian tablets. It is quite possible of course that a migrant Sumerian community adopted an alien script or language, as has frequently happened in the history of peoples.

Success, it has been aptly said, has many fathers. No less true is the dictum that there are far too many claimants to descent from a great people. Numerous groups in modern India have claimed descent from the Indus people. They have been variously described as the ancestors of the Dravidians, or as pre-Āryans. There are found communities in North India that claim to have preserved memories of migration of their ancestors to the Indus cities. At this juncture, the ancient world once again threw up a puzzle, this time not in the plains of the Indus but in far-away Syria.

In the ancient records of West Asia there is just a passing mention of Ebla. The city that merged from the dusty arid plains of north-west Syria in the late 1960s of this century was the remains of a full-fledged civilisation. Ebla was first uncovered in 1968 by an Italian archaeological team led by Professor Paolo Mathiae. The team came upon ancient palaces and dwellings.[18]

An invaluable discovery was made when the team came upon a collection of clay-tablets stored in the royal library of Ebla. The city had been burned down. Through a mere chance, the fire that had swept through the building had baked the tablets, preserving them for posterity. No fewer than 13,000 such tablets have been recovered.[19]

The findings at Ebla are of great interest to students of the Indus valley civilisation. One of the Indus seals has the figure of a seated person, with eyes half closed, in a *yoga*-like posture and, to all appearance, gorgeously attired. What is striking about the figure is its stunningly exotic headgear. It speaks volumes for the originality and imagination of the designer of what appears to be a crown. The closest description of the crown is 'a winged top-hat'. Discovered at Ebla is a statue of a person exactly in the same posture, wearing identical dress with identical ornamentation on it. Unfortunately one can only conjecture what headgear the person had sported. The statue in its present state is headless. It was smashed probably at the time when the city was captured and destroyed. The inscription on the statue says that it is of Ibbit-Lim, a member of royal Eblaite family.[20] Hence it may not be unreasonable to assume that the Indus seal too represents a royal personage and not a god as has been suggested. The Eblaite script comes closer than any known script to the Indus valley script.

The Eblaite people were a Semitic race and their language has been described as a pre-Canaanite. The Eblaite tablets have not been fully read and studied. The Eblaites had trade with far-flung countries, chiefly with other ancient West Asian peoples. They once controlled the region stretching up to the Persian Gulf.

In speaking of the discoveries at Ebla, have we strayed far off course. We think not. Here is the nub. Of all known ancient peoples, the Eblaites stand closest to the Indus valley people. Were the latter also a Semitic people? If they were, the Indian population received a large infusion of Semitic blood when they were absorbed into it.

At first sight the Indus people appear to have disappeared without a trace. A closer scrutiny of the evolution of Indian society will reveal that they have left their imprint on Indian society. It shows clear signs of inheriting from them. Surely the whole population of the Indus cities was not destroyed. A part of the population may have migrated to other areas; but it is certain that a remnant was assimilated. Various elements from their life and worship may have found their way into what may be called later Hinduism. Among these elements are: temple rituals, the mother goddess, sacred baths, the *yoga* posture, the sacred bull, weights and measures, cotton spinning and weaving, use of coins, irrigation techniques and trading skills. D.D. Kosambi believes that the merchant community in the Indus cities passed into Indian society as *banias* and suggests that the '*bania*' may have been derived from '*pani*' one of the tribes inhabiting the Indus plains at the time of the invasion of the region by Indo-Iranians.[21] Kosambi also maintains that the custom of constructing temple tanks (*puṣkara*) was borrowed from the Indus people. His view is based on the presence of the Great Bath at Mohenjodaro believed to have been used for rituals. Some scholars believe that the work-force of the Indus cities found a place among the śūdras of the Vedic people. There can be no doubt that the cities possessed a large work-force, considering the vigorous commercial activity of which we have some evidence. Metal workers, weavers, potters, toy-makers, brick-kiln workers, agricultural workers and construction crews must have constituted a substantial part of the population.

What were social conditions like in the Indus city population? One thing can be stated with confidence that there existed noticeable differences in the economic levels of various strata of society.[22] Some lived in cramped quarters, while others in commodious, comfortable houses. Trade must have created a class of merchant barons. All social groups found a niche in the society that was forged out of the many ethnic groups. The question naturally arises – where did the priestly class of the Indus cities finally find its place? Surely the Mother Goddess who was worshipped must have had her priests. It is logical to conclude that those men with their pretensions to esoteric knowledge joined the priestly class.

There is reason to believe that some of the founders of the brāhmaṇic *gotras* were non-Āryans. Vasiṣṭha was one of them. There seems to have been a long-standing tradition of the uncertain origin of Vasiṣṭha. At first he was portrayed as having had no father. The implication may very well be that he came of a matrilineal tribe where descent on the mother's side only counted.[23] Manu himself alludes to the dishonourable antecedent of Vasiṣṭha when he makes him the ancestor of the śūdras (*Manusamhita* 3 : 198). It also seems that the priest-magician-medicine man of many a tribe was inducted into the brāhmaṇa coterie. A special ceremony accepting him as a member of the class was all that was required for legitimation.

At the beginning of historical times the attitude towards alien and aboriginal groups was markedly different from what came to be the policy in later periods. At that time there did not obviously exist the near paranoia that was to grip some of the upper castes in Hindu society regarding the 'purity' of the Aryan blood. There exists a close parallel to the evolution of the early Vedic society. The evolution of

Hebrew society in Palestine followed the same pattern. Both were pastoral nomads and were strongly patrilineal societies. Both conquered peoples vastly superior in civilisation. The Hebrews conquered their enemies on the strength of their guerilla warfare tactics, while the Vedic people obtained the same results on their numerical advantage, better weaponry and greater mobility.

They are joint heirs of many ancient traditions and myths. Their myths of origin exhibit many similarities. The story of the *Matsya Purāṇa* is obviously of West Asian origin.

They had many superstitions in common and held similar views with regard to the woman's monthly period or an involuntary emission of semen. Their laws on slavery, levirate practices and bride-price (*śulka*) probably had a common source. Both had to contend endlessly with 'degenerate' native religions. The Vedic people nearly lost the battle. But for the uncompromising stand of the Old Testament prophets, the same fate would have overtaken the Hebrew religion. The Canaanite fertility cult and 'high places' exerted a tremendous pull on the Hebrews. Many of them were drawn into the worship of Baal and Astarte. The Vedic people probably borrowed their fertility cult from the Indus people and gave it a very respectable place in their religion. The story of the sacrifice of Isaac appears to be basically the same as the legend of Śunahśepha of the Hindus. In both stories the Deity asks for the supreme sacrifice of the only son born after many prayers had been offered. The story of Isaac sticks out of the pages of the Bible like a sorethumb.

It is also worth noting that the early Vedic people and the ancient Hebrews saw themselves in the role of giant-killers. What credit is there in killing small fries? Hence the size of one's victims had to be magnified. And so they became *rākṣasas* and giants. The physical strength and size of Bhïma, one of the Pāṇḍava brothers, had been so magnified that giant victims had to be invented to match his strength to present the semblance of a fair contest. A court scribe may have invented the story of the killing of Goliath by David to glorify the king. The ruddy-cheeked boy killing a giant, armed to the teeth, makes a good story.

Both the Hebrews and the Vedic people in their early stages of settlement in the new land showed remarkable flexibility in assimilating alien peoples. The Hebrews on their entry into Palestine had already assimilated other groups. This social tolerance was in sharp contrast to their strong intolerance of any alien religious tenets and practices. On the contrary the initial social tolerance of the Vedic people would give way to forms of intolerance which would make that society the only specimen of its kind. Yet mysteriously it would retain its religious tolerance, absorbing beliefs and practices that were, not infrequently, at variance among themselves. The attitude of the New Testament writers to non-Israelite peoples is shown from the fact that several non-Israelites figure among Jesus' own ancestresses.

Few myths in any religion have been so tenaciously clung to or so assiduously promoted as the myth of the Promised Land by the Hebrews. The myth was created probably after the occupation of Palestine by the Hebrews. The belief in the right to the Promised Land lay behind their determination and self-imposed commission to exterminate the nations that inhabited the region. Closely akin to the myth of the Promised Land is the myth of the Chosen People. When political developments did not fit their self-image as Chosen People they simply dismissed it as a punishment from God for their sins. Thus, they could interpret the humiliating experience of the Babylonian exile as the just retribution from God. The Vedic people too had their Promised Land. They called it 'Āryavarta' which was the region between the Himalayas and the Vindhyas.

The ideas of 'a chosen people' is not the exclusive possession of the Hebrews. The term 'Ārya' frequently approximates the sense of 'a chosen people', a people apart. The Hebrews, however, never claimed racial superiority. The use of 'Ārya' was not altogether free from it.

Women in Early Indian Society

Women in all pastoral societies have occupied a subordinate position. While they did not enjoy full equality with men in the early times, there is nothing to suggest the near total isolation and segregation of women that was to characterise later Indian society. In the *Ṛgvedic* society women appear to have enjoyed some freedom of movement. They could participate in public assemblies. They could chant the Vedic hymns and perform certain sacrifices by themselves.[24] They also enjoyed some freedom of choice of their life-partner. We also hear of women going astray.

They contributed to the economic life of the community as might be expected in a primitive society where women were never regarded as mere ornaments. Such view of women would be the result of growing civilisation. Dowry had not become a problem yet. The girl's father received a pair of bullocks as a present from the bridegroom. This was the standard bride-price. Obviously girls were not regarded as a great liability as was to happen in later ages. It seems that the *upanayana* ceremony was performed for girls too.[25] Child-brides were unknown. Widows were permitted to re-marry.

In the epic period women continued to enjoy some freedom of movement as well as freedom of choice of their partner. They did not confine their choice to their own particular *varṇa.* The custom of *swayamvara* is one of the examples of the freedom of choice enjoyed by women. There is altogether no reason to believe that the practice was restricted to the royal families. In fact our so-called wild tribes have always granted this right to women. The *swayamvara* is probably an ancient aboriginal custom. And for aborigines, girls were never looked upon as liabilities. Their life, however, was anything but a bed of roses, being full of hardships and hunger. Yet they could call their soul their own. Thus, outside the brāhmaṇic cultural milieu, there existed many communities where women held their heads high.

India has had a history of numerous groups that followed from ancient times the matrilineal form of inheritance. The Nairs of Kerala in the deep South, the Khasis and Garos in the North-East are but a few of the examples. The story of the legendary kingdom ruled by women will accord the position of honour which women held among the Nairs. Such a kingdom was no great curiosity in the milieu.

What the ancient sacred books of the Hindus have to say about Indian society is not necessarily universally applicable, but at best reflects the cultural values of a particular community or region.

Who were the śūdras?

We have observed earlier in the chapter that the word śūdra was an importation, brought over by the Vedic people and is reminiscent of their sojourn in Iran. We have rejected the theory that the śūdras as a distinct division of Vedic society arose at a somewhat late stage. The *Puruṣa Sūkta*, therefore, did not offer a theory of the origin of the four-fold division of society but was an attempt to rationalise it. Such an attempt could not be made unless the division was an established fact. We suggested that the term 'śūdra' was applied to all alien peoples. It is not inconceivable that originally the term was the actual name of a tribal group and the Indo-Iranians continued to use the same name for the people of the new homeland. Hence it need not have carried any connotation or contempt arising from performance of menial jobs or servitude. The idea of pollution was a later development.

A slave people, unlike their masters, have no options regarding their status. Thus, status of a group is an index of their political power. The śūdras had to take what they got. The inhabitants of Palestine were subjugated by the conquering Hebrew people and reduced to virtual slavery.

Like 'śūdra', 'dāsa' was also an importation. Perhaps these terms were interchangeable. It is not clear when the transition from the 'dāsa *varṇa*' to 'śūdra *varṇa*' occurred. The former was abandoned at an undetermined period.

There must have been vast differences in the degree of development of the various groups in the subjugated population. There were, and continued to be, numerous groups in an extremely primitive stage of development. Some of these were never subjugated. Even Aśoka, with all his military might, would find it difficult to bring them under control. They held themselves aloof and followed their own fancy and ancient practices. Cannibals and head-hunters existed till modern times in many parts of the subcontinent.

It is not quite reasonable to suppose that the early Vedic people did not count among themselves artisans, craftsmen, and various types of skilled and unskilled workers and that they would depend upon some subject people for various services. A people on the move could not afford to do so. A primitive tribe produced the skilled workers it needed. All these workers must have been included in the *viś*. Thus, the term 'śūdra' could hardly have been applied to a class of workers.

At this stage a question may be posed; what became of the skilled and unskilled workers of the Vedic community? In later times all categories of artisans and workers were classified as śūdras, with the sole exception of goldsmiths. In some regions of the country the goldsmiths were accorded a higher status. Were the former relegated to the status of śūdras? This possibility cannot be ruled out, considering the change in the work ethic that took place in that community. The term 'śūdra' is more likely to have been applied to people on the fringe of Vedic society, not fully belonging to it. Some contacts with alien tribes were inevitable. At first, some distance would be maintained between the members of the community and the outsiders. In the course of time the latter would be gradually drawn into it. Such appears to be the sequence of events in the interaction between the Vedic people and the śūdras. As the work ethic in that community deteriorated, the mass of skilled and unskilled workers were probably relegated to the status or the śūdras.

The New Phase

Societies interacting with other societies manifest a variety of symptoms. Extreme aggressiveness, withdrawal, over-zealousness for their traditions and way of life, regimentation of ranks, cultivation of its special identity as a matter of religious creed are some of them. It is usually in a period of comparative peace that these symptoms manifest themselves. At these times, the defences, created during a period of conflict, break down and an unconscious assimilation of customs and beliefs takes place eventually leading to reactionary trends within a society. Something akin to this situation was experienced by the Vedic people. The period is represented by the Brāhmaṇa and Sūtra literature.

The new phase generated a mass of literature by way of commentaries on the older Vedas. Ritualism gained ground; sacrifices became so all-important that even the gods themselves were described as performing them.[26] The power they wielded was derived from these sacrifices. The new emphasis led to the growth of the influence of the priests in the life of the community. Their emoluments increased to make the calling attractive and rewarding. New sacrifices and ceremonials were invented for all types of need and occasion, requiring the service of the priests. Priesthood in every society has the uncanny quality of making itself indispensable. It will create the type of literature that will in turn promote its cause by attributing to it uncommon powers and special insight into mysteries.

In the sphere of the life of the members of the Vedic society, we may note several interesting developments. The distinctions between various functional groups become sharper. They drift apart and tended to become hereditary groups. It was in the Brāhmaṇas that the term'*varṇa*' was first used to denote the four divisions of society. The term thus undergoes its first major alteration. A term that was at first used to distinguish outsiders from the Vedic people was now employed to designate its own ranks. The foundation of the future *varṇa* system was being laid now.

Priesthood had become a specialised profession with the growth of the scope and number of priestly services. When heredity becomes the key factor in the adoption of a profession or trade, mobility is greatly constrained. The term 'brāhmaṇa' would take on new meanings. Serenity, gentleness, virtue, knowledge, compassion and self-control would be regarded as his characteristics. The priestly functions could be restricted to a particular group or class of people. Yet the ethics that were regarded as characteristic of the priests could not be confined to them. Good virtues, erudite compassionate individuals were not limited to any particular group. These qualities were not hereditary. They could be found even among the śūdras.

It was also no longer possible to apply the designations of the first three *varṇas* exclusively to any ethnic or racial groups. Diverse elements had been merged into these *varṇas*. For instance, there were many dark-skinned persons among the brāhmaṇas. 'All sorts of men', said Yudhiṣṭhira, 'are continually begetting children on all sorts of women'.[27] Yudhiṣṭhira rules out birth as the deciding factor in determining one's *varṇa*.

The theory of *varṇa* based on heredity had broken away completely from the concept of *varṇa* which had found acceptance in many circles. The new approach was probably adopted to stem the merger of aboriginal groups into the higher *varṇas*.

The more enlightened individuals had consistently rejected birth as the criterion for determining a person's *varṇa* and status. Nor did it have any racial or ethnic basis. The more restrictive criterion of *varṇa* came to be accepted. It also became part of the religious lore and was written into the sacred laws of the later Vedic period. The concept struck at the root of social mobility and was to determine the very future of Indian society. Yet, there would be individuals throughout the coming centuries who would reject it as a hollow pretension and ruinous to social progress, since it was a divisive principle. There are two principles at work in human society – one of unity and the other of divisiveness. There will never be wanting individuals who will uphold the ideal of unity and emphasise the common bonds of humanity. This was so even in ancient India.

The restrictive view of *varṇa* was further reinforced by the concept of *dharma* that was developed in this period. The term was to assume a variety of meanings. G.H. Mees distinguishes as many as 13 different meanings that the term is capable of conveying.[28] They range from: the morally proper, virtue, religious duty, good deeds, a universal law or principle, Divine justice, code of customs or traditions, common law and rules laid down by authorities.

Birth assigned to everyone a place in society and a specific role. The newly emergent vision of society saw the membership of a *varṇa* as *dharma*. It was an inescapable fact of life, an inviolable duty. Along with *āśrama*, *varṇa* became a *dharma*. Henceforth, the law of *varṇāśrama-dharma* would hang like the sword of Damocles over the heads of the Indian people. Later, the awesome discovery would be made that it was not the mortals alone who were governed by the *dharma* of *varṇa* but the gods themselves were subject to this inexorable law. The discovery would enhance the sacredness and inviolability of the *varṇa-dharma*.

The body of legal literature known as the *Dharma Sūtras* probably came into existence during the Brāhmaṇa period. It would seem that various law schools flourished independently which developed their own legal tradition. It is clear from the Buddhist tradition that the *Sūtra* style had been developed by the time of Buddha. The method was extensively employed by Buddhist and Jaina writers.

The later *Dharmaśāstras* would carry on the tradition and spirit of the Dharma Sūtras. There can be no doubt that the *Dharmaśāstras* have grown out of the more ancient Dharma Sūtras. Gautama is believed to be the first of the compilers of Dharma Sūtras. Baudhāyana, Vasiṣṭha and Āpasthamba are the other well-known compilers of Dharma Sūtras.

It would seem that by the time of the Brāhmaṇas, the śūdras had fallen in their status. They had lost much of their independence and civic rights. There is evidence of their economic dependence on other groups. According to a well-known passage of *Aitareya Brāhmaṇa* the śūdras are '*yadhā-kāma-vadhya*' or fit to be thrashed at will.[29] They had no gods. The masters of the houses where they served were their gods.[30] Yet we have evidence to show that many brāhmaṇas continued to teach the Vedas to the śūdras on payment of a fee and rewards. Many śūdras would even ascend the throne, especially in the South. A substantial amount of gold could and did nullify the injunctions of the *Śāstras* banning teaching of the Vedas to the śūdras. Money could make black into white and *vice versa*. It was only the poorer śūdras who were affected by the prohibition. In brāhmaṇas the position of women also appears to have deteriorated markedly. They were being increasingly segregated and discriminated against. Like the śūdra, the woman is described as untruth.[31] She has also become the source of defilement. The *śata-patha Brāhmaṇa* lays it down that the performer of the *parivargya* ceremony should shun contact with women.[32] Same Brāhmaṇa states that the woman has no right to her body or to inheritance.[33] These views were never universally accepted at this time.

By the end of the Brāhmaṇa period we encounter a new class of people called *caṇḍālas* from whom the high castes were to keep their distance. The *caṇḍālas* were by no means the only group so shunned. The origin of this class of people is not known for certain. One opinion holds that they were an extremely primitive aboriginal tribe who because of their barbarous manners and customs evoked contempt and revulsion.

Another theory has it that the *caṇḍālas* were a mixed group sprung from the union of brāhmaṇa male and an aboriginal female. A combination of these two theories may provide the more plausible explanation. The illegitimate progeny of the superior classes may have found a place among the aboriginal communities. In the past, the peripheral groups have been the dumping ground for unwanted children. The practice has spilled over into the present day. It was a convenient arrangement for the superior classes. They could embark on their amorous adventures without the risk of responsibility for their actions.

The frequent references to *caṇḍālas* may mean nothing more than that the Vedic people were coming in contact with groups whom they were not prepared to incorporate into their own communities. There was obviously a wide gulf between them. At the moment the gulf appeared unbridgeable.

It is indeed ironic that the *caṇḍālas,* despised and ostracised as they were, should have made a valuable contribution to the welfare of the very people by whom they were thought unfit to associate with. It is evident from the testimony of Uśana, an ancient writer, whom Kauṭilya has frequently quoted, that the *caṇḍālas* were employed as street cleaners.[34] In later times they were assigned other occupations. They were to act as hangmen and keepers of cremation grounds. In Uśana's day the *caṇḍālas* lived outside the villages. They were allowed to enter the villages in the first half of the day only to perform their duties. By taking on themselves the various odious tasks, the *caṇḍālas* helped others to retain their respectability, besides, of course, keeping the environment clean. This was no small contribution.

NOTES

1. G.S. Ghurye who holds this view of twin *varṇas* is quoted with approval by M.N. Srinivas in his *Caste in Modern India and Other Essays*, Bombay, Asia Publishing House, 1962, p.63.
2. G.S. Ghurye, *Caste and Race in India*, Bombay, Popular Prakashan, 1969, p.12.
3. *CHI*, I, p.536 Bhattacharya, Calcutta.
4. M. Winternitz, *A History of Indian Literature*, I, Calcutta, University of Calcutta, 1962, p.105.
5. *Ibid.*, p.671.
6. Romila Thapar, *Ancient Indian Social History*, New Delhi, Orient Longman, 1978, p.220.
7. *The Gazetteer of India*, II, ed. by P.N. Chopra New Delhi, Govt. of India, 1973, p.43.
8. C. Rajagopalachari, *The Mahābhārata*, Bombay, The Bhartiya Vidya Bhawan, 1971, p.80.
9. *The Mahābhārata of Vyasa*, translated by P. Lal, New Delhi, Vikas Publishing House Pvt. Ltd., 1980, p.288.
10. *Ibid.*, p.319.
11. *Ibid.*, p.307.
12. *Ibid.*, p.322.
13. James B. Pritchard (ed.), *The Ancient Near East:* An Anthology of Texts and Pictures, Princeton, Princeton University Press, 1958, p.30.
14. Thor Heyerdahl, '"Tigris" Sails Into the Past', *National Geographic*, September, 1978, p.748 ff.
15. *Ibid.*, p.755.
16. On the excavation at Ur, cf. Leonard Woolley, *Ur of the Chaldees.* Harmondsworth, Pelican Books, 1938, p.81 ff.
17. L. Woolley, 1938, p.115.
18. Howard Lezy, 'Ebla', *National Geographic*, September, p.730 ff.
19. *Ibid.*, 1979, 1978, p.740.
20. *Ibid.*, 1978, p.432.
21. D.D. Kosambi, *The Culture and Civilization of Ancient India in Historical Perspective*, New Delhi, Vikas Publishing House, 1970, p.80 ff.
22. Stuart Piggot, *Pre-Historic India*, Harmondsworth, Penguin Books, p.160.
23. D.D. Kosambi, 1970, 1961, p.83.
24. *CHI*, I, p.222.
25. *Ibid.*
26. M. Winternitz, 1962, p.171.
27. G.H. Mees, *Dharma and Society*, Delhi, Seema Publications, 1980, p.116-17.
28. *Ibid.*, p. 8-9.
29. VII: 29. For a discussion on the passage, cf. R.S. Sharma, (1980 A). *Śūdras in Ancient India*. Delhi, Motilal Banarsidass, p.65.
30. VII: 29 *op cit.*, p.49.
31. *Ibid.*, p.131.
32. *Ibid.*, p.131.
33. M. Winternitiz, 1962, p.179.
34. G.S. Ghurye, 1969, p.89.

2

THE AGE OF PROTEST

WE NOW enter a period in the history of Indian society marked by new socio-religious trends. These trends had already set in much before the time of Lord Buddha. The new wave of non-conformism in religious thought appears to have arisen as a reaction to the formalism and inflexibility of religious observances and rigid code of behaviour. It was as though the human spirit was trying to free itself from the gods the religious imagination had created and to assert its innate freedom. Along with religious non-conformism there sprang a social revolt against the artificial barriers that separated people. Humanity, it seemed, was re-asserting the common bonds that knit it together.

Birth of Heterodox Sects

The ritualism in religious practice and ossification of social institutions inevitably created a reaction. Serious doubts began to be cast on the utility of sacrifices and ceremonies. Many questioned even the reality of the world of gods. Severe criticism of the prevailing norms of social conduct was publicly voiced. It was all refreshingly new. Nothing of the kind of new teaching had ever been preached before. A variety of views on man, the world and the world beyond was aired. The period saw the birth of the sects which rejected the doctrines propounded by the brāhmaṇas. The ascetics who advocated heterodox doctrines were called 'śramaṇas'. The Jains and Buddhists also fell under this category.

The śramaṇas held vastly differing and frequently conflicting views. Their doctrines ranged between total futility of all human efforts, rejection of the distinction of good and evil, advocacy of unrestricted freedom, of extreme austerities and denial of even innocent pleasures of life.[1] Wandering ascetics, known as *parivrājakas*, *maskarin* or *tāpasas*, propagated these new-fangled doctrines. The air was thick with them.

Some account of a few of the well-known personalities of the period has come down to us. One such ascetic was Pakuddha Kaccayana (Prakuddha Kātyāyana). According to Buddhaghosa, he never touched cold water, crossed a running stream or a marshy land, lest his vow should be broken.[2] One of the most important non-brahmanic sects was that of the Ājīvikas. The sect continued to flourish along with Jainism and Buddhism. Gośāla Ājīvika, founder of the sect, is believed to have been a contemporary of Buddha, and probably belonged to a low caste. On account of the Ajıvika's low origin, the sect must have held a special appeal for the lower classes.

Emperor Aśoka befriended the Ājīvikas too and made them several gifts and grants, as recorded in his inscriptions. It is well-known that Aśoka honoured monks and ascetics of all sects and was tolerant to a wide range of doctrines and practices. The Ājīvikas could hardly have been pleasant company as they abjured all washings and baths. They also abstained from the use of *ghee*, regarding it as a luxury. The followers of the sect earned their livelihood by their practice of medicine and astrology. The sect acquired the name on account of their insistence on earning a livelihood.[3]

With the rise of Jainism and Buddhism, we observe a refreshing change in the attitude towards social relationships. An ethical dimension is introduced into all human actions and relations. The emphasis is no longer on the correct performance of sacrifices and rituals. In fact these are rejected as unavailing towards attaining the goal in life. The Jain doctrine holds that the belief in the efficacy of baths and pilgrimages as a means of liberation is an obstacle to liberating oneself from the misery of human existence. The belief in gods and goddesses is another kind of ignorance.

The only effective remedies for the miseries of transient existence are: Right Faith, Right Knowledge and Right Conduct. These three are known as the 'Ratna-Traya' or the Triad of Jewels, and constituted the basic principles of *dharma*. Jainism not only condemns all animal sacrifices but regards all life as sacred. *Ahiṃsā* or non-injury is one of the cardinal doctrines of the sect. Jainism placed little value on nobility of birth or superiority of caste. Among the eight types of arrogance a householder is asked to shun include nobility of birth and caste superiority. Temple worship, magical powers and *Yoga* also figures in the list.[4]

The foundation of the teaching on non-injury in Jainism is the intrinsic equality of all living beings. The purpose of religious conduct (*carita*) is to remove the condition of inequality. Non-injury embraces not only actions but thoughts and words as well. The householder was asked to limit the use of worldly goods and luxuries. Wealth, he was told, was not a great value to be cherished, nor a goal in life. Non-covetousness was commended to him as a virtue and a *vrata* (vow).[5]

Jainism was a striking departure from the teachings of the brāhmaṇas. The Vedic religion laid much stress on external observances. It lacked inferiority and left the inner spirit untouched and unmoved. This shortcoming must have contributed largely to the growth of heterodox sects.

Buddhism was another sect that staged a powerful protest against the socio-religious practices of the day, Lord Buddha denounced the pretensions of the brāhmaṇas and had many personal confrontations with them, if we are to believe the Buddhist traditions. He rejected birth as the measure of man and recognised personal merit as the sole measure of a person's worth. He dismissed all claims to hereditary merit and holiness of the brāhmaṇas. A person's merit, he held, was determined by his worth, his conduct (*caraṇa*) and his character (*carita*).[6] *Dhamma*, Lord Buddha's gospel, was addressed to all and was comprehensible to all. The *sangha* he founded was open to members of all four *varṇas* without any distinction. Upāli, one of Buddha's closest disciples, is believed to have belonged to the śūdra class. But he played a prominent role in the first Buddhist Council held at Rajagrha during the reign of Ajātaśatru.[7] The lower classes may have made use of the *sangha* to shake off social deprivation, as entry into it brought with it a rise in social status.

Buddhism must have come as a great relief to many who had been repelled by doctrines requiring total withdrawal from the world and extreme austerities. It preached a middle path between severe austerities and licentiousness. Buddhism was thus more acceptable to a large number of people.[8] The philanthropy, Buddhism taught, stood in sharp contrast to the self-centeredness of the brahmanic religion. Within the space of a few centuries the new teaching had spread beyond the borders of India. The spread was partly due to the missionary spirit of its adherents.

Buddhism's mass appeal is proved by the language of its early scriptures which was invariably vernacular. Thus Buddhism made a valuable contribution to the growth of vernacular literature. At first

Buddhist scholars were not enamoured of Sanskrit as was to happen in later centuries.

Buddhism's greatest appeal lay in its social teaching. Its emphasis on the basic equality of all humans was strikingly new. Tribal cultures which showed greater regard for egalitarianism responded more eagerly to Buddhist teaching.

Women were not excluded, as in the brahmanic religion, from the full enjoyment of the benefits of religion. They were also admitted to the monastic order, not without some questioning in some circles. Women would become missionaries for the new faith.

In spite of its lofty principles of equality and universalism, Buddhism did not bring within its ambit such peripheral groups as the caṇḍālas. Buddhists may have found the popular prejudice too strong to overcome and dared not ignore it. The position of the latter remained unchanged in Buddhist kingdoms. But the opinion that the caṇḍālas were a creation of Buddhism is certainly not warranted. Caṇḍālas were the product of an age when social elitism was the great pre-occupation. Their habit of meat-eating reportedly set them apart. Even in Aśoka's reign, killing of animals and meat-eating was never totally forbidden. Manu himself would permit it. Hence killing of animals or meat-eating could hardly have been the cause of the social degradation or of the origin of caṇḍālas.

Some scholars see in the rise of Jainism and Buddhism the revolt of the kṣatriyas as their founders are believed to have belonged to that class. Several other leading figures of the heterodox sects may also have been kṣatriyas.

A revolt against the power and dominance of the priestly class would not have found much support and patronage in that class which stood to gain most from religion and ceremonials. Upaniṣadic thought seems to have burgeoned among the kṣatriyas independently of brāhmaṇas. This development must have occurred at a time when kṣatriyas had plenty of leisure to engage in philosophical discussions. They even claimed to be the highest *varṇa*. 'Verily, in the beginning', says *Bṛhad-āraṇyaka Upaniṣad*, 'this world was Brahman one only. Being one, he was not developed. He created still further, a superior form, the Kṣatrahood, from those who are Kṣatras (rulers) among the gods: Indra, Varuna, Soma, Rudra, Parjanya, Yama, Mrityu, Īśāna. Therefore, there is nothing higher than Kṣatra.[9] Kṣatras, then, are the first-born among the creation. The unequivocal declaration of the Kṣatrahood of the chief gods could have been made only by a circle of kṣatriyas. They were foremost in pioneering philosophico-theological speculation. We are told that Ajātaśatru, king of Banaras who cannot with certainty be identified with Ajātaśatru of Magadha, carried on a learned discussion with an erudite brāhmaṇa named Driptabalaka who was no match for Ajātaśatru in the exchange that ensued.

Bālāki, a brāhmaṇa comes to Ajātaśatru with fuel in hand to be instructed by him about Brahman. Approaching a teacher with fuel in hand meant that one wished to sit at his feet as a pupil. However, Ajātaśatru thought it odd that a brāhmaṇa should come to a kṣatriya to learn from him. Yet he duly instructed the brāhmaṇa.[10]

We also learn from *Bṛhadāraṇyaka Upaniṣad* (3, 1, 1) that Janak, king of Vedeha, cultivated the company of learned brāhmaṇas and arranged discussions among them where fabulous gifts were offered, as much as of a thousand cows.

A brāhmaṇa named Gautama presents himself before Pravahana Jābāla, a prince, to learn from him how creatures are reborn.[11] Pravahana tells Gautama that this knowledge has never before been the possession of the brāhmaṇas. Five learned brāhmaṇa householders led by Uddālaka Aruṇi come to a prince Aśvapati Kaikeya to learn about the Universal Ātman.[12]

It is interesting to note that the kṣatriyas claimed to have developed the theory of transmigration. In the course of centuries several tribes with uncertain ancestry have been designated as kṣatriyas. The doctrine of transmigration had much in common with the animistic beliefs of aboriginal peoples. Some new elements have been added to these beliefs, such as the Karma doctrine. The combination of the life-theory of the aboriginals with the Karma doctrine was overlaid with the *varṇa* theory. The heady mix that resulted from the combined beliefs was highly addictive.

King Bṛhadratha was a seeker of knowledge and answers to the multifarious questions of existence. Having crowned his son on the throne, he betook himself to the forest, and there he stood with outstretched arms, gazing up at the sun. Sakayanya, a Brahma-knower, comes on the scene, 'Sir', said Bṛhadratha, 'in this ill-smelling, unsubstantial body which is a conglomeration of bone, skin, muscle, marrow, flesh, semen, blood, mucous, tears, rheum, faces, urine, wind, bile and phlegm, what is the good of enjoying of desires?'.[13] Bṛhadratha saw the whole universe decaying around him. He drew a very gloomy picture of human existence. Bṛhadratha had obviously been brooding over the uglier side of life. He wasn't the only one to do so.

From the above examples it is abundantly clear that progress in Upaniṣadic thought owed much to the prince-philosopers. For reasons not known to us, the great tradition would disappear from the midst of the kṣatriya. The brāhmaṇas would not only take the lead but monopolise intellectual life, leaving the princes to their petty wars, the chase and other mundane interests.

Women in the Upaniṣads

In the intellectual circles of the Upaniṣadic period, we come across an attitude that is at variance with that of the Brāhmaṇas and the Dharma Sūtras. Women were not only not barred from acquiring knowledge, but a few of them even distinguished themselves with their erudition. They participated in public discussions and even took a leading role at public debates. One of the scholars who examined Yājnvalkya on his knowledge of Brahman at the court of Janak was a woman named Gargi Vācaknavi.[14] Yājnvalkya himself had two wives – Maitreyi and Kātyāyani. Maitreyi, we are told, was a discourser on Brahma-vidya.[15] No doubt it was Yājnvalkya himself who instructed her. Yet in Dharmaśāstras, a wife is never mentioned as one of the suitable candidates to whom one may impart the knowledge of Brahman.

The *Bṛhadāraṇyaka Up.* (6, 4; 17) has a recipe for couples who wish to obtain an erudite (panditā) daughter. They should prepare rice boiled with sesame and eat it with *ghee*. It is remarkable that anyone should desire a daughter. In later times girls would be mentioned so rarely that one begins to wonder how the race multiplied. The desire for an accomplished daughter is consistent with what was said above showing that at least in certain circles women enjoyed equality with men. But we also come across such superstition as the prohibition of women in their 'monthly sickness' drinking from a metal cup.[16]

Śūdras in the Upaniṣads

The brāhmaṇas of *Chāndogya Up.* do not appear to have been aware of the prohibition of imparting Vedic knowledge to a śūdra. The example of Jānaśruti the śūdra (4:1:1) has often been quoted in support of this contention. Jānaśruti, son of Janaśruta, was a pious dispenser, a generous giver, a preparer of much food. Apparently Jānaśruti was quite rich. He had built rest-houses. 'People everywhere,' he said to himself, 'will be eating my food.' Jānaśruti was also a lover of knowledge. He sought out a learned brāhmaṇa named 'Raikva'. The śūdra offered Raikva a thousand cows, a gold necklace and a chariot drawn by a she-mule in return for teaching him the divinity that Raikva reverenced. The brāhmaṇa, however, spurned the offer 'off with your cows, necklace and the carriage', Raikva told him. Thereupon Jānaśruti threw in a village and his own daughter as a bait for the brāhmaṇa. That clinched the issue. It is worth noting that a śūdra damsel was quite welcome to the brāhmaṇa's household and was to become the brāhmaṇa's wife.

According to the author of *Bṛhadāraṇyaka Up.* (4:3:22) the discovery that 'I am the world-All' is not beyond the reach of even caṇḍālas and Paulkasas. A caṇḍāla or Paulkasa could not make this discovery unless he was instructed, sitting at the feet of a guru. Logically one should conclude that instruction was not denied to caṇḍālas and other peripheral groups.

In the Upaniṣads we have irrefutable evidence of a comparatively open society where interaction between various sections was clearly possible. Disabilities arising from births were not insurmountable. Social exclusiveness was not cultivated sedulously yet. There is, however, little doubt that even at this time there were groups that held rigid views on social relations. As has frequently happened in the social history of India, the more obscurantist views and practices have prevailed. Yet the liberal voices would not be stilled completely. They would ring out like voices in the wilderness, unheeded and lonesome.

A View from Outside

India owes it to Buddhism that it abandoned its near total isolation from the outside world. Thanks to the missionary spirit Buddhism generated, its messengers travelled to West Asia and the Far East, carrying the torch of the new faith. Before this period India's contact barring a Persian military interlude was limited to trade through her ports on the west coast.

The Persians were lured by the stories of the fabulous wealth of India. Herodotus tells us that the Persian King Darius sent an army under Scylax to explore the land. It would seem that the Persians occupied the region west of the Indus. Scylax sailed down the Indus and returned by sea. Herodotus also tells us that the Indians brought tribute to the Persian court and describes the amount of tribute, part of which was in gold dust.[17] We possess independent evidence that corroborates the testimony of Herodotus on the Persian occupation of Sind. This evidence comes from the Aramaic Aśokan inscriptions in the Taxila province of the Mauryan empire.[18] We know for certain that the Achemenid kings had adopted Aramaic as the diplomatic language. It can be asserted without the fear of error that Aramaic was brought to north-west India during the Persian occupation.

At this time Aramaic was understood in the area stretching from the eastern borders of Persia in the east to as far as modern Turkey in the west. That language occupied virtually the same position that English has today in the same region. There is a passage in the Bible that suggests that even Assyrians spoke Aramaic.[19] It continued to be widely used in north-west India even after the Greek invasion. If Thomas Didymus, a disciple of Jesus, ever visited the court of the Bactrian King Gondophornos, as many believe, he did not need an interpreter. He could make do with his native Aramaic in its Palestinian variant. With the Muslim conquest of Iran and north-west India, Aramaic was dislodged by Arabic, another Semitic language. Yet India's sacred books give no inkling of the politico-cultural winds that blew in from the West. Their authors, in their forest retreats, were either unaware of the winds blowing outside or they simply ignored them.

We happen to know of the results of the cultural contact the Persians had with the Hellenic people. We are told that Greek historical thought owes much to the civilisations of West Asia particularly the Persian.[20] The Greek historians were to excel in the science historiography. Their historical writings are an eloquent proof of it. Persian influence was not confined to historiography. The Greek kings borrowed court etiquette and dress from the Persians. Once Alexander the Great was castigated by one of his young officers for his blind imitation of Persian ways. The Indians do not appear to have profited greately from their contact with the Persians, least of all from the Persian science of historiography.

The invasion of India by Alexander opens up a new chapter in the history of ancient India. Its importance lies in that it has produced some accounts of India by visitors to this land. The first accounts were prepared by Alexander's officers who had accompanied him on his whirlwind expeditions to the East. Though these accounts are no longer available to us, they have been quoted by later Greek writers. The references to conditions in India are limited to a region the writers were acquainted with, namely, the region west of the Indus. The eastern-most point Alexander advanced to was the Sutlej River.

There was a group of ascetics in the vicinity of Taxila. Since Alexander expressed a desire to meet them, an officer was dispatched to conduct them to Alexander's presence. But the ascetics refused to oblige the conqueror, saying if the king wanted to meet them, he might as well come to them. Accordingly Onesikritos, Alexander's general, was deputed to talk to them. He found the naked ascetics in a variety of postures. After the preliminary greetings, Onesikritos proceeded to ask further questions. At this one of the ascetics, Kalanos, told him that if he wanted to know more he should divest himself of his clothes and be like them. The Greek was debating with himself on what course of action to take, when an older ascetic upbraided Kalanos for his insolence. This older ascetic praised Alexander for seeking wisdom and said that the king was the only philosopher in arms he had ever heard of.[21] According to Strabo both ascetics later went to Alexander's camp. Kalanos grew addicted to the royal table. He was to accompany Alexander to the west. Unaccustomed to the rich fare served at Alexander's table Kalanos fell ill and died at Susa and was cremated there.[22]

Ancient writers have also told us about the custom of women burning themselves on the funeral pyre of their dead husband. Diodorus, a Roman writer and a contemporary of Julius Caesar and Augustus Caesar, has narrated an actual incident. He obviously owes the information to the earlier Greek writers. A soldier, who had died in battle, left behind two wives, one of whom was young and recently married. On examination by a midwife, the older wife was found to be pregnant. The younger wife now proceeded to distribute her jewellery among her friends and servants, and then lay down by the dead husband's side. The by-standers were variously affected. Some were moved with pity for her, some praised her but some Greeks condemned the practice as barbarous and inhuman.[23]

Diodorus goes on to speak of the origin of the practice. It was the ancient law of the Indian, says Diodorus, that young people chose their own partner and did not follow the wishes and judgement of their parents. But they frequently made unsuitable matches at an immature age. When young women regretted their choice, they became incontinent and fell in love with other men, but could not be separated from their first choice. Some got rid of their first husbands by poisoning them. When punishment failed to stop the crime, a law was enacted that a woman, unless she was pregnant or already had children at the time of her husband's death, should burn herself along with him. There is little doubt that Diodorus' source of information is one of the early Greek writers on India.

Among the Greek writers Megasthenes is our best informant on the conditions in the Mauryan empire. He was qualified to write about them since he had lived at the court of Sandracottos (Chandragupta) as the envoy of Selucas in the last quarter of the 4th century B.C. Though his original report has been lost, he has been extensively quoted by such writers as Strabo, Arrian and many others. Since the quotations show remarkable agreement, we are justified in assuming that Megasthenes has been correctly quoted. During the years he spent in India, he was not confined to Patliputra, the Mauryan capital. He also visited other kingdoms under the Mauryan suzerainty. He points out that the city administration of Patliputra (modern Patna) was able to ensure cleanliness of the streets; it penalised the citizens who threw garbage on the streets. (Modern Patna, however, is most unlikely to bag a prize in a contest for the title of the cleanest city.) The Greek ambassador has also given us much valuable information about the city administration, the working of the various departments and of the officials in charge of them.

Megasthenes tells us that there was a law among the Indians that not one of them should ever be enslaved.[24] Even of the time Megasthenes' writing quotes about, India was not wholly free of slavery. Buddhist records refer to it. Megasthenes, possibly, was referring to the injunction of the *dharmaśāstras* that no Ārya was to be enslaved. Megasthenes further testifies to the honesty and truthfulness of the people. He thought it most remarkable that though no written documents were kept on contracts, an orally given pledge was as good as law. Some scholars have doubted Megasthenes' statement on the absence of writing, pointing out the Aśokan inscriptions as proof of the people's literacy. Far too much has been read into the presence of the Aśokan edicts. Nothing can be concluded regarding the ability of the people to read. The edicts were meant to be read out aloud by the officials and explained to the people. Moreover, the Aśokan pillars were erected at cross-roads and on important highways. It was only the officials, merchants and itinerant monks and ascetics who were likely to read them. The chances of the large majority of the people coming across one of these pillars was rather tenuous. Megasthenes' remarks about the illiteracy of the masses cannot be dismissed without strong proof to the contrary. And these we sorely lack. A city's administration could not have been carried on without the use of written documents. Hence, the city officials, one may be certain, were at least literate.

Megasthenes speaks of two types of philosophers, the brāhmaṇas and the śramaṇas. There was an annual convention of philosophers. The Greek diplomat met a group of brāhmaṇas living in a grove outside the city.[25] His statement that brāhmaṇas pursued studies for 37 years has intrigued many scholars. *Chāndogya Upaniṣad* has three allusions to a 32-year long *brahmacharya*.[26] No less an authority than Manu himself (35:1) speaks of studentship period as being 36 years or half or quarter of that period. Hence a 36-year *brahmacharya* was not unknown. Megasthenes obviously had a reliable informant. But it is difficult to explain why he added an extra year.

What interest us most in Megasthenes' report on India are his observations on the structure of Magadhan society. He tells us that society has a seven-fold division. The first division is made up of the philosophers. Husbandmen constitute the second. The third division is that of shepherds and hunters who alone are permitted to hunt or to keep cattle and sell beasts of burden. In return for clearing the land of wild animals and birds, they receive an allowance from the king. The fourth division consists of those who work at trade, vend wares, or those or ors are employed in manual labour. Some of them pay tax to the State and render certain prescribed services. But armour-makers and shipwrights receive wages and provisions. The fighting men constitute the fifth division. The sixth consists of the inspectors to whom is entrusted the superintendence of everything. The best and the most trustworthy men, Megasthenes tells us, are appointed to these posts. The seventh division consists of the counsellors of the king. To them belong the affairs of the State and the tribunals of justice and the general administration of public affairs.[27]

Megasthenes' omission or ignorance of a four-fold division of society, which is believed to have been in force at that time, has puzzled not a few students of Indian social history. There is no sign whatever of *cāturvarṇya* in his account. Had not Megasthenes heard of the four-fold division? Considering that he had interviews with the brāhamaṇas of Patliputra, it seems unlikely that he had not. Some scholars maintain that Megasthenes had at best a superficial knowledge of Indian society and had moreover to rely on second-hand sources. Romila Thapar has an even less satisfactory explanation. 'The numerical confusion,' writes Thapar, 'may be due to the fact that in writing his account, possibly some years after his visit to India, he may have accidentally arrived at the number seven, forgetting the facts as given to him'.[28] This view is poor tribute to a man who has shown himself to be a keen observer and of more than average intelligence. It would be rather inexplicable that a man who discovered the widespread use of spies and of the ways of prostitutes of Patliputra should not have been able to obtain information on the prevalent social system in Magadha. Possibly the explanation lies elsewhere.

Magadha had only recently been organised. A semi-aboriginal culture still prevailed where the laws of brāhmaṇas were not in force. Nor did brāhmaṇas exercise control over society as in later times. Moreover, Magadhan society was a pluralist society where heterodox sects wielded great influence. Megasthenes describes the Ājīvikas without naming them. He says that some śramaṇas practised medicine.[29] Besides Ājīvikas, there were Muṇḍakas, Jains and Buddhists. *Cāturvaṇya* may have been known at this time as a social theory. But it could not have been enforceable in the prevailing religious atmosphere. It is then highly improbable that Megasthenes' forgetfulness lies behind the omission of the four-fold division of society.

There has existed elsewhere a closely similar situation which corroborates the argument just adduced. A social situation akin to that of Magadha prevailed in 12th century A.D. Kashmir. Kalhāṇa in his *Rāja-taraṅgiṇi* has described Kashmir society which was not organised on the principle of *cāturvaṇya*.

Society of Kalhāṇa's time was divided according to professions. The *cāturvaṇya*. if known, was ignored. This is most remarkable considering that the writer, Kalhāṇa, was a brāhmaṇa. Kashmiris also ignored rules on inter-caste marriages. Even a Domba (Dom) could become the queen of Kashmir. In short, all brahmanic views were completely disregarded in the observance of caste rules.[30] Kashmir society of Kalhāṇa's a day was not really different from the Magadhan society of Megasthenes' time. The aboriginal or 'Naga' elements dominated the Kashmir scene. So too the brahmanic law did not operate there.

Megasthenes has something to say about the women of Magadha. He observes that brāhmaṇas did not impart the knowledge of their philosophy to their women lest in their weakness they should divulge it to others or leave their husbands.[31] But we are told that among the heterodox sects women studied philosophy along with men.[32] It is Megasthenes who has told us about the legendary kingdom ruled by women in the Pandya country.

Strabo has charged Megasthenes with exaggerated account. The charge refers to the latter's account of such curiosities as gold-digger ants and a race of one-legged men, who inhabited a region in central India. In fairness to Megasthenes it needs to be pointed out that such stories appear to have been current in India in his time. Arrian, on the other hand, regards Megasthenes as a 'man of approved character'.[33]

It is not possible to draw definite conclusions from Megasthenes' testimony. Though his observations on non-brahmanic sects and on the city administration of Patliputra are fairly accurate, Megasthenes has not presented us with a complete picture of Magadhan society. Even if we admit that Magadhan society was divided professionally, still it is difficult to concede that no class consciousness existed then. Buddhist traditions attest to such class consciousness. Megasthenes treats Magadhan society as though it were a homogeneous people. We have no solid reason to believe it was. The only heterogeneous groups, he mentions, are the 'wild tribes'. He makes no reference to outcastes who were to be found at that time.

Life in Magadha According to Kauṭliya

Kauṭliya in his own well-known work the *Arthaśāstra* has depicted a society that had notable differences from what Megasthanes offers us. Kauṭliya or Cāṇakya was believed to have been the minister of Candragupta Maurya and is credited with having assisted him in conquering Magadha from the Nandas. Considerable doubt, however, exists about the identity of the author of the *Arthaśāstra*. Among his Indian curiosities, Megasthenes fails to mention this extraordinary minister of Candragupta. The author of this work is identified in the work only in its colophon. Some scholars believe that Books IX to XIV are later additions. It seems rather odd that

Kauṭliya, who is fond of quoting his teacher, has completely forgotten him in these books. There is no indication even that the author was a resident of Patliputra. What is rather more surprising is that though Kauṭliya was closely associated with an imperial administration, he omits any mention of it.[34] Surely the relations between the governors and the emperor would be a matter of great importance to one who sets out to write a manual on statecraft. A linguistic problem is presented by the occurrence of several Dravidian words in the work. The Dravidian words pose, by no means, the greatest difficulty against authorship by a contemporary of Candragupta.

Kauṭliya gives us the impression that deceit, fraud and all kinds of dishonest practices were rampant in Magadha. This apparently contradicts what Megasthenes has told us about the same people. Kauṭliya makes Magadha a kingdom of thieves, crooks of all varsities and abilities, quacks, tricksters, spies disguised as ascetics, agents, provocateurs, conspirators, embezzlers and adulterators – all seeking whom they could devour. It has been said that Kauṭliya was dealing with possible crimes and not with those usually committed. In that case he did not have a model in mind. If that is so, the work can have little relevance in a discussion on the actual situation in Magadha in the early Mauryan period.

Kauṭilya's view of law and *dharma* needs to be pointed out. In fighting crime and an enemy, any means may be employed. Kauṭilya's notion of *dharma* does not seem to stand in the way. False rumours may be circulated against a suspect citizen. False witnesses may be recruited. *Dharma* thus has little reference to righteousness. But the king, Kauṭilya insists, is the protector of *dharma*. Agreements made by a king rising to power, may be broken at will (VIII: 17).[35] When someone declares another person as enemy, he becomes liberated from the rule of law. The line between righteousness and unrighteousness begins to blur. Kauṭliya seems clearly to believe that one may resort to '*adharma*' (unrighteousness) in defence of *dharma* or righteousness. A king may adopt fair or foul means in extorting money from the citizenry to replenish the treasury (V: 2).

The Indian police have borrowed more than a couple of tricks from Kauṭliya, especially regarding the use of ascetics and wandering holy men (*cakradhara*) in intelligence work (IV:4). Kauṭliya recommends administering poison to the sentries to free an imprisoned prince (VII:17).

Kauṭliya describes no fewer than 40 ways of embezzlement (II:8).

Besides the use of poison to destroy your rival, black magic may also be employed for the same purpose. Among the various methods to destroy a rival kingdom, Kauṭliya advocates the principle of 'Divide and Rule' (VII:17). Spreading disaffection among citizens of that kingdom, poisoning of river waters and spreading panic of all kinds are some of the other methods recommended.

What shocks a reader is Kauṭliya's total disregard of ethics. In the struggle for power no holds are barred. The end justifies all means.

The socio-political atmosphere that the *Arthaśāstra* writes about is of extreme political uncertainty and breakdown of peace and stability. Such was the post-Mauryan period. Following the eclipse of Mauryan imperial power, there was prolonged and deadly struggle for supremacy. The author of the work may actually have had a model in mind. Kauṭliya had many ancient manuals to draw upon. On statecraft he had Uśana's manual. The use of ancient manuals would explain many terms of the Mauryan times. Among many terms are the names of state officials. But it is extremely doubtful if industries and crafts had reached the state of specialisation suggested by the *Arthaśāstra*.

Kauṭliya assigns different quarters of the capital city to different *varṇas*. Yet military service was open to the four *varṇas* (IX:2). Even wild tribes were employed to guard the frontiers. Kauṭliya lays it down that the king should regulate the numerical strength of each of the *varṇas* in the village. We are not, however, told how the balance was achieved. Śūdra women were also recruited as spies (I:12). Kauṭliya pays lip service to the '*varṇadharma*', just as he upholds the principle of *dharma* in society. If the author of the *Arthaśāstra* lived in a period of political upheaval, he could not have witnessed a strict observance of the *varṇa* rules. Unlike some *Dharmaśāstras* Kauṭliya does not exempt the brāhmaṇa from the death penalty. For crimes such as inciting wild tribes, he may be drowned (IV: 2). Sutas and Magadhas are of greater merit than the brāhmaṇas and kṣatriyas (III: 7). But Manu would not recognise any group higher than the brāhmaṇas. It is worth nothing that both Kauṭliya and Manu carry virtually the same catalogue of mixed castes.

The caṇḍālas do not seem to have been the object of hatred. They are mentioned along with hunters archers and wild tribes. The caṇḍālas may be employed for lashing erring women (III:3).

What Kauṭliya says about the condition of women is very significant. He permits marriage of widows (III:2). Women whose husbands have been long absent are permitted to remarry. Women enjoyed freedom of choice of their husbands (IV: 12). Girls reached majority at twelve and boys at sixteen (III: 3). Girls were married only after they attained majority.

Women enjoyed property rights. A married woman's property was known as '*śulka*'. It was neither a dowry nor bride-price. Neither the woman's father nor her husband had any right over the *śulka*. In an emergency she had the right to its use. After a woman's death, her wealth was inherited by her daughters. The *śulka* seems to have been made up of the wealth given to her at the time of the marriage by the bridegroom's father as well as the things she brought with her from her father. The father-in-law appears to have had some say in the choice of a new husband, if the first husband died. She lost her claim to the *śulka* if she did not follow his wishes. In effect, the *śulka* was regarded as a deposit.

If a master begets a child by his female slave, both the mother and child are to be recognised immediately as free (III:13). If a master violates the daughter of his slave, he is fined, and he must offer an adequate *śulka* at her marriage (IV:12). Kauṭliya lays down safeguards against sexual exploitation of female slaves by their masters. A female slave is not to be asked to attend on her master during his bath. It is clear that slaves in Kauṭliya's time were better off than the females of the untouchables in later Indian society. There was no guarantee against their exploitation by the upper classes. Anyone employing a slave to carry the dead or excreta forfeited the value paid for him (III:13).

Many customs are alluded to by Kauṭliya that lost currency in later times. Meat eating was quite common. Slaughter of animals was banned only during certain periods of the year. Brāhmaṇas also consumed alcoholic beverages. They may also take up military service. For the funeral Kauṭliya mentions both burial and cremation.

Brāhmaṇas may have many wives one of whom may be a śūdra. The interpretation given to the levirate (*niyoga*) practice is very broad. If a king is too old to beget a son, he may appoint a maternal relation or any blood relation, or even any king of the neighbouring kingdoms 'to sow the seed in his own field' (I:17). Levirate in West Asia, as well as among the Hebrews, was intended to help perpetuate the lineage of a man who died without issue. That is why a brother or a near relation of the dead man was to marry the widow and beget children in his name. In Kauṭliya's view it was not necessary that the male appointed to beget a child on the wife of a living man should be a relation (I:17). West Asians would have been horrified at the practice.

It appears that even 'Āryans' were sometimes enslaved. But the children of such a slave were to be free.

In speaking of contemporary society, Kauṭliya accords some importance to the *varṇa* system. To whatever period we may ascribe his work – early, late, or post-Mauryan – it is evident that society was not organised strictly on *varṇa* principles. We need only point to the rise of the Nandas to imperial power to support this contention. The Nandas were of śūdra origin. But the Nandas were by no means the only example. The Kosalan kings were also of humble origin, and no doubt there were others too.[36]

In early Mauryan period as well as later, sections of society did not conform to the norms of *varṇa*. Many śūdras embraced the monastic life. The *varṇa* order was unenforceable owing to the influence of the non-brahmanic sects. But being a brāhmaṇa, Kauṭliya must have felt obliged to declare his faith in the system. For reasons given above, his observations on contemporary society cannot be taken on their face value.

Aśokan Vision of a New Society

One of the most impressive attempts to rebuild society on humane and just principles was made by Emperor Aśoka in third century B.C. He had a close acquaintance with the heterodox sects popular in his day and had assimilated the spirit of dissent from the brahmanic theory of society. Though professedly a Buddhist, he equally honoured followers of other sects favouring them with gifts and grants. Drawing upon the ethical teachings and insights of the time, Aśoka evolved a theory of socio-religious reconstruction. He had been weened away from the destructive cult of conquest involving mass scale slaughter of human beings and unspeakable suffering. The new ideology was called '*dhamma*'. Compassion towards all beings and concern for the welfare of all were its very foundation.

Aśoka set the ideal of *dhamma* before the whole population.[37] It was not meant only for the followers of Buddhism. There was a place for everyone in it, both Buddhist and non-Buddhists. It could, therefore, be called a basic code of conduct. He did not even appeal to Buddha for authenticity of his *dhamma*, since he was an eclectic in-his beliefs.

The rock edicts and other inscriptions of Aśoka are an eloquent witness to his idealism and the sincere and earnest efforts he made to realise the goal of building a humane society. In them we possess the most reliable records which can be dated with certainty. Aśoka's earnestness in carrying the reform forward touches us deeply.

Aśoka speaks of mercy, forgiveness, reconciliation, respect for all living beings, neighbours, friends and servants, regard for the welfare of prisoners and respect for the followers of all sects. His is an all-embracing vision. It is something the people of his time were quite unaccustomed to see in rulers.

There was a freshness about it. *Dhamma* will be endorsed, Aśoka declared, in the form of mercy, charity, truthfulness, purity, gentleness and virtue.[38] Aśoka was setting forth nothing less than a new ideal in human relations.

Nowhere in his inscriptions does Aśoka refer to the *varṇa* order in society. He recognised no such order of the things. He mentioned śramaṇas and brāhmaṇas side by side and made no distinctions between them. Aśoka wasn't the only one who held this view in his day. A yearning for a social order founded on equality of all men and women was the common heritage of many sects. Hence Aśoka was stamping his seal of approval on this yearning of a section of the people.

His views on the treatment of servants and slaves are even more striking. Coming as they did from a sovereign, these could be termed epoch-making. They set aside the injunctions of the *Dharma Sūtras* and *Dharmaśāstras*. Aśoka has mentioned the subject in several of his edicts. In the 13th major rock edict he lists servants and slaves along with friends, relatives and acquaintances towards whom one should behave well and devotedly.[39] Aśoka established the principle of equality of all citizens before the law. While some enlightened individuals may have believed in this principle, it never had the force of law. The judicial officers were to act according to the new norm of justice.

Aśoka was not content to issue the edicts which embodied the ideas of *dhamma*. He appointed officials called *dhamma-mahamatta* with wide powers to supervise the promulgation of *dhamma*. They periodically read out the edicts and explained them to the people. All groups, even śramaṇas and brāhmaṇas, came within their jurisdiction. They even had authority to enter homes in the course of their duties. Some officials were appointed exclusively for certain groups such as women and the *sangha*. The relations between the sects were very much the concern of the officials. Thus, they were to maintain peace and harmony among various sections of the population. This was part of the programme envisaged by *dhamma*. We see that all aspects of the life of the people were to be imbued with the spirit of *dhamma*. Aśoka believed in persuasion rather than compulsion. In spite of his advocacy of respect for all living things, he did not impose a blanket ban on killing of animals. In fact he did not forbid meat eating in his own palace. But certain animals were protected.

Though Aśoka spoke repeatedly of regard for servants and slaves, it is difficult to show that he planned to abolish all social distinctions. Even before the time of Aśoka, the lower classes must have seen new opportunities with the growth in trade and the stimulus given to agriculture. It is quite reasonable to assume that members of the lower classes figured among the new cultivators. Aśoka's liberalism would further strengthen their gains. The śūdras in particular stood to gain most from the new liberalism.

Modern states can learn much from Aśoka. He was keenly aware that the state could be guilty of naked violence against the citizens. He took steps to reduce the chances of its occurrence.

Aśoka attempted to lay a solid moral foundation for the functioning of the organs of the state. In this matter he was quite unlike Kauṭliya who found nothing wrong with the principle of expediency usually followed by sovereigns. But expediency is the source of moral degeneracy and corruption of the state.

The kings and emperors of laṭer periods failed to learn anything from Aśoka's convictions on the futility of wars. The Aśokan experiment with *dhamma* was a bright patch in a mass of black clouds. At the decline of Mauryan power the country would be plunged into a blood-bath.

Buddhism would largely disappear from the land of its birth. But Aśoka has been termed the finest flower of Buddhism that bloomed in the land. The flower wilted and died away. Yet future generations would with gratitude recall the exquisite fragrance that lingered after the flower was no more.

There were two other Buddhist kingdoms in north India which have left their mark on history. The first was ruled by King Menander in the first century B.C. and the second by King Kaniṣka in the first century A.D. King Menander (Menandras in Greek) was, according to Buddhist tradition, converted to Buddhism. He was bold enough to carry his conquests as far as Sāketa (Ayodhya). Patanjali, in his *Mahābhāṣya*, refers to an attack on Sāketa by Yavanas.[40] He established his capital at Sagala (modern Sialkot) in Punjab. Menander is the subject of Nāgāsena's work, *Milinda-panna*.[41] Buddhism naturally received patronage and encouragement from Menander. The period is important for the closest contact between the Hellenic and the Indian cultures. Yet this contact was limited to Punjab and the North-West, and was to leave no lasting impression on India.

The Kuṣāna king, Kaniṣka, ruled over a much larger territory of northern India. The Kuṣāna period is marked by the cultural ties India forged with Central Asia and China. Buddhist missionary ventures to these parts of the world gathered momentum.[42] Apart from the patronage Kaniṣka is believed to have extended to Buddhism, there is nothing to suggest that he tried to mould society according to the teachings of Buddha or the lines of Aśoka's *dhamma*.

The Jātaka and Contemporary Society

The Buddhist *Jātaka* furnishes us with much information on the conditions prevailing in the country. The society, the work portrays is not one rigidly compartmentalised. There appears to have been some freedom of choice of professions. What the *Jātaka* tells us on this point is confirmed also by many epigraphic records. Brāhmaṇas adopt such occupations as land tilling, cattle tending, hunting, snake-charming, carpentry, weaving, driving of carriages and escorting of caravans.[43] Social barriers were not strictly observed. There appears to have been easy interaction between various castes. According to the *Dharmaśāstras*, a brāhmaṇa may turn to trade or agriculture or tending of cattle only in distress. This injunction was very broadly interpreted or wholly ignored. There were few occupations at this time too contemptible for brāhmaṇas. Weaving is regarded as a lowly trade. Weaving of rush baskets is still more lowly. Even this was not scorned by the brāhmaṇas.

The kṣatriyas too enjoyed the freedom of choice of occupations. A prince works as a trader, a potter, a florist, a cook and a menial servant in succession.[44]

In the *Jātaka* we encounter people engaged in a variety of occupations traditionally assigned to the śūdras. We meet tailors, potters, carpenters, peasants, servants and artisans of all types. There is nothing in this collection of stories to suggest that these occupations were looked down upon. There was a village of 500 carpenters situated not far from Varanasi where they carried on their trade and earned an honourable living.

They accepted contract work for which they obtained the needed timber from the forest. The carpenters in this tale exuded an air of dignity and freedom.[45]

What strikes one is the variety of occupations, crafts and services alluded to. It is logical to conclude that there was a lively demand for goods and services.

It is the folklore image of women that emerges from the pages of the *Jātaka*. They are not devoid of wit and resourcefulness.

When a woman's husband, brother and son were charged with crime and condemned to be hanged, she protested that she would be left without any support in this world and pleaded for the life of one of them. Given the choice between the three, she picked her brother. She could, she explained, replace her husband and son but not a brother.[46] A housemaid borrowed her mistress' ornaments, while heading for the public garden. There a trickster lures her to a corner of the garden and gorges her with food and drink. Then he suggests a more secluded spot. Suspecting him of nefarious designs on her, she decides to make a pre-emptive strike. She then complains that her throat has gone dry and asks the man to draw some water from a well nearby. As he bends down over the edge of the well, she gives him a hefty shove and sends him tumbling to the bottom of the well. 'That won't kill you,' she shouts after him. So she drops a stone after him, which hits the man on the crown of his head, killing him instantly.[47] This maid was blessed with a strong physique. Surely maids in those days were not undernourished. The mistress-maid relation appears to have been very cordial.

Women frequently appear as unfaithful partners and tempters. There is the story of the queen who extracts a reluctant promise from the king that he would never cast eyes on another woman. He had to lead an expedition and had to absent himself from the palace. In an ironic twist, the queen had sex with all the 64 messengers sent by the king to enquire after her. She does not stop there but goes so far as to seduce the royal chaplain who is none other than Bodhisattva who resists her lustful advance. On the king's return the chaplain is predictably denounced to the king who promptly had the chaplain led to the place of execution. But the truth is revealed to the king's utter chagrin.[48] The moral of the story, of course, is that women are insatiable in their desires.

A young woman acts treacherously towards her husband on their honeymoon trip. A young man from Varanasi had acquired all the arts at the famed centre of learning at Taxila. His teacher, immensely pleased with him, gave his own daughter in marriage. On their way to Varanasi the accomplished youth has an encounter with a dacoit gang. But the woman falls for the dacoit chief and has her husband killed.[49] The *Jātakas* present many such stereotype images of the woman.

Undoubtedly, untouchability prevailed in the *Jātaka* period, and *caṇḍālas* were its victims. A brāhamaṇa, meeting a *caṇḍāla* on his path, shouts to him to move to the leeward side of the path. This refers to the old superstition that the breeze that brushes by a caṇḍāla is defiling to the twice-born. But the *caṇḍāla* in this story turned out to be a learned man and the brāhmaṇa fails to answer the questions put to him by the learned *caṇḍāla*.[50]

What is most extraordinary about the attitude towards the caṇḍālas, Buddha in several of his former births was born as a despised *caṇḍāla*. The famed *caṇḍāla* seer, Mātanga, who lived near Varanasi was one of them. The above examples go to show that some *caṇḍālas* did manage to acquire not only elementary but good education.

In the *Jātaka* there are many references to slaves and slavery. The position of slaves remains ambiguous. Some of them appear to have been confidants of their masters. A man nearing his death, seeing his wife was young, reveals the location of his treasure to his slave with instructions to divulge the location to his young boy when he grows up.[51]

The son of a slave grew up with the son of his master. When the latter was being taught, the slave boy sitting beside him picked up crumbs of learning. But on growing up, he forged the signature of his master to marry a rich merchant's daughter.[52] These instances may have been exceptional cases where slaves reached positions of strength. If slaves were employed as valets and domestic servants, they could not have been viewed with horror and revulsion. They were not treated, it is obvious, as untouchables. Slaves were probably prisoners of war or their descendants.

Buddhist writings show no sign of the prohibition of travel abroad which brahmanic circles tried to enforce. We are told of trade with and voyages to distant lands. These contacts were, no doubt, facilitated by the Greek incursion into the North-West. It opened the door to the countries of the West.

The South in the Ascendant

The centre of political power had now shifted to the South. The Sātavāhanas with their capital at Paithana (Pratiṣṭhāna), on the Godavari, were the paramount political power. They not only controlled the greater part of the Deccan, including the Maharashtra region, they carried their conquests across the Vindhyas up to Ujjain and beyond. At the decline of the Mauryan power, the Sātavāhanas (or Salivahanas) had established themselves. They would dominate the political scene for several centuries to come. The Sātavāhanas were probably of Naga (aboriginal) stock, as also were the Āndhrabhṛtyas, their successors to the imperial power in the Deccan.

The Sātavāhana rulers were tolerant of the religious sects popular at the time. Buddhism in particular thrived in Andhra during this period. Excavations have confirmed the wide diffusion and popularity of Buddhism in the region. Prākṛt was the medium of literacy works. The inscriptions too were composed in Prākṛt. The authorship of the *Saptaśati*, a love poem in Prākṛt, is attributed to Hala, a Sātavāhana ruler.[53]

Even before the birth of present era, Buddhism, Jainism and probably Ājīvikas had established themselves in the South. Aśoka attempted the propagation of the *dhamma* in the peninsula. The influence of heterodox sects is clearly visible in the didactic poems of Tiruvaḷḷuvar, who is undoubtedly one of the greatest teachers of India.

We are not quite certain to what sect Tiruvaḷḷuvar belonged, nor are we certain of the time he lived. His period has been tentatively placed somewhere between 1st century B.C. and 3rd century A.D. His work, the *Tirukkural*, a collection of couplets on a variety of subjects, has been the source of inspiration for countless millions for many centuries.

Tiruvaḷḷuvar was, as the name suggests, a Vaḷḷuvar, a caste of drummers who stood low on the social ladder. Whatever may have been Tiruvaḷḷuvar's social status, he did not recognise any social distinction or hierarchy. 'By birth', he declared, 'all men are equal; it is by the differences in their actions that their worth is rendered unequal'.[54]

In a land where xenophobia was promoted practically as a virtue, Tiruvaḷḷuvar's universalism marks him out as unique. He has been called 'the bard of Universal Man'.

Tiruvaḷḷuvar stands apart in his espousal of love as the underlying principle of all human relations. The Indian tradition, whether brahmanic or non-brahmanic has no parallel to Tiruvaḷḷuvar's emphasis on love. The loveless ones, said he, belong all to themselves. The loving ones belong to others-their bones and all.[55]

Nowhere does Tiruvaḷḷuvar speak of dhamma or of *varṇas*. To express the idea of duty, he preferred the Tamil word, '*aram*'. Nor was Tiruvaḷḷuvar obsessed with the question of transmigration. Karma held no terrors for him. He did not believe in the cessation of all activity but upheld freedom from all desires as of supreme value.

It is abundantly clear that the main ideas of the sects of the times were circulating in the South. Many brahmanic values had penetrated to the land of the Ceras, Colas and Pāṇḍyas. The traditional Dravidian society was not yet organised on hierarchical lines. There is no evidence to show that any disability was attached to anyone by reason of his birth. Tiruvaḷḷuvar was merely giving expression to the egalitarianism that was the hallmark of Dravidian social order.

We see similar ideas of universalism espoused by other Tamil writers. 'Every country', said Pūn Kundrānār, a contemporary of Tiruvaḷḷuvar, 'is my native land, and every man my kinsman'.[56]

The Philosophers and Society

Since long before the birth of Jainism and Buddhism, Indian thinkers had been deeply engrossed in seeking answers to numerous questions regarding man, the universe, the unity and plurality of beings, and the world within. They had gained many wonderful insights into reality. Yet the search continued relentlessly to produce a variety of answers, which speaks volumes for the courage, sincerity and earnestness of the seekers. The various opinions would later crystallise into systems of thought. The insights of pioneers would be pondered over, further refined and handed down. The classical systems of Indian philosophy were born in this way, not at the same time but in the course of centuries. These philosophies concern us here only insofar as they have something to say on society and social relations.

The *Mīmāṁsā* is one of the most orthodox schools of Indian thought. The *Mīmāṁsākas*, the followers of this school, faithfully uphold the authority of the *Vedas*. They formulated their own system of interpretation of the *Vedas*. Their understanding of *dharma* has had enormous influence on later Hinduism. Good action, according to the *Mīmāṁsākas*, is what has been enjoined by the *Vedas*. Hence the *Mīmāṁsā* ethics is solidly anchored on *Śruti*. The Vedic injunctions must be accepted on their authority and are of permanent value.[57]

The *Sāṁkhya* system struck a dissenting note with its theory of three *guṇas* or constituents. It sought to explain the differences between beings in their conduct, attainments, and virtues by postulating the three-fold constituents of *sattva, rajas* and *tamas*. Human beings differ among themselves owing to the variation in the proportion of these constituents. It is not only human beings who are so constituted but all corporeal beings as well.[58]

The *Sāṁkhya* school thus cast serious doubts on the theory of inherited charisma of certain social groups. Individuals of the same group would not possess the same qualities. The claim to excellence by all members of a particular group would not thus be sustainable. Logically, the *Sāṁkhya* school did not withold its esoteric doctrine from any of the four *varṇas*.

The *Sāṁkhya* system was to leave its mark on the *Bhagavadgītā* which made an attempt to integrate the *guṇa* theory, just as it tried to assimilate the principles of the Yoga system.

For Patanjali, author of *Yogasūtra, ahiṁsā*, though expressed by a negative term, was a positive doctrine. Its foundation was amity with all beings. Logically, Patanjali taught that the Vedic injunctions on animal sacrifices should be abjured.[59]

In its early stages of development the Yoga school believed that the conquest of self was attainable by all, irrespective of their social status. In latter stages the school became exclusive in its approach to self conquest.

Indian society has displayed through the ages varying tendencies and attitudes towards social relations. Aśoka, the heterodox sects and some of the philosophers represent the class of opinion advocating an open society. The *Dharmaśāstras* generally mirror another opinion. The question may now be posed which of these reflects the actual situation, and which is the more authentically historical.

According to Nikunja Vihari Banerjee, divergent and conflicting trends have prevailed in India. Two parallel lines of thought have continued to exist. One favoured animal sacrifices, restricted interaction between social groups and curbs on the freedom of women, and the other promoted *ahiṁsā*, free social intercourse and freedom of women.[60] It would seem then that more orthodox views have prevailed and came to be accepted as the authentic teaching.

NOTES

1. *TYB*, p.13 ff.
2. *CHI*, I, p.389.
3. *Ibid.*, p.394.
4. *Ibid.*, p.341.
5. *Ibid.*, p.430 ff.
6. Bhikhu Sangharakshita. 'Buddhism' in *A Cultural History of India*. ed. by L. Basham. Oxford. Clarendon Press, 1975, p.98.
7. *TYB*, p.58.
8. D.D. Kosambi. 1970, p.105.
9. *BRAU* 1:4:11. This passage as well as other direct quotations from the *Upaniṣads* on the following pages are taken from *Thirteen Principal Upaniṣads*, tr, by R.E. Hume. Madras. Oxford University Press, 1965.
10. *Aitareya Up.*, 4:19.
11. *CHAU* 5:3:1.
12. *Ibid.* 5:11:2.
13. *Maitri Up.* 1:3 ff.
14. *BRAU* 3:8.
15. *Ibid.* 5:1.
16. *Ibid.* 6:13.
17. W. M'Crindle, *Ancient India as Described in Classical Literature*, Westminster, Archibald Constable & Co. Ltd., (1901), pp.3-4.
18. For details of these two Aramaic inscriptions, see Romila Thapar, *Aśoka and the Decline of the Mauryas*. Delhi, Oxford University Press, (1980), pp.7, 21.
19. 2 Kings 18:26.
20. *Greek Historical Thought*. introduction and translation by Arnold Toynbee, New York. The New American Library. (1962). p. xii.
21. W. M'Crindle. 1901, p.72.
22. *Ibid.*, p.78.
23. *Ibid.*, p.204.
24. J. W. McCrindle (tr), *Ancient India as Described by Megasthenes and Arrian*, Calcutta, Thacker Spink & Co., (1877). Fragment IB (39).
25. W.M'Crindle. 1901, p.57.
26. 8:7:3; 8:9:3; 8:11:3.
27. W.M'Crindle. 1901, p.47 ff.
28. R. Thapar. 1980, p.57.
29. W. M'Crindle, 1901, p.87.
30. Somnath Dhar, *Kalhana*. New Delhi. Sahitya Akademi, (1978), p.21.
31. W. M'Crindle. 1901, p.66.

32. *Ibid.*, p.67.
33. J.W. M'Crindle, 1877, p.222.
34. For a brief discussion of the *Arthaśāstra*, see A.B. Keith, *A History of Sanskrit Literature*. London, Oxford University Press. (1961), p.xviii ff.
35. All references to the *Arthaśāstra* are to the translation by Shamasastri, *Kauṭliya's Arthaśāstra*. Mysore. Mysore Printing and Publishing House, (1967).
36. D.D. Kosambi, 1970, p.128.
37. R. Thapar, 1980, p.149.
38. The seventh pillar edict. See R. Thapar, 1980, p.265.
39. R. Thapar. 1980. p.256.
40. P.V. Kane, 'Ancient Cities Mentioned in the *Mahābhāṣya*', in *Journal of the Bombay Branch of the Asiatic Society*, Part I, (1951), p.40.
41. *TYB* p.196.
42. *Ibid*. p.199.
43. Radha Kumud Mookerji. *Hindu Civilization*. Bombay. Bhartiya Vidya Bhawan, (1977). p.320.
44. *Ibid*., p.319.
45. *Jātaka* No.156. All references to the Jātaka stories are to: *Jātaka or the Former Births* ed. by E.B. Cowell. London Luzac & Co. (1957).
46. Jātaka No:67.
47. *Ibid*. No:415.
48. *Ibid*. No:120.
49. *Ibid*. No:374.
50. *Ibid*. No:377.
51. *Ibid*. No:39.
52. *Ibid*. No:125.
53. Nilakanta Sastri. *A History of South India*. Madras, Oxford University Press, (1981). pp.43-4.
54. *Kural* No: 972. cf. Maharajan. *Tiruvaḷḷuvar*. New Delhi. Sahitya Akademi. (1982).
55. Kural No:75.
56. Maharajan. 1982. p.93.
57. Radhakrishnan. *Indian Philosophy*. IV. New York. Macmillan Co., (1962), p.375 ff.
58. *CHI* III. pp.42-3.
59. Nikunja Vihari Banerjee. *The Spirit of Indian Philosophy*. New Delhi, Arnold Heinemann. (1979). p.272 ff.
60. *Ibid*., p.291.

3

OF LAW-GIVERS AND MEN OF LETTERS

NO OTHER class of literature has so deeply influenced and moulded the social thinking of the Indians as the body of legal writings known as the *Dharmasamhitās* or *Dharmaśāstras*. They are best described as codes of sacred laws. Though these *samhitās* are only *smṛitis*, that is, a collection of traditions and usages, they have had a far greater influence on the day-to-day life on an average Hindu than the Vedas themselves. While the average man may have been ignorant of the contents of much of the Vedic writings, this was not true of the *Dharmasamhitās*. The latter had something to say about every detail of his life. They laid down what he must do and avoid. He also knew the sanctions of the laws. He could ignore the Vedas, but not the *samhitās*. It was no small risk he ran ignoring the latter.

The voluminous legal literature is a proof of the advance the science of jurisprudence had made during the course of many centuries. Some of the *samhitās* like the *Manusamhita* have ancient roots. But they have been revised to meet the needs of the changing times. The result is not always a happy one. The new elements introduced into the test have not been fully harmonised. For instance, the ancient text of Manu could not have expressed a serious concern for small crawling creatures which might be hurt by such articles as a water pot, the broom and the pestle. Manu says: A householder has five places where animal lives are destroyed; they are: the hearth, the grinding-stone, the water-pitcher, the pestle and mortar. These five when performing their functions kill animal life (3:68).[1] Manu goes on to prescribe the *'Panca Yajna'* for the expiation of the sin committed in the destruction of life in these five places. Yet, strangely enough, he permits meat-eating. In fact, Manu permits animal sacrifice. A brāhmaṇa may also kill animals for the maintenance of his dependents as did Agastya of old did (5:22). Concern of small creatures must have been incorporated under the influence of Jainism and Buddhism, but no such concern was expressed for the larger creatures killed for meat.

The ancient legal works express a variety of opinions on important subjects. Gautama and Baudhāyana, reputed authors of law codes, permit *niyoga* (levirate). But Apastamba condemns the practice. Vasistha permits *niyoga* as well as remarriage of child widows. But Apastamba roundly condemns the taking of bride-price from a bridegroom.[2] Though Parāśara clearly permits widow marriage, it is Manu's prohibition that has been frequently appealed to as the genuine *śātraic* teaching. In general Parāśara is more liberal towards women, compared with Manu. The great latitude permitted by various schools point to the freedom that once existed regarding social customs.

The existence of many law schools contributed to a wide range of opinions backed by authority. The schools were associated with or named after well-known teachers. No particular opinion could be claimed as authoritative. This freedom of opinion was to disappear in later times. Frequently, it was not the liberal view that prevailed. As the differing views often contradicted one another, they could not claim the authority of the Vedas. It was not till modern times when Manu became the authoritative *Dharmasamhitā*. It is not difficult to see why this happened. Manu is one of the most comprehensive among all *Dharmaśāstras* in its very range of subjects treated. It was thus a fairly complete code of laws. Other codes fell short of this requirement. As time passed, the text grew longer and incorporated more subjects and accommodated new trends to bring it up to date.

All śāstraic injunctions were supposed to have a corresponding Vedic text. To find Vedic texts justifying all śāstraic laws was a clear impossibility, because some of these laws contradicted Vedic texts. To overcome this difficulty, it was argued that where Vedic texts in support of śāstraic injunctions did not exist, these may have been lost in the course of time. Thus *smṛti* (traditions) was allowed in an insidious manner to supersede *śruti* (revelation). This interpretation was a great achievement for the law-givers or redactors. They would no longer feel inhibited now, as it was rendered practically unnecessary to seek any Vedic authority for *śāstraic* laws.

The *Dharmaśāstras* are a bewildering mix of sense and nonsense, the highest forms of religion and crass superstition, a keen sense of justice and naked class interest. Manu, for example, is a mirror of a bygone era. For Manu, a cross-road is an object of superstition. A brāhmaṇa is asked never to go through a cross-road but around it. A brāhmaṇa should not look at his own image in the water (4.38).

Mushroom is unfit for eating as it originates in impurities (5:5).

It should be noted that Parāśara considers the codes of Manu, Gautama, Sankha and Likhita outdated. Manu's code was valid only in the Satyayuga, Gautama's in the Tretayuga, Saṅkha's and Likhita's in the Dvāparayuga. Parāśara's own code is the proper code to be followed in the Kaliyuga.[3] Yet Parāśara quotes Manu with approval (9:51) and calls him a man who knew all the scriptures. Parāśara seems to have forgotten what he had written at the beginning of his code on Manu being outdated. Later redactors or editors of Manu probably did not read the entire text at one stretch. There are times when a reader bemoans not only their poor memory but doubts their sanity.

What strikes a reader of the *Dharmasamhitās* is the unshakably pre-eminent position that has been accorded to the brāhmaṇa. The brāhmaṇa has risen from the level of the mere mortals, leaving them far below, into the realm of gods themselves. The phenomenon is a sociological wonder. We have said above how the *Dharmasastras* were frequently updated. The brāhmaṇas have gained in the updating efforts. This is hardly surprising, since the law-givers were mostly brāhmaṇas themselves. And they had a fairly free hand. Few groups in any society have been so privileged as the brāhmaṇas. It was as though the gods themselves had dropped the basket of privileges right into their lap. It was given to few to determine their own social position, their own prerogatives, to determine the position of other groups, to create by a mere flip of the pen a class of servants who would regard it as a great privilege to serve them and to be rewarded with heavenly bliss, and to award themselves tax exemptions. They turned themselves into a special species of humans on whom it was a religious duty to lavish gifts. Brahmaṇas had all these and a great deal more besides.

There is no evidence to show that legislative authority originated from or exclusively rested or the brahmaṇas in the early times. Later on, this authority was claimed by the brahmaṇas. By reason of being the eldest born and of being the repository of the Vedas, brāhmaṇa is the ruler of all creation inasmuch as he lays down the duties of all social orders (1:93). The basis of the claim for pre-eminence was the brāhmaṇa's origin from the mouth of Puruṣa. Purity of the organ of origin was not the issue here. Anatomically the mouth is only slightly more pure than the opposite end of the alimentary canal. What was indicated by the mouth was probably the brāhmaṇa's function as the chapter of hymns and prayers. As we have said earlier, the brāhmaṇas were not always the most respected *varṇa*. At certain times the kṣatriya occupied this position. For reasons not fully known, the kṣatriya's position deteriorated. One of the contributory factors to the deterioration may have been the kṣatriya's neglect of and indifference to the pursuit of studies. This facilitated brāhmaṇa's rise to pre-eminence. At first his right of primogeniture was taken for granted.

Manu stipulates that a brāhmaṇa should be merely exiled, while the members of the other three *varnas* should be punished and exiled.

The basic of a brāhmaṇa's greatness is not his erudition. Just as the fire, said Manu, whether consecrated or unconsecrated, is the great deity, so a brāhmaṇa, whether erudite or not is a great deity (9:317). Hence an ignorant brāhmaṇa, even if bereft of the virtues of his order, is to be preferred as a judicial officer, to a śūdra (8:20). Presumably, such a brāhmaṇa would better protect *dharma*.

Few have surpassed Paraśara in his glorification of the brāhmaṇa. Whatever a brahmaṇa enjoins is the law. One who disobeys the dictates of a brāhmaṇa should be regarded as a brāhmaṇa-killer (6:57). The word of a brāhmaṇa is the word of a god. A brāhmaṇa is a moving pantheon. His word can never be falsified (6:61). Riding in the chariot of scriptures and wielding the sword of Vedas in his hands, a brāhmaṇa, whatever he may speak, even in jest, is to be obeyed (8:33). The punishment for killing a brāhmaṇa devoid of the rites of his *varṇa* is the same as that of killing a devout sudra. The killer should carry out the *candryana* now and make gift of thirty cows to a worthy brahmaṇa (6:17). For Parāśara, a brahmaṇa without the Gāyatri *mantra* is worse than a sudra.

Śūdras in the Dharmaśāstras

Of the four *varṇas* it is to the śūdras alone that the scriptures have not assigned an occupation, that is, the kind of occupation allotted to the three higher *varṇas*. The śūdra, of course, has a solemn duty, that of serving the higher *varṇas*. Even so, the scope of this duty came to be greatly restricted. Towards the close of his *Samhitā*, Manu stipulates that the śūdras should serve the brāhmaṇa for the acquisition of heaven or a living or both (10:122).

A śūdra is so vile that he should assume a name that denotes vileness (2:31). His life has no more worth than the life of a cat, owl, crow, or lizard. The expiation prescribed for killing any of these creatures is the same as that prescribed for killing a sudra.

The scales of justice were heavily weighed against the śūdra. A crime committed by members of the various *varnas* drew differing punishments. A śūdra got the worst of it, as one might expect. If a śūdra uses abusive language at a twice-born, his tongue shall be severed, inasmuch as he has originated from a vile part of the Supreme (8:270). The myth of the origin of the four *varṇas* is being adduced here to justify the inhuman punishment. For the offence of using abusive language, while the twice-born are fined, a śūdra is flogged. The sudra has even to pay higher rates of interest than the members of the higher *varṇas*.

Manu condemns the practice of brāhmaṇas giving religious instruction to the śūdra students. That some brāhmaṇas did give such instruction is clear from the fact that brāhmaṇas who instructed śūdra students were declared unfit to be invited to a *sradha* ceremony (3:162). A professional astrologer, a horse dealer and animal-tamer are also considered unfit.

Manu condemns a brahmaṇa accepting gifts from the sudras, even from a sudra king. But the sudra's gold was too tempting to refuse. The prohibition was circumvented through a conjuror's trick, as it were. The *hiraṇyagarbha* ceremony transformed a sudra into a brāhmaṇa and nothing less. The ceremony was double-edged. The king gained by being transformed into a brāhmaṇa and thus a boost in social ranking and the brāhmaṇa gained by walking away with the golden vessel used at the ceremony. This was how many śūdra kinglets of South India put away their sudrahood.

According to Manu a kingdom where the sudras abound or one infested with atheistic, non-brāhmaṇa population is soon destroyed, stricken with famine and pestilence (8:22). Manu reduces many tribes and people to the sudra status for the ostensible reason that they had not kept in touch with brāhmaṇas. Even the Sutas and the Magadhas, whom Kauṭilya classifies as superior to the brāhmaṇas, are relegated by Manu to the śūdra status. Among the tribes he has so relegated are: Paundrakas, sakas, Dravidas, Kambhojas, Yavanas, Pandavas, Chinas, Kiratas and Daradas (10:45). Manu seems to make little distinction in status between the Yavanas, Pandavas and Kiratas. Apart from the status the Yavanas and Sakas have been accorded, their very mention is significant. It is now evident that in

Manusamhitā, the award of śūdra status was quite arbitrary, even somewhat whimsical.

It is worth noting that in the course of time certain occupations came to be assigned to 'mixed castes'. The Carmakaras are the result of a mixture of Karacaras and Nisadas. The Carmakaras are the traditional shoe-makers or Camars. The professions of musicians and chariot-drivers have also been assigned to mixed castes. One gathers the impression from Manu that there was a proliferation of mixed castes. These mixed castes arise, it would appear, not from a mixture of *varṇas*, but from a fusion of tribes or aboriginal groups. All lower-ranking occupations have been distributed among the mixed groups. Some ingenuity has been exercised to create these groups. That is why the fusion of various groups always takes place according to strict rules.

Parāśara has carried strictures against the śūdras a step further. What Parāśara enjoins is unmitigated untouchability. The twice-born are forbidden to touch a śūdra. They should not carry or cremate a dead śūdra. Even a casual glance at a deceased śūdra must be expiated by looking at the sun (3:54). A brāhmaṇa visiting a śūdra woman even for a single night must atone the sin by living on alms for three years. The knowledge acquired from a śūdra, partaking of a śūdra's boiled rice, sharing his bed or seat and his touch drag down a brāhmaṇa to the level of a degraded śūdra (12:32).

Yājnavalkya also enjoins that the duty of the śūdra is to serve the twice-born, but adds that if he cannot maintain himself in this manner, he may take up trade or the arts. However, he should always be good to the twice-born (1:20). The sudra is exhorted to be pure in conduct, to be devoted to his wife and to be a protector of servants. It is of interest to note that the śūdra is thought of as having servants of his own.

A father, dividing his property, is free to give a share of his property to his śūdra son. But after his death, his sons must give half of their share to their śūdra brother (2:37). In the absence of such brothers, the śūdra son is entitled to the whole property. Yet, in principle, Yājnavalkya does not approve of a śūdra as wife for the twice-born.

To the śūdra, Yājnavalkya assigns certain *mantra*, and reciting these, he should perform the five *yajnas* (1:121). Thus, the śūdra is not deprived of all religious rites. But the prohibition of performing sacrifices with articles borrowed from a śūdra holds good for

Yājnavalkya too. Yet food can be accepted from one's servant, a share-cropper and a barber (1:168). These three types of workers were presumed to be sudras.

Yājnavalkya is of the view that no one should be made a slave against his will (2:185). If anyone is so enslaved, he should be freed forthwith. The law-giver rejects all forms of bondage, even of one who sells himself into slavery merely to be fed. In Yājnavalkya's time, slavery must have come to be viewed with disfavour.

Parāśara agrees with Manu in the latter's view that the service of the brāhmaṇas is the noblest virtue accessible to the śūdra. Any other virtue practised by him is fruitless (1:61).

The śūdra is barred from drinking the milk of the 'Kapila cow'. He is threatened with hell fire for violating this prohibition as well as for knowing a brāhmaṇa woman carnally and for reciting the Vedas (1:64).

Parāśara has a curious explanation for the word '*dāsa*'. He maintains that a son begotten by a brāhmaṇa of a śūdra woman and duly consecrated is called a *dāsa*. A son so begotten but unconsecrated is a 'nāpita'. It must be noted, however, that brāhmaṇas had affairs with śūdra women, considering the frequent imprecations poured on such brāhmaṇas. But the imprecations failed to put an end to the affairs. What is surprising, Parāśara, who has shown the greatest zeal in upholding the dignity and status of the brāhmaṇa, has admitted brāhmaṇa's liaison with the śūdra females.

Manu does not recognise a class known as the *pancamas*. That was logical, if one took the myth of the creation of the *varṇas* seriously. The śūdras had originated from the feet of the Puruṣa. That was as low as you could go. Where would the *pancamas* originate from? Manu stipulates that the caṇḍālas should eat from broken pots, wear the clothes taken from corpses and lead a nomadic life (10:52). A brāhmaṇa expiates the sin of carnally knowing a caṇḍāla woman by living on alms for three years and by the recitation of the *Sāvitṛ mantra*.

Even Manu permits great latitude in extreme situations. Viśwāmitra, though he accepted, when he was famished, the flesh of [illegible] leg from the hand of a caṇḍāla, was not associated with sin (10:108). When it is a matter of saving one's life, the *varṇa* laws are held in abeyance.

Parāśara forbids a brāhmaṇa to walk the same road with a caṇḍāla. This sin is expiated by the recitation of the *Gāyatri mantra.*

The sin of drinking from a well polluted by the touch of a caṇḍāla's water pot is expiated by drinking cow urine for three days (6:24).

It would seem that the Nambudiris of Kerala have strictly followed the injunctions of Parāśara on untouchability. They would not allow untouchables to walk on the public roads. The very sight of an untouchable was abhorrent to the Nambudiri. Needless to say, a caṇḍāla could not approach a Nambudiri within a certain distance. For the lower castes there was a gradation of approachability to the Nambudiri, who has been termed 'a brāhmaṇa among the brāhmaṇas'. There is a falsetto note in their cries of horror at the sight of untouchables. Over-enthusiasm is proverbially the trait of a neophyte or a new entrant to a group. The Nambudiri brāhmaṇa and the elite brāhmaṇa castes of Maharashtra were probably once inducted into the brāhmaṇa fold from alien cultures. Anthropometric data on the castes of Maharashtra and Kerala support this contention. If we take the cephalic index and nasal index into account, the Desastha and Citpavana brāhmaṇas of Maharashtra stand in close proximity to the lower castes of the same region than to the brāhmaṇas of the Gangetic plain. Similarly, the Nambudiris of Kerala have a greater affinity to the Ceramar than to their fellow castemen of the North. This observation holds good about the affinity between the brāhmaṇas and the lower castes of Bengal. These stand in the same relationship as that between the brāhmaṇas and the lower castes of Maharashtra.[4]

Scholars believe that ancient India witnessed many migrations from West Asia at different periods.[5] One of the waves of migrations, it is said, struck the Maharashtra region and later swept eastward into the Andhra country. The dominant physical type represented by the Desastha and Citpavana brāhmaṇas and the lower castes may have originated from such a migration.

Woman in the Dharmaśāstras

If there was anyone even more disadvantaged than the caṇḍāla in the *smṛtis*, it was the woman. The caṇḍāla was master at least in his own home. But frequently the woman was a caṇḍāla in her own home. She was often grouped with dogs and caṇḍālas. A parturient woman or one in her menses was worse off than a caṇḍāla.

The woman in Manu is a great deal more disadvantaged than the woman in Kauṭilya. Kauṭilya's woman has property rights, while woman in Manu has no such rights. A widow in Kauṭilya can remarry. Permanent widowhood is the lot of a widow in Manu, except when she has to conform to the rules of levirate (*niyoga*). She can take few decisions of her own. She has no right to choose her life partner. She does not deserve any independence. She is treated as an immature person, incapable of taking decisions for herself or looking after herself. She is a dangerous creature for a male. Manu advised a man never to remain alone with his mother, sister or daughter in a solitary place, lest his passions should overpower him (2:315). This view of the woman is a great deal more alarmist than that of the Jews, who permitted a man to remain alone with his mother but not his daughter. A brāhmaṇa should not eat in the company of his wife. Needless to point out that he should not eat food touched by a woman in her menses or by a newly parturient woman.

A wife has no religious rite or vow other than to serve her husband unflinchingly. She must serve him even if he is unfaithful. A wife cannot acquire property (8:416).

Manu makes no secret of his disapproval of the practice of '*śulka*'. It is clear that a somewhat different meaning than what was given to it by Kauṭilya is attached to the word by Manu. It amounts to bride-price, and that is why Manu condemns a father for selling his daughter by accepting a price for her in the form of *śulka* (9:100).

In a woman's purificatory rites, no Vedic *mantras* are to be used. In being so disqualified from the use of Vedic *mantras*, 'women are like unto inorganic things' (9:18). Manu holds that women are sexually insatiable (9:14). This view has passed into Indian literature and is the subject of many popular sayings among the country folk.

Manu permits *niyoga*. If a widow has no son, though having daughters, she is permitted to have a son procreated on her by a younger brother or a near relation of her deceased husband. Manu, however, strongly disapproves of the practice for brāhmaṇas and adds that the beastly custom was introduced during the reign of King Vena (9:66).

The husband of a sterile woman, or a woman who gives birth only to girls or one whose children have died in infancy or a harsh-tongued woman may remarry. There need be no delay over the last mentioned type (9:8).

In the society visualised by Manu, the most pathetic figure is the widow. For the widow, there is nothing to look forward to and much to bemoan. She was forbidden to wear ornaments and good clothes.

Worse still, she had to shave her head. She was thus reduced to a scare-crow. She would be constantly exposed to the barbs from the relations of her husband. Heartrending descriptions of the conditions of widows have come down to us from the last century.

A widow was barred from attending the sacred rites of the family, because her presence was considered inauspicious. Thus abandoned by both god and man, so it seemed, the widow ground out her days. The irrational in Manu shows through clearly here. First the widow was denied her right to remarry. Then she was denied her right to live a normal life and was reduced to an object of derision, a mere scare-crow. Then she was declared unfit for human company. Her very presence brought bad luck. The villainy of the logic behind the oppression of the widow dismays a modern reader.

Manu appears to have forgotten the lot of the widow when he wrote: 'Prosperity reigns supreme in the family where the females do not grieve' (3:47). Nevertheless, the mental torture that many young brides are subject to in modern Indian society has little justification in Manu. With all his anti-women stand, there is nothing in Manu that permits bride-burning the modern horror perpetrated in the name of dowry.

One is happy to note Āpastamaba's injunction in his *samhitā* (1:34): Two fingers' width of woman's hair should be clipped where a complete shaving of her head would be found to have been enjoined in the regulations'. The symbolic gesture of cutting two fingers' width of hair did not meet general approval, as has happened to many other liberal interpretations of the law.

The woman in Yājnavalkya is in a happier position than the woman in Manu. It is fairly certain that Yājnavalkya's *samhitā* is a post-Gupta work. Yet the woman's property rights resemble those of Kauṭilya's *Arthaśāstra.* If these rights had not disappeared even in Yājnavalkya's time, it is strange that Manu did not recognise them. After her death, a woman's property is divided among her daughters, after the debts on it are paid off (2:219).

Even Yājnavalkya holds a woman responsible for producing girl babies. On that score, a husband is permitted to take a second wife. Yet Yājnavalkya does not omit to remind a husband to maintain the childless, chaste wife properly. He also permits levirate.

Yājnavalkya accords women only a low ritual status. He puts them in the same category as the śūdras in the matter of purification (1:21). But he adds that a wife must be honoured by her husband and his near relations including her father-in-law and mother-in-law (1:82). A woman whose husband is absent is not permitted any entertainment or sports or laughter. She leads a life, Yājnavalkya appears to say, like one in mourning. This is the traditional image of the woman who has no existence of her own. The woman is one of those to whom one should yield the right of way. Others are: a king, a bridegroom, one carrying a load, an aged person and a cartman. Caste and social rank step aside here.

Parāśara represents a liberal attitude towards women. He shows greater sensitivity to the rights of women. For one who forsakes a chaste, innocent wife, Parāśara assigns re-birth as a woman in seven successive incarnations to suffer the pangs of widowhood in each. Parāśara allows a woman to remarry in the following emergencies: her husband becomes an ascetic; he becomes a degraded person (*patita*), loses his virility; he is not heard from (4:20). At the death of her husband, a woman has a clear option between *brahmacarya*, remarriage and *satī*. Parāśara, no doubt, praises *satī*, but it is not obligatory.

Parāśara still clings to the superstition regarding menstruation and parturition. For a brāhmaṇa, the period of expiation for the sin of touching a caṇḍāla woman is two days, while it is three days for touching parturient woman, and six days if the woman so touched is in her menses.

Parāśara devotes a great deal of space to the subject of the expiation of all manner of crimes that could be committed against the cow. He is simply unsurpassed in the exhaustive treatment of the subject. In contrast to a whopping 112 verses he devotes to the cow, Parāśara dismisses the matter of the murder of one's wife with a solitary verse.

From the foregoing analysis it is clear that the law-givers held a great diversity of views on several matters of importance such as the status and freedom of women, śūdras and untouchability. The society the *smṛtis* visualised was sharply compartmentalised, with each group having its own clearly defined duties and privileges, with limited interaction between the groups. In spite of the strictures against inter-*varṇa* marriages, such marriages were quite common. The frequent references to the brāhmaṇa's śūdra wife point to their occurrence. Sanctions imposed against brāhmaṇas contracting marriage with śūdra women failed to stem the practice. The brāhmaṇas had taken up occupations once considered taboo. We find brāhmaṇas horse-dealers, traders of all kinds and snake-charmers mentioned even in Manu. The repeated references to the disabilities imposed or those engaged in non-conventional professions point to the widespread departure from the norm. The trend towards adoption of non-conventional professions was in fact irreversible. It would become worse later on.

Since the Mauryan times both agriculture and trade had witnessed a boom. The Mauryan expansion of power greatly facilitated the movement of goods, thus creating a demand for them. As the communication lines opened up between the different regions of India, trade was the first to benefit from the new opportunities. The boom in trade in turn led to greater productivity in agriculture. Trade had also become more remunerative. It was natural that *varṇas* other than the vaiśyas should want to have a slice of the cake. The *Dharmaśāstras* allow even the śūdras to deal in certain articles. All this point to a change in the environment of economic relations and in the attitude towards business activity.

The shift in economic relations was bound to affect social relationships. On top of all this, the social policy of Aśoka had left its mark on society. The brāhmaṇas were in no position to enforce the traditional restrictions on social relationships. The *Dharmaśāstras* reflect the reactions of the orthodox sections of society towards the changing conditions. Their reactions are at times alarmist, but even they had to concede that some changes were inevitable.

The *śāstras* were the outcome of the bid to restore the old-time value. They rejected the new-fangled ideas of social egalitarianism of Aśoka. Equality before the law was not a principle the *śāstras* subscribed to. Justice, according to them, was conditioned by such contingent factors as the social position of the offender, his learning and his virtuousness. The same offence by different social groups drew differing punishments. The *śāstras* uphold the principle that the same excellence of behaviour cannot be required of all members of society. There is a sound argument to justify the principle. Not all had same education, training in good conduct, the benefit of good teachers. Therefore, it was unrealistic to expect the same refined conduct from so far so good.

According to the above principle, deviations from the norm set for each group would call for more stringent punishments on those who were expected to show refinement in their conduct. Those who enjoyed privileges on the strength of their refined behaviour should also be required to display a greater sense of responsibility. But this was not so. The elite were gainers on both counts. They had the privileges and they did not have to pay any price for them by way of greater obligations.

However, there are to be found in the *Dharmaśāstras* vestiges of another legal tradition which laid down the principle that the higher the *varṇa* of the offender, the greater the penalty inflicted on him.[6] Such injunctions may have been altered in subsequent revisions. The changes understandably benefited the higher *varṇas*.

The *Dharmaśāstras* are reminiscent of a particular vision of man and society. The law-givers handed down their understanding of reality. In so doing they thought they were rendering a service. But the generation following them have idealised the vision of their forefathers and put a value on it that it did not possess. We have attributed to a particular age in the history of religion and society a comprehensiveness of understanding and a depth of perception of reality that does little credit to our forefathers or to ourselves. Followers of all religions have promoted the dubious fiction that God spoke definitively to the men and women of a particular age. The generations that followed had only to preserve and transmit these 'revelations' to the generations coming after them. This view of religious insights and 'revelation' leads to the glorification of the past and an abject form of religious obscurantism. The age-old laws are looked upon as the last word on a given topic. The laws then become a great millstone around man's neck.

Many of the provisions of the *śāstras* originated in brahmanic circles and were intended for the brāhmaṇas only. These were later applied to other groups as well. Thus an unbearable burden was laid on the shoulders of vulnerable segments of the population. They were vulnerable because they had little say on laws that were made for them. The door to the acquisition of learning had already been closed in their face. It was then easy enough to convince them that it was their God-given duty to serve others. History will judge the law-givers harshly for depriving the mass of population of the right to education. One cannot help adverting to the fact that the will of God determined for the class of servants was identical with the interests of the elite classes.

History provides another example of how mundane laws acquired the status of revelation and explicit divine will. The Mosaic Law is rooted in the Code of Hammurabi and other ancient laws. Some of the provisions of the Mosaic Law have been copied verbatim from the Code of Hammurabi. Yet we are repeatedly told in the *Bible* that the Lord directly revealed the whole law to Moses in the desert. Whenever priests wanted to invest any law with authoritativeness, they put it in the mouth of God. It then not only carried authority but became immutable. In this manner such primitive tribal customs as the obligation of blood vengeance and circumcision took on the character of divine commands. It is difficult to believe that the Lord was so heartless as to set down solemn injunctions on agriculture for a people who were then blundering among sand dunes of the Arabian desert.[7] The liturgical rules which came into force during or after the time of King David were also put in the mouth of God. Laws enacted centuries after the Hebrews settled in Palestine were attributed to Yahweh himself and thus they assumed an aura of inviolability and unchangeability.

Jesus, born and bred a Jew, who claimed to have come to fulfil the scriptures, rejected what was irrational and anachronistic in the Mosaic Law. Being a layman, Jesus was not competent to interpret the law. This does not seem to have troubled him at all. Is it only the founders of great religions who enjoy this right to reject and change what is irrational? Every discerning person can claim that right. A mere attribution to God does not make any law inviolable or unalterable. A law purported to have the divine sanction cannot cancel the inalienable right of an individual to follow what his conscience approves or to reject what it abhors.

The Jewish law had a redeeming quality, namely, its egalitarianism. The law explicitly states that there is only one law for all. Its treatment of slaves was humane. No Israelite was to be enslaved. All slaves were to be set free in the Jubilee year, which fell once in every 50 years. The prospect of a slave living long enough to see a Jubilee year dawning was extremely slim.[8] Few could have benefited from this special provision. Anyone harbouring a runaway slave was not only not penalised but was told not to surrender the slave to his master.[9] A slave could become by adoption an Israelite. Several of the patriarchs had slave wives and had children by them who were reckoned as legitimate heirs and Israelites. Contrast this with the many disabilities to which the children of a śūdra wife were subjected to in the *śāstras*.

The Mosaic Law counselled the Israelites to show kindness to aliens who lived in their midst. Justice towards labourers was stressed. The employer was told not to withhold the wage of a labourer. Yet there was one class of people to whom the Jews denied humane treatment. They thought the Samaritans unfit to associate with, practising a gross form of untouchability against them.

The Hebrew law-givers had visualised an egalitarian society. A family could not be deprived of its land. No section of the community except women had to suffer any disabilities. There was clear provision against the oppression of the poor. Yet the best intentions of the law-givers would be powerless against class interests. With the advent of monarchy in Israel, a class of bureaucrats came into being that was the cause of much oppression, bringing into existence an in-built system of exploitation. Unbearable tax burdens were imposed on the peasants to pay the salaries of the officials. Peasants could not meet the new exorbitant demands made on them. Apparently it was King David who first appointed the new class of officials.[10] This had become necessary as he had decided to model his administration on the Egyptian pattern. Solomon's reign put even heavier burden on the peasantry. As a result, many peasants lost their land which the law had tried to protect. For the peasants, monarchy had turned out to be a curse. The landless peasants slipped gradually into a marginal existence very nearly approaching slavery. The exploitation of the poor drew fire from the Hebrew prophets. The Hebrew dream of egalitarianism had vanished, replaced by yet another dream of the Hebrew empire.

The class of people in Hebrew society known as the *Anawim* was made up of the poor and the landless. They gradually turned into a social class, whom the highbrows despised.[11] They were the śūdras of Jewish society. The term *Anawim* did not have any ethnic connotation. The Jewish law had made no provision for a low social class.

In contrast to the Hebrew law, the *śāstras* were wholly innocent of any intention to forge an egalitarian society. They clearly set out to create a class of servants. As we have seem, man does not need any legal sanction to create institutions of exploitation and oppression. He does it despite unambiguous legal strictures against his doing so. Hebrew society further had an institution that fiercely militated against exploitation. The Hebrew prophets came into conflict with the forces of exploitation. It was not only the grasping rich who came under fire but also the priests who cared only for their fees, the judicial officers who throttled justice for financial gains and all those who were far too comfortable in their palaces. Like the saints of other cultures, the prophets proclaimed that God was the friend of the poor and the afflicted. The unpalatable social message of the prophets did not make them popular. Prophets have always been inconvenient people who disturbed others. They not only denounced exploitation, but were also careful to nurture hope in the heart of the downtrodden. They dreamed of a day when the hills would be levelled, all valleys filled, the rough paths smoothened and all tears wiped away from every eye. This was the refrain that would echo through the centuries.

Though Indian society did not possess the institution of prophets, it had its dissenters from the traditional social philosophy of the brāhmaṇas. But the voices were less strident than those of the Hebrew prophets. And the gods were against them, while the Hebrew prophets had God on their side. The gods of the brāhmaṇas had willed the social system. Hence it was not possible to reform the system; one could only reject it outright. The founders of heterodox sects chose precisely that path.

An indepth psycho-social study is yet to be attempted of the origin and growth of the *Dharmaśāstras* and related literature. We stand to gain immensely from such a study. It could reveal how certain groups manipulated legislative power to their advantage, to ensure privileges, to exempt themselves from penal sanction, to ward off all threats to their own authority, to raise themselves to semi-godly status and how they managed to do all this by controlling the system of education. None could better exemplify the truth of Edmund Burke's saying that power corrupts and absolute power corrupts absolutely. Leaving the destiny of any society to be decided by a particular group within a community is fraught with perils. The group is likely to create new myths to safeguard its interests. The heavens bend before the one who has the ability to create myths. History teaches us that the groups that possessed power have rarely surrendered it willingly. Those who refuse to learn from history, it has been well said, are condemned to repeat its mistakes.

The Men of Letters and Society

The view of society that the classical writers have projected is not uniform. For the most part, these authors uphold the brahmanic view of society and their value system. Their society is organised on the *varṇa* pattern with severely restricted interaction between the different sections. The rules of intermarriage are adhered to. The classical writers dealt with only a stratum of society with which they were familiar. Their characters and their lives centred around the king's court. The protagonist was invariably a royal personage or a nymph. Kālidāsa is a representative of the period.

There is yet no consensus on the exact time Kālidāsa lived. A majority of scholars seem to favour 5th century A.D. In Kālidāsa's time the Gupta empire had reached the pinnacle of its glory. The period was one of economic prosperity, comparative peace and luxurious living by the upper strata of society. These strata enjoyed leisure and benefits of economic growth. It was they who mattered in the eyes of the authors of the period, and they figured prominently in their works. Kālidāsa can be hardly credited with having portrayed the society of his day.

The world of Kālidāsa is peopled with heavenly nymphs, who shuttle between heaven and earth. *Yakṣas*, kings who are inexplicably struck with debilitating amnesia and mythical characters. There is an air of unreality about the world in which Kālidāsa's men and women move.

One does not hope to learn form Kālidāsa how the majority of the population lived and worked and struggled. We do not hear of the men who built the beautiful palaces and temples, not of the men who wove the fine garments or fashioned the precious stones and ornaments. We know nothing of a regular army of servants which every *nāgarka* seemed to command. It was the duty of a court poet to keep his patrons amused. This he did with finesse. The *nāgarka* had little interest in knowing what it cost to keep him amused. He had of course very refined tastes in clothes, food, arts, literature and women. The poet could find a ready ear if he spoke of these things.

Kālidāsa appears to believe that Manu's code is fit to be followed to the last iota. His ideal king observes Manu's code in letter and spirit. Every female willing to contract a 'love marriage' eventually turns out to be a nymph or of royal blood. This stratagem absolves the poet of the duty to follow caste rules governing marriage. The poet dare not depict an open violation of caste rules. The society of his day would not brook open disregard of accepted norms.

Kālidāsa seems to favour free sex for both men and women in his *Meghadūta*. One wonders if the youths of Nicala mountain, where the Cloud Messenger was requested to tarry, and whose amorous exploits the city elders fondly related, observed caste restrictions. One should like to ask about the women of Ujjain who were making their way to their rendezvous through darkness, which a needle could not pierce, if they were choosy about their patrons.[12] The Cloud Messenger is asked to light their path to speed them on. Kālidāsa seems to imply that while arranged as well as love marriages had to observe caste restrictions, free sex was unhampered by any such inhibition.

Śūdraka does not occupy himself with the concerns of Kālidāsa. Śūdraka makes no attempt to keep up appearances. In his classic work, *Mṛcchakaṭikā*, Śūdraka has broken the conventions of his time. The hero of the play, Cārudatta, is a merchant-brāhmaṇa. Vasantasena, a courtesan of great charm, falls in love with him. Both have been described as the pride of Ujjain. It is Vasantasena who makes the first move. Though in popular view a courtesan is like a creeper that grows by the roadside and her person is an article for sale as Viṭa tells Vasantasena, the playwright regards Vasantasena a good enough match for a brāhmaṇa. And the story is being played out in Ujjain, the metropolis of India. Yet it is not Cārudatta who wins the heart of the spectator and the reader. It is rather Vasantasena and Maitreya, Cārudatta's confidant, who endear themselves to the spectator. Cārudatta snivels and snuffles endlessly over his lost fortune. He lacks manliness in the face of misfortune. On his way to the place of execution, his executioners, the caṇḍālas, bolster up his courage. One rarely meets such learned caṇḍālas, who prolong the formalities before execution, hoping that some unforeseen event might intervene on behalf of the condemned man. Their hope is realised when the wicked king is overthrown and the liberator stays the execution.

The servants we meet in Śūdraka's play are not the soulless, grovelling creatures we might expect. Kumbhilaka, Vasantasena's servant, has both wit and self-confidence. Maitreya is unable to answer the questions Kumbhilaka puts to him. Madanika, though a harlot and Vasantasena's attendant, has a quiet dignity about her. Incidentally she is being courted by Sarvilaka, a house-breaker, who, while making a breach in the wall, takes care to leave a sample of his skill, as befits a star disciple of Yogācārya.[13] Though a brāhmaṇa, he has only taken to the discreditable profession of house-breaking for the sake of Madanika, the idol of his heart. The two guards watching the exit of the city to apprehend Aryaka, the great rebel who has just escaped from prison, are comradely until a quarrel erupts between them. It is only then that they think of their caste affiliation; 'Camar' is the epithet they fling at each other.[14]

There is a vast gulf between the world of Kālidāsa and that of Śūdraka, though they were not far apart in time. Śūdraka speaks of harlots and thieves, impoverished brāhmaṇa crooks, inept judicial officers and weaklings of all types. In *Mṛcchakaṭikā*, one meets people one can recognise in real life. There is greatness and villainy, nobility and hypocrisy, love and hatred. Harlots are invested with great charm and humanity. Greatness in not the monopoly of any particular class. One meets men and women of flesh and blood, not as if they were characters of another world. Śūdraka obviously rubbed shoulders with a cross-section of humanity.

In *Mālatīmādhava* of Bhavabhūti, who probably flourished in the 7th century A.D., the partners of love marriage turn out to be of the proper caste. Mādhava, 'the dark-hued youth', at first believed to be a commoner, and a student from Vidarbha, is later revealed to have royal blood in his veins, so that he makes a good match for Mālatī, the minister's daughter.

In the play the author assigns Buddhist nuns roles which might strike one as rather unorthodox. They not only show keen interest in the affairs of the heart, unite grieving hearts which cruel destiny keeps apart, but even excite tender feelings in hearts where they are not found. The exertions of the nuns in this matter are so painstaking and so intense that one wonders how they managed to find time for strictly religious pursuits as befits members of *sanghas*. Apart from the nuns, the world of Bhavabhūti is peopled with idle and highly distracted youths who appear to be living on fat stipends from their guardians.

The women of Bhavabhūti seem to enjoy considerable freedom of movement. We see bevies of damsels mounted on elephants, singing songs of joy, interrupted by the chewing of perfumed betels.[15] We come across a form of self-immolation rarely met with elsewhere. Bhurivasu, Mālatī's father and minister in the kingdom, supposing his daughter to be dead, and overcome by grief, prepares to immolate himself in flames.

Many of Bhavabhūti's characters give the impression of being denizens of a make-believe world as it deals with the doings of high society. It is a world most people know of or live in. Its lovers bore us with their incessant and lengthy protestations of love for their loved ones and we rarely meet them in situations other than these pining and moonings.

The works of Daṇḍin, Damodaragupta and Kṣemendra are separated by several centuries, yet they are inspired by a common purpose, namely, to present a critique of contemporary society. They subject their times and manners to merciless criticism. Among their characters are harlots and tricksters, princes and nuns, pimps and courtesans, charlatans and love-lorn lovers. Daṇḍin's *Daśakumāracarita* is an example of the satire the above authors have attempted. In the society that is portrayed here, we see a complete breakdown of traditional morality and ethical values. It is a society which has been corrupted to the core, and an all-pervasive malaise grips the various social strata. It certainly is not a society organised on the principles advocated by Manu.

No institution of society escapes Daṇḍin's censorious scrutiny. Religion, court life, kings and their inane pursuits, the hollow claims of the peddlers of cures for both body and soul – all come in for severe judgement. Brāhmaṇas, Buddhists and Jaina Digambaras and nuns do not appear in the best of light. Religion's lofty teachings are held up to ridicule. The gods themselves are not spared. The pious pretensions of the brāhmaṇas are lampooned. Daṇḍin does all this with great flair, humour and forcefulness.[16]

Daṇḍin is believed to have flourished before the post-Harṣa period. It is during a time of comparative ease and peace that social institutions degenerate and morality declines as we find in Daṇḍin's work. Daṇḍin's is not a historical but a satirical work. His protest was directed against the prevailing values and the hypocrisy of his time.

Damodaragupta belonged to a much later period than Daṇḍin. He has administered blows as powerful as Daṇḍin's on the preoccupations of his time. The title of his well-known work, *Kuṭṭanīmata*, clearly indicates the subject matter, namely, the world of harlots. The author, was a minister of Kashmir king Jayāpīda.[17] The work is a satire on the moral degeneracy of the time the author lived. In the form of 'Advice from a Procuress', it focuses the searchlight on the uglier side of life. The work is a primer on the art of seduction.

Another author who has attempted criticism of society was Kṣemendra, poet-dramatist-didactic writer of the 11th century. In his expose of the morals of his contemporaries, we meet courtesans, harlots, procuresses and the victims of their wiles. His *Kalāvilāsa* is a manual for tricksters, quacks, adulterators and harlots, written in a satirical vein.[18] Kṣemendara has also several didactic works to his credit.

Alberuni was one of the most distinguished visitors to India in the Middle Ages. He accompanied Muhamad of Gazni to India. A great scholar himself, he made a sympathetic and deep study of Indian sciences, religion and philosophy. He has left us much valuable information on medieval society.

Alberuni speaks of the relative positions of the four *varṇas* and adds that there is no great difference between the vaiśyas and the śūdras.[19] Trade was no longer the monopoly of the vaiśyas. All *varṇas* without distinction, including the brāhmaṇas, had taken to trade and this had considerably influenced and determined the fortunes of the vaiśyas. They would virtually disappear from Indian society as a separate group. Adoption of trade by the śūdras had brought them closer to the vaiśyas. At least in certain regions, the distance between them had so narrowed as to make them practically indistinguishable. Even the *Dharmaśāstras* had to concede the inevikable by permitting the śudras to trade. In effect trade was an open profession. This was indeed a great concession but the concession merely demonstrated in which direction the wind of change was blowing.

Alberuni also tells us that people belonging to all the four *varṇas* stayed in the same inns and even dined at the same place.[20] The observation is significant, since the practice differs markedly from what was in force in later times. In Sher Shah's times the brāhmaṇas refused to share inns with others and he had separate inns built for them.

Alberuni further informs us that there were eight groups or 'guilds' as he terms them, of an *antyaja*. They are: the fuller, shoe-maker, juggler, basket and shield maker, tailor, fisherman, hunter of wild animals and birds and the weaver. Except the fuller, the weaver and shoe-maker, all other *antyajas* inter-marry among themselves freely. The *antyajas* live outside the villages of the four castes.[21] Alberuni speaks of another class of people who stand outside any of the classes noted above. This class is made up of the Hadi the Doma (Domba), the Badhatau and the caṇḍalas. These people formed a class by themselves because they were occupied with 'dirty works'. 'In fact', the scholar adds, 'they are considered like illegitimate children'.[22] He then refers to the popular belief that they are descendant and from the union of a śūdra father and a brāhmaṇa mother. In Alberuni's day brāhmaṇas ate meat. What is more, they had the privilege of having the flesh of the rhinoceros reserved for their use.

Alberuni was sincerely appreciative of whatever was good in Indian thought. He especially points out the achievements in mathematics. Nonetheless, he notes that great insights are often hopelessly mixed with legends and myths, like precious gems hidden in a heap of rubble. He remarks on the Indians' inability to separate fact from fiction, scientific data from mere fancy.

Alberuni's testimony goes to show that various grades among the *antyajas* had become sharply distinguishable. The position of the *caṇḍālas* and communities similarly placed in the social hierarchy is clearly marked in relation to the higher grade of *antyajas*, such as the shoe-maker and the weaver. Alberuni's remarks on the *antyajas* reminds us of what Fa-Hien, a 5th century A.D. visitor to India, notes about the caṇḍālas, or *Chan-chelas* as he calls them, that they were viewed with revulsion. Whenever they entered a town or market, they had to strike a piece of wood to make their presence known to the inhabitants, and thus forewarned, they would be on their guard against contact with them.[23]

Bāṇabhaṭṭa, writing two centuries later during the reign of Harṣa, does not show extreme revulsion for the caṇḍālas. In Bāṇa's *Kādambarī* a caṇḍāla girl enters the royal court with a talking parrot.[24] Harṣa himself had strong leaning towards Buddhism and his kingdom is often pictured as a Buddhist kingdom. It is strange that Bāṇa, a contemporary of Harṣa, should not have been fully acquainted with the prejudices of his period.

Kalhāṇa in his historical work, *Rājataraṅgiṇi*, has left us a mine of information on the conditions in 12th century Kashmir. Though he claims to have made a close study of his sources, his accuracy is in doubt when he speaks of the times far removed from his own. Kalhāṇa also helps us to solve many riddles of Indian history with his chronicle of the reign of Lalitāditya Jayāpīḍa who carved out an empire in the 8th century.

Kalhāṇa was the son of a minister. Thus he had a very good opportunity to acquaint himself with Kashmir politics. Kalhāṇa has touched upon a variety of matters relating to Kashmir society which are of great interest to us. He has spoken in details of the Kayasthas. The term, Kayastha, it is clear, did not refer to a particular caste but to the class of officialdom which was not restricted to any particular caste group. People of all communities could join it.[25] The Kayasthas were very powerful, corrupt and their influence was felt everywhere. The basis of the division of Kashmir society was not *varṇas*, but occupation.

Kalhāṇa was equally critical of the brāhmaṇas and sneer at their ignorance and arrogance. Yet because of their easy access to learning and their status, the brāhmaṇas still exercised considerable influence. Kalhāṇa does not think this influence was all to the good of the state. They did not assume the larger-than-life posture they fancied elsewhere in India. We find that there was free intercourse between various sections of the population.

Women enjoyed much freedom and were not segregated. Some of them took a prominent part in the affairs of the state.[26] We may conclude then that women, not merely elite women, received education of a high order. *Satī* was known, but not obligatory. Even a sister would sometimes demonstrate her love for her dead brother by immolating herself along with his body. Unlike the later practice, it was not merely the dear ones of the dead who immolated themselves but courtesans and attendants too did so on the death of their patron. A woman at her husband's death had three options before her; to remain a widow, to perform *satī*, or to remarry. Kalhāṇa also speaks of the widespread immorality among certain classes of women. It must be borne in mind that Kalhāṇa was not kindly disposed towards women. He found them a mystery. 'In no manner', he declared, 'can one be sure of women'.[27]

In Kashmir, the caṇḍālas did not excite intense revulsion as is indicated by the *śāstras* or some Buddhist sources. The Dombas and the caṇḍālas were not treated as untouchables. The curse of untouchability was unknown in Kashmir. King Cakravarman married a Domba girl. According to Kalhāṇa, Dombas were good musicians. The caṇḍālas could join the army; they were also royal bodyguards. These facts show a view of the lower classes vastly different from what we meet with in many other regions of India. The brāhmaṇas did not quite relish the idea of a Domba queen entering the temple. But there was little they could do about the matter. Yet Queen Hansi's visit to the temple speaks much for the tolerance in Kashmir society. We may rest assured, that her visit did not evoke horror in the minds of masses.

That the tolerance in Kashmir was a tradition is shown by the story of the legendry engineer, Suyya. A great famine struck in the reign of Avantivarman in the 9th century. Suyya was able to build a dam across the river and thus irrigate large tracts of land. Thus a catastrophe was averted.

What was remarkable about Suyya was his humble origin. He is said to have been the adopted son of a caṇḍāla, a street cleaner woman called 'Suyyā'. She had come upon an abandoned infant in the course of her duties and had lovingly brought up the child naming him after herself. Bright and lovely, the child grew up to be very learned and full of original ideas. Eventually he caught the eye of the king himself. Suyya was allowed to put his novel idea into execution which resulted in new life for Kashmir and its people. To his great credit, engineer Suyya never disowned his origin, but honoured the memory of his foster-mother by naming a bridge after her, thus immortalising the lowly street cleaner.[28]

We have been presented with an account of 13th century Magadha by a visitor that draws a depressing picture of the situation. Dharmaswāmin, a Tibetan monk, lived in India from 1334-1336 and studied at the Buddhist university of Nalanda. He has told us about the utter confusion that prevailed in the region. The Turuṣkas (Turks) were in control of the region. Bands of these soldiers roamed the countryside. When the marauders came, even the kings took refuge in the forest, emerging from it only when the danger was past. Once while Dharmaswāmin was on a boat crossing the Ganga, a Turuṣkas was bent on dispossessing him of his begging-bowl. Only on the intervention of a lay person did the Turuṣkas desist form the attempt.

At another time while crossing a swollen river he was swept away by the current. Noticing a dark man standing on the bank, Dharmaswamin shouted to him to save him. But the man replied that he was an untouchable and, therefore, was unable to come to his rescue.[29] But the monk lived to tell his tale. It may be recalled here that it was Buddhist country.

The monk was on his return journey to Tibet. When he reached Vaiśālī, he learned that the people of the city were in great panic, hearing that the Turuṣkas were about to swoop down on them. Most of the inhabitants fled the city, carrying what they could.[30]

The period was one of intense political turmoil. There was a breakdown of authority and there was no one the people could turn to for protection. Yet it is precisely such turbulent times that have formed the background for great religious awakening. The 14th and

15th centuries saw the birth of many great saints. The period witnessed the blossoming of the *bhakti* movement.

NOTES

1. All direct quotations from the Dharmaśāstras are from the translation by Manmath Nath Dutta, *Dharam Shastra : Hindu Religious Codes*, New Delhi, Cosmos Publications, 1978, Throughout the present book, the terms Dharmaśāstra and Dharmasamhitā are used inter-changeably.
2. *CHI*, II, p.306 ff.
3. *Parāśara Samhitā*, 1:23.
4. G.S. Ghurye, 1969, Appendix D.
5. K.A. Nilakanta Sastri, 1980, p.60 ff.
6. See *Manu Samhitā*, VIII:137.
7. For directions on agriculture, see *Book of Levitcus* 19:5; 19:23.
8. Roland de Vaux, *Ancient Israel*, New York, McGraw-Hill Book Company, 1965, p.87 ff.
9. Deuteronomy 23:15.
10. John L. McKenzie, *The Old Testament Without Illusion*, New York, Image Books, Doubleday Company, 1980, p.234.
11. One of India's best known Biblical scholars, George Soares-Prabhu has attempted to show that the *anawim* were a social class. See 'The Biblical Poor, a Social Class', *Vidyajyoti*, A Journal of Theological Reflection, New Delhi, 1985, p.322.
12. The two allusions to the *Meghadūta* are to the English Version, *Kalidasa Translation of Shakuntala and Other Works* (Everyman's Library ed.) by Arthur W. Ryder, London, J.M. Dent & Sons, p.192.
13. Act III.
14. Act VI.
15. Act VI, Scene 2.
16. A.B. Keith, 1961, pp.301-3.
17. *Ibid.*, p.236.
18. S.N. Dasgupta (Gen. Ed.), HSL, p.408
19. Edward C. Sachau (tr.) *Alberuni's India*, London, Kegan Paul, Trends Trubner & Co., 1910, p.101.
20. *Ibid.*, p.101.
21. *Ibid.*, p.101-2.
22. *Ibid.*, p.102.
23. Ramusat Klaproth and Landress (tr.) *The Pilgrimage of Fa-Hien*, Calcutta Bangbasi Office, 1913, p.108.
24. *HSL*, p.330.
25. S. Dhar, 1978, p.21.
26. *Ibid.*, p.23.
27. *Ibid.*, p.27.
28. G.S. Ghurye, 1969, p.315.
29. George Roerich, (tr.) *Biography of Dharmaswamin*, Patna, Jaiswal Research Institute, 1959, p.86.
30. *Ibid.*, p.62.

4

THE BHAKTI MOVEMENT AND THE QUEST FOR EQUALITY

THE SOCIO-RELIGIOUS history of the medieval period has been deeply marked by the growth and spread of the *bhakti* movement. It was like a powerful stream that burst upon a parched farmland, irrigating it with its life-giving waters to make it bloom into riotous greenery once again. The stream of the *bhakti* movement was to radically alter the very concept and practice of religion, to enrich it, taking it out of the realm of empty phrases, mechanical rites and sacrifices and bringing the deity down to the world of his devotees. *Bhakti* liberated the god from his lofty heaven, where he had remained inaccessible, supremely blissful in his heavely isolation. Owing to the *bhakti* movement the divinity left his heaven and came to dwell in the image the mortals had made.

Bhakti, Its Ancient Roots

The *bhakti* strain in Indian religion has had a long tradition behind it. We can find elements of *bhakti* in the later Upaniṣads such as *Svetāśvatara* and *Praśna* Upaniṣads. Both are post-Buddha works and were almost certainly influenced by the new current of the worship of Buddha. A personalised religion and the stress on loving attachment to deity owe much to Buddhism and Jainism. The new current was to leave its mark on the brahmanic religion. How widely diffused the trend had become is proved by the work of Aśvaghoṣa, a 1st century A.D. Buddhist writer. Many of his stories centre on the theme of a person surrendering himself and taking refuge in Buddha.[1] The *Bhagavadgītā* extols the surrender of a devotee of Kṛṣṇa as the highest path of religion. Aśvaghoṣa and the author of the *Gītā* may have been contemporaries. Aśvaghoṣa may even have antedated the latter. In the brahmanic tradition, however, the path of *bhakti* was not universally accepted. The *Gītā* itself would be regarded as rather unorthodox by some brāhmaṇas.

How widely known was the way of surrender throughout India is seen from the writings of Tiruvaḷḷuvar in the South. Tiruvaḷḷuvar was deeply influenced by Buddhist and Jain teachings. He did not represent the brahmanic tradition. With his roots in the Dravidian culture, Tiruvaḷḷuvar would have found greater concordance between the Buddhist teachings and the values of his own native tradition.

From what Greek writers tell us, it seems clear that Śiva worship was more popular among the people of the mountains[2]. In fact, Śiva may have been a mountain god. Later the worship apparently spread southward and there it assumed several features of the cult of the Dravidian god Murugan. The trident, Murugan's weapon, was appropriated by Śiva.[3]

Mathura on the bank of the Yamuna had long been established as a centre of the worship of Kṛṣṇa. Kṛṣṇa, the tribal hero, would gradually displace many other gods and would be identified with the all-pervading Brahmaṇ himself. The *Gītā* is a proof that Kṛṣṇa had established an unassailable position.

The Purāṇas were brilliant in their conception. The composition of these works bears ample testimony to the fusion of cultures of the aboriginal peoples and the Āryans. The Purāṇas point to the way an alien creed gradually inculturated itself in the beliefs and myths of a people and thus came to terms with them. Myths of validation were created to lend justification to totemistic cult. These myths were also a tacit recognition of the power of the popular beliefs. The totem animals found their way into the pantheon of the brahamnic religion. The composition of Purāṇas marks the final phase of the incorporation of tribal religion and its myths. Native gods would continue to find a place in the brahamnic pantheon, either as incarnations of the traditional gods or as their alternative forms.[4]

The Purāṇas filled a genuine need of the masses. They presented the gods not as dwelling in their isolation but revealing themselves and taking a lively interest in human affairs. The Purāṇas show forth a new face of the gods, not as jealous unpredictable powers taking arbitrary decisions affecting the earthly beings but as superior beings concerned about their spiritual conditions. This concern is expressed through his appearance in the form of historical human personalities. The great gulf between the deity and human has never been so effectively bridged or reduced. The Purāṇas were to have a profound influence in shaping the *bhakti* movement and thus the religious life of the masses.

The medieval *bhakti* movement that was to transform the religious practice of the people had its origin in South India. The Nayanār saints sang the praises of Śiva in songs that grew into the *bhakti* literature. Many of these saints were constantly on the move, singing ecstatically of their god. This cult would grow into a powerful movement.

The Āḷwārs of the Tamil country gave a great impetus to the *bhakti* movement. A succession of twelve poet-saints founded and nurtured the new tradition of total absorption and emotional attachment to the incarnations of Viṣṇu.[5] *Bhāgavata Purāṇa* that has provided the inspiration for much *bhakti* literature probably had its origin in the land of the Kaveri and the Tamraparni.[6] The twelfth century philosopher Madhava was deeply influenced by this work. Among the Āḷwārs are found members of lower castes. They didn't turn away even outcastes. Karaikkal Ammal (A.D. 6th century), whose writings have been included in the Śaiva literature, was an untouchable woman. It would be rather simplistic to assume that all distinctions in castes vanished from the midst of the adherents of the new cults. The reality was far from it. Other influences were being brought to bear on an individual which frequently proved stronger. The great philosopher Śankara is a case in point.

Śankara spearheaded a revivalist movement in the brahmanic religion. For this purpose he established a chain of centres of learning in different parts of India which were to be the rallying points in the revival campaign . If we are to believe some scholars, Śankara did not confine himself to merely popularising his ideas. In his zeal for brahmanic religion, he is believed to have used great violence and probably had a hand in the destruction of the Buddhist centre at Nagarjunkaonda in Andhra Pradesh. Śankara could not have perpetrated the deed without the connivance of the rulers of the region. The Cālukyas ruled Andhra at that time. Śankara is credited with having perfected the philosophical system known as Advaita (Non-Dualist) Vedanta. The system upholds the identity of Brahman and other beings. The plurality of beings is an illusion. Śankara held in his hand the most powerful instrument for forging a society founded on the principle of perfect equality of all humans. His heart seems to have overruled his head. He denied to śūdras the right to study the Vedas. Śankara explains away the case of Jānaśruti.[7] Śankara maintains that if a śūdra shows the capacity to understand the truth, he must have studied the Vedas in a previous existence.[8]

According to Śankara salvation is not gained by the Vedic sacrifices and rituals. He taught the sufficiency of the path of knowledge (*jnāna*). If salvation was not attainable through Vedic sacrifices, the śūdra lost nothing by a ban on his performing them. Nothing stood in his way to prevent him from acquiring the highest merit. But now Śankara stepped in. Like the compilers of the *Dharmaśāstras*, he never winced at the thought of undermining the Vedas. Śankara declared that the people of lower status were not entitled to the saving knowledge unless they rose to a higher status through the path of *samsara*.[9]

Sankara was nevertheless an ardent devotee of Śiva. Śankara must have come under the influence of the *bhakti* movement during his sojourn in the Tamil country and his association with Kanci.

Śankara allowed his passion for orthodoxy to get the better of his philosophical principles. While in theory he was prepared to grant that anyone was capable of attaining the highest knowledge, he denied the non-twice-born the right to aspire to it. A great philosopher had failed to be consistent.

Despite Śankara's efforts to bolster orthodoxy, the *bhakti* movement was sowing the seeds of a new attitude towards social relations. Birth as a determinant of one's eternal destiny, as Śankara held, would cease to be the all-important factor in one's quest for a more intense religious life. The trend was irreversible. There would be much opposition to the liberal view even within the *bhakti* movement, not to speak of those outside.

Madhava taught a religion founded on the *Bhāgavata Purāṇa*. Its essential feature was adoration of Kṛṣṇa. The way of *bhakti* was the way of salvation. Madhava vigorously opposed Śankara's theories. For his pains he was persecuted by the followers of Śankara. Madhava had his satisfaction by portraying Śankara as a reincarnation of Manimat, a mythical demon.[10]

It was the Vaiṣṇavas who first introduced the use of vernacular singing into temple worship. The lyrics of the Āḷwārs added a new quality to worship, making it more appealing to the devotees.

The *bhakti* movement would make a valuable contribution to the growth of vernacular literature. An enormous volume of writings would be produced by the followers of the twin streams of *bhakti* – Saiva and Vaiṣṇavism.

The life and writings of Rāmānuja marks the full blossoming of

Vaiṣṇavism. Rāmānuja gave a philosophical foundation to the movement of *bhakti*. He was the spiritual heir to the tradition of the Āḷwārs. His reputation of being a scholar, the respect he commanded and the authority he wielded helped him to strengthen the movement.

Unlike Śankara, Rāmānuja, the 11th century philosopher saint, taught that salvation is to be gained not through knowledge but through *bhakti* and grace (*prasāda*).

Bhakti is man's reaching out to God quietly and meditatively. Through *bhakti* the soul becomes more and more conscious of its relation to God until it surrenders itself totally to him. Hence *bhakti* is not an emotional state but it entails the fuller knowledge of God.[11]

Rāmānuja maintained that no distinction should be made between the lovers of God. Love requires no sanction of scriptures. He defended the equality of all in worship. While he held that only the twice-born should study the Vedas, the path of *bhakti* was open to all, even to the untouchable pariahs. He is believed to have opened the doors of the temple at Melkote to the pariahs.[12] Thus even though Rāmānuja upheld a measure of equality in worship, he still regarded the *varṇa* system sacrosanct.

The *bhakti* movement generated surge of good fellow-feelings. Philanthropic activities were also begun under its impact. Alms giving, houses for wayfarers, digging of public wells and of course building of temples were the visible outcome of the new spirit.[13] Land-grants to temples was an expression of munificence of the rulers. Grants of land were also made to brāhmaṇas and agrahāras (brāhmaṇa settlements).

Strangely enough, these grants were to lead to the concentration of land in the hands of the brāhmaṇas. As a result brāhmaṇas became owners of large landholdings. The new phenomenon of brāhmaṇa landlords appeared on the Indian scene. Large holdings naturally necessitated the expenditure of much time and energy in their management. Power came with wealth and the brāhmaṇas became an economically strong group. We have many epigraphical records of brāhmaṇas being settled adjacent to temples or brought in from elsewhere to perform temple services. The period thus saw the strengthening of the hold of the brāhmaṇas.[14] Temple worship once regarded as unorthodox practice, proved the saving of the priestly class, ensuring it economic security. Vaiṣṇavism laid great emphasis on communal worship. The new interest led to the construction of many new temples. Large investments were made in the renewal and constructions of shrines of popular gods and goddesses. Even private individuals took to building temples and this enabled them to receive an honourable mention in the contemporary inscriptions.

Bhakti and Social Mobility

Social reform or reconstruction of society on the principle of equality was never one of the aims of the *bhakti* movement. What the advocates of the path of *bhakti* conceded was that no group should be barred from adopting it. Everyone is free to approach the Lord through the path of devotion. They made this concession even while upholding the *dharma* of *cāturvarṇya*, which, according to them, was the basic social order enjoined by the scriptures. This was the position taken by Rāmānuja and other Vaiṣṇavas. Imparting of religious instruction to the lower classes was a natural corollary to the liberal attitude towards socially backward groups. Epigraphical records show that some temples did organise religious instruction on the temple premises. That instruction may not have been of a high order and was probably limited to the Epics and the Purāṇas. The temple schools, we may assume, did meet the basic educational needs of those sections of the population which aspired to rise socially. The śūdras were the chief beneficiaries of the new educational opportunities. The untouchables of course would have been excluded from the group gathered at the temple premises. Even before this time, many śūdras did acquire some education. But now there were greater opportunities for doing so.

Education naturally opened up more avenues of occupations. The śūdras had already entered the profession of trade. As a result many śūdras managed to acquire landed property and improve their economic situation. We saw earlier how the gap between the vaiśyas and śūdras had narrowed in Alberuni's time. Yet the identification of the śūdras as a landed class was much later development. Some śūdra communities manage to shed their śūdrā status and moved upward. This seems to have been true of the Kayasthas. They enjoyed a low caste status at first. The phenomenal rise of the Kayasthas was a post-ninth century development.[15] Their metamorphosis into an upper caste may have been linked to their entry into administrative service. The Kayasthas had become quite a respectable people by the 11th century. Candella King Kīrtivarman (1070-90) gifted a prosperous village to a Kayastha.[16] Kṣemendra, an 11th century writer of Kashmir speaks of the Kayasthas as a group of officials invested with great power and equally great capacity for wickedness.[17] In the following century, Kalhāṇa employs the term Kayastha as an equivalent of State official.[18] This non-casteist use of the term did not gain currency elsewhere in India.

Later the Kayasthas entered the service of the Muslim rulers. Quick to grab the opportunities, they went on to improve their position, both politically and economically. The Maratha leader Shivaji had Kayasthas among his top military officers. In modern times in States such as West Bengal they claimed a status inferior only to the brāhmaṇas. They hold a position of great advantage in other States too of North India, especially U.P., Bihar and Rajasthan.

Today the Kayasthas are looked upon as a progressive community with a somewhat liberal attitude towards women and their education. Education has in fact been the key to their rise in society.

Other groups also rose in society, perhaps on a less impressive manner. Migration to a new locality, adoption of a new occupation or a combination of both and adoption of new name were some of the methods used to climb socially. According to a fifth century Mandso (Madhya Pradesh) inscription, some silk-workers who migrated there from Gujarat adopted a new occupation.[19]

The *Viṣṇu Purāṇa* states that in *Kaliyuga* the vaiśyas will give up their traditional calling of trade and raising of cattle to take up occupations in the arts, such as acting and music.[20] This is an official recognition of the changes that were taking place in the occupational pattern of the *varṇas*. The vaiśya now had no occupation that was specifically his. The change in the occupation of the vaiśya had occurred long before Alberuni's time and it was noted in *Viṣṇu-Purāṇa* believed to be the first of the Purāṇas.

The expansion of the kṣatriya community was a striking development of the early medieval period. Many ambitious tribal chiefs succeeded in the post-Harṣa centuries to hew out a niche for themselves. The next step was to claim kṣatriya status. The Pratīhāras in Gujarat, the Ceddis in Bundelkhand and the Kalacuris in Upper India, the Seuna-Yadavas in the Deccan and the Rāṣṭrakūṭas on the Konkan coast established themselves at this time. An illustrious ancestry had to be found for them linking them with either Solar race or the Lunar race.

For legitimation of their position, the upstart princes had to lean heavily on the brāhmaṇas whom they had to placate. The price often was heavy. It consisted of substantial gifts in the form of land grants, cash and, of course, the indispensable feastings. So it was that the Solar and the Lunar races swelled rapidly. The new princes posed as the guardians of the traditional religion. Their zeal in this role compensated for any feeling of inadequancy, arising from their humble origins. They had no option but to play up to the brāhmaṇas. As the kinglets were illiterate they had to rely heavily on the brāmaṇas.

In the medieval age we come across a form of deification of the brāhmaṇas at which the gods themselves would blush. He was now the ruler of the universe, because he was the very source of law. He was above the law, as the king's law did not apply to him. He was above punishment. Metādhiti, a medieval commentator of Manu, would go so far as to say that not even monetary fines could be imposed on a brāhmaṇa.[21] There was only one kind of power that was not accessible to him. The brāhmaṇa began to cast greedy glances at that too. Even that the kingly bastion would fall before him.

In most cultures a symbiotic relationship has existed between the priesthood and the monarchy. The symbiosis worked for the good of both. It was so in Indian society too. The kings needed the priest-brāhmaṇas to legitimise their positions, defend their kṣatriyahood. The priests needed gifts and stipends from the kings.

The brāhmaṇas frequently created a geneology for the upstart kṣatriya kings. The art of poetry was prostituted to glorify the person of the king with the court poets vying with one another in lavishing praises on their patrons.

It was not merely the art of poetry that suffered this fate at the courts. All arts were vulgarised in idolising the monarch. The wealth of the kingdom was at his disposal to achieve this. Today when tourists view the mementoes of yesteryear in the palaces, they may not suspect that all arts existed solely for the glorification of the divine person of the king.

The king owned all wealth. He could take anything from his subjects when fancy gripped him. The fiction of divine origin of kingly authority had been invented just for this purpose. All pretty girls too were his for the asking, not infrequently without the formality of asking.

The *varṇāśrama* suited the kings perfectly. The system ensured the existence of a permanent servant class, and it enshrined the principle of division. What the king feared was the principle of unity. The population was most unlikely to unite and rise against whatever injustice he might perpetrate, as long as *varṇa-dharma* prevailed. Hadn't the brāhamṇas made him the guardian of all *dharma*? The most important part of his duties was to safeguard the *varṇa* system from being sullied. The priests were not worried over his failure on other fronts. He might loot the people and thrive on the unrequited labour of the working classes whose *dharma* was to enhance his happiness.

Rise of Feudalism

The post-Harṣa period saw not only the rise of many kingdoms throughout the land, it also witnessed the ominous growth of feudalism. This development would have far-reaching consequence on socio-economic fronts and the institution of feudalism would remain for centuries to come apart of the Indian scene.

The practice of making grants of villages by monarchs was knowr as far back as the Mauryan times.The monasteries to which the villages were gifted were probably entitled only to the income from them. The Sātavāhana rulers too granted villages to brāhmaṇas and other sects. But feudalism took on a far more vicious form later.

Feudalism in the strict sense is believed to have had its origin during the Gupta period when the power to collect taxes was transferred from the central authority to the feudatory chiefs. They thus became intermediaries between the emperor and the subjects.[22]

The custom of paying salaries to officials in form of land began about this time. Such payment may have become necessary owing to an acute shortage of cash and thus it marks the weakening of the economy.

Medieval feudalism first arose in central India, but is soon spread to the Kingdoms of the Kalacuris of Gorakhpur, the Pālas of Bengal, the Pratīhāras of Gujarat, the Rāṣṭrakūṭas of the Konkan and the Gāhaḍavālas of Varanasi, displaying some variations. In the Pāla kingdom the beneficiary of a village grant did not enjoy the right to administer justice but enjoyed exemption form the taxes. The right to administer justice was included in grants made in central India.[23] The surrender of administrative rights would have serious consequences. The beneficiaries could levy taxes in villages under their jurisdiction, or impose new taxes. These villages were immune to inspection by state officials or the visit of state troops. To top it all, the beneficiaries had the power to extract *viṣṭi* or forced labour. The practice was known in ancient India. Kauṭilya mentions it. But now the scope of *viṣṭi* was widened. Peasants and artisans were its victims. Peasants were reduced to a virtual serfdom.[24] The artiṣans fared no better, being obliged to render free service to the holders of the grants. They were also restricted in their choice of residence and were forbidden to migrate to other villages.

Chief beneficiaries of land grants or village grants were brāhmaṇas, temples and monasteries. Religions grants predominated in the grants made buy the Rāṣṭrakūṭa rulers. They gave away hundreds of villages. A break-up of 31 grants from eastern India made between the third and eighth centuries shows that two were made to Buddhist monasteries, three to Hindu temples and the remaining 26 to brāhmaṇas.[25] The credit for making the most religious grants goes to the Gāhaḍavālas of Varanasi.[26] Among their beneficiaries are found several Kayasthas who appear to have risen to prominence in the region by this period.

Besides legitimate grants, there were forgeries too. A 13th century Khayarvāla inscription from Palamau district of Bihar carries a warning against forged charters.[27] There must have been many instances of forgery. It may also be pointed out here that the brāhmaṇas stood to gain from land grants to temples. Feudalism was at its worst in the two centuries preceding the establishment of Delhi Sultanate. More land grants, both religious and secular, were issued then than ever before and more tax burdens imposed.[28] The institution of feudalism had grown very oppressive. This situation must have led to the decay of medieval Indian society. The modest gains the lower classes had made in the wake of the *bhakti* movement were wiped out. They were worse off than before. In this state of demoralisation of the masses, society was very vulnerable. The lower classes would have little interest in defending the interests of the upper classes.

Birth and Growth of Vīra Śaivism

The appearance of Vīra Saivism was a notable development in Indian religion. It was to leave its permanent impression on the caste structure. The sect of Vīra (Militant) Śaivism is believed to have been founded by Basava in the 12th century. Basava was the prime minister of the small kingdom of Kalyāṇa on the Konkan coast. Basava's was powerful protest against brahmanic ideas on several important matters. No brahmaṇa priest was allowed to officiate in the sect. He denounced the caste system, rejected the ideas of ritual purity and pollution, and pleaded for widow marriage. The members of the sect were required to renounce caste.[29] Vīra Śaivism subsequently established a strong base in Mysore where it became known as the sect of Lingayats.

Vıra Śaivism also took deep roots in the Andhra region. A movement towards egalitarianism was set afoot there. Many reformers like Brāhamnaidu and poet-saints like Vemana were vigorous advocates of equality of all men and women.

Vemana lived in 17th century in Andhra. He did not belong to any particular sect and was a wandering ascetic. In his writings he attacked social inequalities and distinctions, for which, he said, there was no ethical ground. These social practices, Vemana warned, would sap the strength of society and pave the way for its disintegration. He showed great concern for the poor and the disabled.[30] Vemana was a pioneer in the creation of vernacular literature. He initiated a trend in the use of popular language in writing. His memory is cherished today both for his contribution to Telugu literature and for his courageous views on the need for social regeneration.

The Lingayats of Karnataka embody the spirit of Vīra Saivism. They are clearly marked off by their doctrines and practices. The fierce antagonism to caste has been softened. The Lingayats worship Śiva as the Supreme Being. Child marriages were forbidden and widows were permitted to marry. In contrast to the more common practice among the Hindus, the Lingayats bury their dead.

What is to be specially noted about the Lingayats is the genuine concern for equality of all members of the community. All discrimination against women at worship was removed. The Lingayat was asked to make no distinction between one member and another of the community. Marriages were to be contracted freely among them.

The same rule held good regarding inter-dining. All were required to earn their living by honest work. The Lingayats were told to share their earnings with those in need.[31]

Vīra Śaivism in Karnataka may have been influenced by Jainism which once had a solid base in that region. There could have been other influences too.

The larger Hindu community came to terms with the dissent of the Lingayats. There was place for yet another distinctive group within it. But it could accept it only in terms of the caste category. The Lingayats gradually turned into another caste group and found a place among the upper castes of the region. They wield great power both in political and economic life. A movement that was designed to further social reform had only succeeded in giving birth to another caste. Yet as a social protest the sect cannot be regarded as a total failure. The example of the Lingayats disproves the theory that it is ritual purity and observance of pollution that determines the status of a group in Hindu society. The Lingayats reject both concepts but the rejection has not affected their caste status. In the course of their history the Lingayats were able to secure political patronage. Thus the community came to have much clout and their unorthodox teachings have not stood in the way of their enjoying an honourable position in society. The caste status is, therefore, determined by mere clout.

The Medieval Saints of North India

Rāmānanda is perhaps one of the best known of the saints among the Vaiṣṇavas who have made a contribution to the regeneration of society. He has done much to promote devotion to Rāma, the incarnation of Viṣṇu. Rāmānanda was also the founder of a sect named after him. What interests us about the saint is his stand on the inequalities in contemporary society.

He is said to have been a brāhmaṇa. Yet he accepted disciples from different communities.[32] Even untouchables and a woman found a place in the circle of his close disciples. What Rāmānanda opposed was imposition of any disability on any group of people and discrimination of all kinds, not so much the caste system itself. He was a champion of the masses. Giving up Sanskrit, promoted vernacular to serve the common people better.[33]

There is a story which says that Kabīr, the poet-saint, was instructed by Rāmānanda. Their times were close enough to make it possible for Kabīr to have received instruction from Rāmānanda. The latter had his base at Varanasi where Kabīr was born and brought up. Kabīr was the adopted child of a Muslim couple who were weavers by profession. Kabir's couplets reveal that he did receive not only religious instruction but philosophical knowledge as well. Kabīr's humble origin must have been the cause of much discrimination at the hands of the high-brows. This could explain the strong stand he took towards the arrogance of the brāhmaṇas. He was the meeting point of two religious traditions, Hindu and Muslim.

Kabīr minced no words in ridiculing the claims of the brāhmaṇas to special status. He believed in the absolute equality of all human beings. Some of his sayings on equality found their way into the *Adi-Granth* of the Sikhs. One such verse declares:

'The Lord the Maker hath moulded one mass of clay.
Into vessels of diverse shapes.
Free from taint are all the vessels of clay.
Since free from taint is the Divine potter.'[34]

Kabīr's blistering criticism of the brāhmaṇas and their practices brought down on his head the ire of the brāhmaṇas. They couldn't swallow his diatribe, coming as it did from a mere weaver upstart.

Some of Kabīr's most pointed barbs were aimed at idolatry and religious obscurantism of all varieties. He scoffed at observance of vows, fasts and pilgrimages.

'Hindus kill themselves by worshipping idols,
Muslims going for *Haj*;
Long-haired yogis perish,
Your mystery eludes them.'[35]

Kabīr pleased neither the brāhmaṇas nor the mullahs. Why pack one month with good works and let slip eleven months without them, Kabīr asked the mullahs.

Kabīr developed his own method of *nirguṇa bhakti* or devotion to an attributeless God. He used several names for God, such as Harī and Rāma . But his Rāma was not the Rāma of the *Rāmāyaṇa*, nor his Harī the god of the Purāṇas. He rejected all incarnations of God.

Ravidās is believed to have been a disciple of Rāmānanda. He was a cobbler by profession. Of himself he said that he had carried dead cattle in Varanasi. He attained such high reputation that even brāhmaṇas bowed low before him. Ravidās' couplets have also been incorporated in the *Adi Granth*.

Ravidās, cobbler-saint, has become a symbol for the *Camar*

community. The name holds out the hope to them that they too can rise to great heights. No saint has perhaps enabled a community to take vicarious pride as Ravidās has done for the Camars. Many of them proudly sport the saints name.

The Saints of Maharashtra

Many great names emblazon the history of the *bhakti* movement in Maharashtra. The region has come under many movements directed at renewal of religion regeneration of society. The Caitanyas (Mahānubhāvas) and the Vārkarīs are the chief sects that arose out of the *bhakti* movement.

Rāghava Caitanya (not the Caitanya of Bengal) was a saint revered by both Hindus and Muslims. His religion transcended the distinction of sects and creeds. needless to say that he attached no importance to caste, Caitanya originally came from Gujarat but was more popular in the Deccan. The Caitanya cult cast its influence on Tukārām. The sect of Mānubhāvas (Mahānubhāvas) which arose in the 13th century rejected the Vedas and the Hindu *varṇa* system.

The Vārkarī movement was to bring about a new spirit of brotherhood and openness in social relations. Jnānadeva is believed to be the originator of the movement. It was not a new sect but a new approach to the practice of *bhakti*. In this tradition of *bhakti*, great emphasis was laid on purity of life and self discipline. The Vārkarī was required to give up the use of liquor and flesh meat. He had to go on pilgrimage regularly. He wore a garland of Tulsi beads.[36] There was much fasting too. He did not observe caste distinctions. The epicentre of the movement was Pandharpur where the worship of Viṭṭhala prevailed.

Jnānadeva (Dnāynadeva) was the son of an ex-ascetic. His father, Viṭṭhalapant, was a one-time disciple of Rāmānanda, the great Vaiṣṇava saint of Varanasi. Rāmānanda came to know that Viṭṭhalapant had adopted the life of asceticism without obtaining the consent of his wife and sent him back to his wife. Subsequently three sons and a daughter were born to the couple. Jnānadeva was the second of the boys. The children were treated as illegitimate by the brāhmaṇas.[37] Though born in a brāhmaṇa family they were ostracised and persecuted. This humiliating treatment at the hands of his fellow castemen left a mark on Jnānadeva.

When towards the end of the 13th century Jnānadeva came to live at Pandharpur, he began to draw many people towards him with his personality. Pandharpur would become not merely a well-known place of pilgrimage but also a centre of religious learning.[38] It would play a part in the cultural revival in Maharashtra.

Jnānadeva in his *Jnāneśwari*, the most important mystical work of the saint, speaks of the futility of the path of *Jnāna* (knowledge). The only way to liberation is *bhakti*. Thus he rejected rituals, Yoga and the Vedas as means of attaining *mokṣa*.[39] Jnānadeva bequeathed to the Vārkarīs his idea on caste distinctions. His own experience had shaped his teaching on the subject.

Nāmadeva further strengthened the Vārkarī movement. Though springing from a low caste, he too attained great fame as a teacher and saint. Ekanātha, born a brāhmaṇa, was a dissenter. He was ostracised for his non-conformity with caste rules. His crime seems to have been his feeding a hungry Mahār. God, it is said, revealed to him that it was more meritorious to feed a hungry Mahār than to feed thousands of brāhmaṇas. Sadly, this revelation was vouchsafed to so few of his fellow castemen.

Tukārām, the 17th century poet-saint, is one of the best known products of the *bhakti* movement in Maharashtra. By birth and background he was an unlikely candidate to play the role as a dissenter or challenger of the authority of the leader of the community. Tukārām's father was a petty trader, a śūdra in the social hierarchy. On his father's death, Tukārām inherited the small grocery store in the village. He wasn't quite fit for business, even a very modest one. Today this unsuccessful shopkeeper of Dehu, near Pune, is a legendary figure. His father had married him to two young girls. During a terrible famine he was unable to feed his hungry wife. The image of his wife dying of hunger, crying for food, would haunt Tukārām for years.[40] He was thus purified and trained in the school of personal loss and sufferings. He is believed to have been initiated by an ascetic of the Caitanya sect. Tukārām spent much time along on the hills among the rocks and the wild animals. He received light, and with the light came new strength.

Tukārām's generosity and trust in God was legendary. His generosity quite exasperated his long-suffering wife. Many stories have grown around her helplessness, some of which are quite imaginative though obviously fictitious. One such story says that Tukārām once gave away his wife's clothes while she was bathing.

In his well-known *abhangas* (lyrics) Tukārām has given expression to his convictions on a variety of topics. The equality of all human beings was part of the new vision he had acquired. He spoke of the futility of ritualism, the hollowness of the claims to purity by the brāhmaṇas, their pride and fraudulent ways and the meaninglessness of caste distinctions.[41] For a devotee of Vithoba, his favourite deity, there was no caste, he asserted.

Tukārām's denuciation of the brāhmaṇas expectedly brought down on him systematic persecution and the fury of the brāhmaṇas. To them it was insufferable cheek on the part of the upstart Kumbi of Dehu to criticise them. They would take him down a peg or two, they decided. What they could relish least of all was Tukārām's new role as a teacher of the people. How could a śūdra be a teacher? What was worse, Tukārām was writing things. The brāhamṇas of the place, it is said, collected Trukārām's writings and threw them in the river. But through divine intervention, they did not sink and were later found floating in the water. Gradually he received a measure of sympathy from some of the brāhmaṇas. A few of them are said to have become his disciples. Men and women of all classes joined the circle of his disciples.

Few had challenged the authority of the brāhmaṇas as courageously as Tukārām. He mercilessly attacked caste privileges. In a region where caste was the sacred religion, this was no small matter. It was the triumph of the human spirit over artificial barriers that had stifled the innate sense of freedom and unity of the human family. Like many others, Tukārām reasserted this unity in emphatic terms. His reassertion of the faith in the unity of man would echo down the centuries, especially through the Maharashtra region.

There can be no doubt that the *bhakti* movement brought about certain democratisation of society and the practice of religion. The path of *bhakti* was open to all the lower classes. This is borne out by the background of many great saints. Nāmadeva belonged to the tailor caste, Tukārām was a Kumbi. Among the less known saints there were barbers, potters and even untouchables. Of this last group was the Mahar-saint Cokhāmeḷa. When one day Cokhāmeḷa entered the sanctuary at Pandharpur, the brāhmaṇas were incensed. When ordered to leave, the wouldn't oblige, but instead he replied that he did not enter the temple on his own choice, but that God had forced him into it. Of course, that did not satisfy the brāhmaṇas.

Cokhāmeḷa told the brāhmaṇas that a man's caste is pure, if he has faith in God and regards all others as he regards his own self.

Birth counts for nothing.[42] Here was Mahar telling the brāhmaṇas what was right and wrong.

Cokhameḷa was denounced to the Muslim ruler for his crime of entering the sacred place where he was forbidden to. To mollify the brāhmaṇas the ruler ordered him to be published by being dragged by a team of bullocks. It is said that the bullocks refused to move.[43]

Cokhāmeḷa undoubtedly had received much religious instruction. He was able to confront the brāhmaṇas and he was not overawed by them. That some untouchables could attain these heights was in fact due to the *bhakti* movement.

The resurgence among the masses resulted to a great extent from the wealth of vernacular literature now available to them. Sanskrit was no longer the repository of all knowledge and wisdom. True, most of this literature was religious.

Bhakti Movement: An Overview

The *bhakti* movement left its mark on social relations. It was never intended to be a reform movement. It clearly aimed at religious renewal. The movement did attempt to create an environment of brotherhood and fellowship of all men within the *varṇa* system. The first flush of fervour would soon lose its glow. Reversion into older forms of caste practices would begin. Some Vaiṣṇavas would be guilty not only of casteist practices but even of the grossest forms of untouchability. Ultra-orthodox elements in the sect would take control of the sect and its policies.

The movement lacked a solid theoretical foundation. The bias for a liberal attitude towards all men was never spelled out. A kindlier treatment of the lower classes was more in the nature of a concession made by the upper classes. It smacked of an upper class approach to human equality.

Nevertheless, the path of *bhakti* added a refreshingly new dimension to the practice of religion. It made God seem accessible even to the lowest. He was no longer the special property of the learned as in the path of knowledge (*Jnāna*).

Bhakti is said to have been the main cause of the popularity of image worship, which had once been viewed with disdain. It became an indispensable part of popular religion.

Devotees became absorbed with eyes fixed on the image of their favourite deity, contemplating its divine and ineffable beauty. Many writers were inspired to fill pages in praise of the image of their god or goddess. Lakṣmaṇa Ācārya surpasses them all. In a whopping eighty verses, he describes the beauty of Caṇḍi's breasts.[44]

The *bhakti* tradition promoted by the Bhāgavatas and the followers of Caitanya of Bengal had a high emotional appeal. The charge of accesses in this respect is not wholly unmerited. This *bhakti* operated at times on an erotic level, using highly charged religious language. The demarcation between the erotic and religious was difficult to determine.

Apart from the spirit of goodwill the *bhakti* movement exuded towards all men and women, it was in many ways a stabilising force. It preached many upper class values, such as loyalty to powers that be, alms-giving and respect for authority.[45] A feudal society could have no quarrel with a cult preaching these values. In fact, communities ranged themselves on the side of Saivism and Vaiṣṇavism, the upper castes and the princes siding with the former and the peasant castes and the artisans supporting Vaiṣṇavism. There was little love lost between the two groups.

One of the greatest contributions made by the *bhakti* movements is the stimulus it gave to the creation of vernacular literature. The volume of literature it inspired is quite impressive. A strong foundation was laid by the Āḷwārs of South India. Names like Rāmānanda, Jnāndeva, Tukārām and many others will be long remembered for their pioneering efforts. The iconoclastic poems of Kabīr are still being sung and relished by the masses. The lyrics of Tukārām and the *dohās* (couplets) of Kabīr have caught the fancy of the masses. Even the illiterate can enjoy them and are influenced by the thought content.

Unlike the brahmanic religion, the *bhakti* cult permitted the full participation of women in religious rites. It helped a few representatives of the suppressed sex to emerge from their isolation and to take a more active part in worship and other public expression for religion. Owing to the more liberal treatment of women in the movement, some women managed to rise to great heights among the devotees. The *bhakti* tradition can point with pride to many great woman saints who had drawn inspiration and strength from it. Mīrābāī, the Nightingale of Mewār, is one of the best-known of woman poet-saints. Āṇḍāḷ, the Mīrā of the Tamil country, is yet another product of the *bhakti* movement. Muktābāī, Jnānadeva's sister, achieved fame as a spiritual teacher. Janābāī, who styled herself a servant of Nāmadeva, was a well-known poetess of Maharashtra.[46] Tukārām had a brāhmaṇa woman named Bahiṇābāī among his disciples. She had braved the displeasure of her caste to sit at the feet of Tukārām. Among the followers of Caitanya of Bengal women were not behind men in their ecstatic singing and appeared in the streets as witness to their faith.

The *bhakti* movement has a close parallel in the origin and development of the Pentecostal movement in 20th century Christian churches. Both movements appeal to the heart and their teachings and preachings have a strong emotional content. Both trends developed as reaction to formalism in religion. Both advocated a return to the sources. For *bhakti*, the sources were the Purāṇas while for the Pentecostals it was the Bible. Both preached goodwill and fellow-feelings but were lacking in any worthwhile social criticism or attempt to rebuild society and thus ignored the social reality.

Both movements display pronounced streak of anti-intellectualism. *Bhakti* tended to see some opposition between devotion on the one hand and knowledge and works on the other. It set itself against one or the other or both. Pentecostalism was fundamentalist in its approach to the Bible. It spurned and ridiculed all Biblical studies and modern scholarship. Under the thin veneer of newness, both trends were establishmentarian and stabilising forces.

Both *bhakti* and Pentecostalism emphasised the miraculous and the supra-normal in religion. Just as the devotee of a deity expected to manifest himself to Him, so did the Pentecostal expect the spirit to manifest himself through signs and wonders. While the devotee awaited this manifestation, the god dwelt in his Vigraha (image) and the spirit in his heaven, everything was right with the world.

Yet there is no doubt both movements assisted their advocates to attain great personal purity and goodness of life. The devotee appeared to live in an ethereal world, untouched by the harsh realities of this life.

The *bhakti* movement failed to bring about any lasting changes in society. It was smothered by contrary forces. The *bhakti* movement proves that euphoria is an uncertain foundation on which to build a movement. Euphoria is transitory. There is nothing to nourish it, while a movement must be nourished constantly.

Egalitarianism in Sikhism

During 14th and 15th centuries the followers of Hinduism and Islam were being thrown together and interacting with one another. Kabīr himself was a product of such interaction. The contact was not made on an intellectual plane but the level of the common people. The contact was given a fillip by the Sūfī saints. Guru Nānak appeared in a period and in a region which was the meeting point of two religions. The spirit of Sikhism can be appreciated only in this background of social and religious environment. Before Guru Nānak formulated his teachings and became a *guru*, he undertook a tour of many countries, including the West Asia, in company with a Muslim called Mardana from his native village, Talwandi, near Lahore. Obviously Nānak had occasion to observe Islam at close quarters. This contact was to have deep impact on his own teachings.

Guru Nānak did not accept the ideas of his contemporaries regarding the treatment meted out to women. He said:

> 'Why should we consider woman cursed and condemned,
> When from woman are born leaders and rulers?
> From woman alone is born a woman. . .'[47]

Woman, he says, is the true companion of man.

Nānak had some harsh things to say about the religious leaders of his day. He called them purveyors of falsehood. Themselves deluded, they delude all who follow them, he said.

Nānak had a horror of begging. He had cured his friend Mardana of the habit of begging and had persuaded him to sing the praises of the Lord on his rebeck. Only he, said Nānak, knows the true way of life who lived by the sweat of his brow and gives a part of his earnings in charity too.

Nānak's attitude to begging was a notable departure from that of his society where begging had been elevated to the status of great virtue. Thus Nānak laid the foundation of new work ethic. The love of hard work would mark his followers. This new attitude in itself was a great contribution the Sikhs made to the Indian society. In an environment where all physical labour was looked upon as fit only for the lower classes, the stress on earning one's bread was refreshingly new. The positive approach to work was the secret of the Sikh community's economic progress.

Guru Amar Dās, the third Guru, was a courageous social reformer. He organised members of the scattered Sikh communities into a kind of 'dioceses' and appointed a mentor for each of them.

Some of the mentors were women. He made communal dining compulsory for converts from different Hindu communities.[48] For his time this was no small step and it was directed against the prohibition of co-dining, which was then one of the most sacrosanct rules of the observance of caste at meal time. Amar Dās also banned *satī* in the community. He denounced the pride that arises from caste superiority. He declared in no uncertain terms:

'Let no man be proud because of his caste,
For the man who graspeth God in his heart
He, no other, is the true Brahmin.
So, O fool, about the caste be not vain glorious,
From vainglory emerge, many of mind's evils'.[49]

Amar Dās was echoing Kabīr when he said that though there are four *varṇas*, the same Potter has moulded all of them from the same clay.

The *Ādi Granth* has incorporated the works not only of the Gurus but also of many saints such as Nāmadeva, Kabīr, Ravidās, Rāmānanda and Sūfī saints like Sheikh Farid and Bhīkan. Besides being a tribute to these men, it is also a recognition of the universality of the experience of God. The inclusion of the hymns of these saints emphasises the common bonds that bind men of divergent faiths. All these saints, it must be pointed out, have rejected all forms of exclusicism and upheld equality, of all humans. It is this spirit that animates their writings.

The Impact of Sufism on Indian Society

The growth of Sufism in India is an important phenomenon on the Indian scene. Sufism is not of Indian origin. Yet it took on a special character of its own in the peculiar conditions existing in the country. Through the personality and teachings of the Sūfī saints, Islām presented a new face to those outside its fold.

The Sūfīs did not offer a uniform teaching or promote uniform practices. Their teachings show varying degrees of orthodoxy. Some of them were influenced by the Indian theory of *ahimsā*, transmigration and the oneness of all beings. With the adoption of Indian ideas, there came not a few new superstitions.[50] In one respect, their teachings had a salutary influence on society. This was their emphasis on the brotherhood of all members of the community of their followers.

It was inevitable that the Sūfis should have attracted towards them the people of other faiths on the strength of their holiness and the spiritual atmosphere that enveloped them. Those so drawn could not fail to notice the spirit of brotherhood and the absence of caste distinctions among the Muslim followers of the Sūfis. They would be struck by the vast gulf that existed between the members of the Hindu and the Muslim communities in this matter. The great veneration in which the common people held men of spiritual attainments end the great value attached to associating with holy men were additional reasons in drawing the people to the Sūfis. It was the lower classes, especially the depressed classes, who were drawn into the circle that gathered around the Sūfis. Some of them were thus converted to Islam. Many of the converts retained their traditional occupation.[51] That is why even today in some regions of North India tailors and weavers are Muslims.

That all conversions to Islam during the Muslim period were brought about through force is the fond theory of some Indian writers. This is not borne out by historical facts. Some of the Sufi saints were also great bridge-builders between two religions. They displayed a large measure of tolerance towards religious insights and beliefs of other faiths such as Buddhism and Hinduism. They refused to absolutise the values and insights of their own religious tradition. This was one of their most laudable contributions.

Social Reform in the Muslim Period

The practice of *satī* was a matter on which several rulers thought it necessary to take some action. Mohammed Bin Tughlak is known to be an idealist. Though he was motivated by good intentions some of his economic reform measures were utter failures. Tughlak was the first Muslim ruler who decided to act on *satī*. To ensure that no widow was compelled to become *satī*, he issued orders that a licence had to be obtained before a *satī* was performed. Akbar too was much concerned about the problem. Though he did not ban the practice, he issued instructions to the law-enforcement authorities that no widow was to be burned against her will. Akbar refused permission for *satī* to even willing widows, who had children of their own. He intervened to save the lives of several widows. Once he jailed a young man who compelled his mother to perform *satī* at her husband's death.[52] Akbar even offered a monthly allowance to widows. He also expressed himself strongly against the practice of child marriage.

Aurangzeb was another ruler who took steps against *satī.* He decreed in 1664 that no *satī* should be performed in his kingdom.[53] Aurangzeb has often been made out to be the villain of Indian history – a charge he did not fully deserve. It is not known if the ban succeeded in putting an end to the execrable custom.

By the late medieval period there existed a host of sects which had been founded with the avowed purpose of bringing about socio-religious rejuvenation. Such sects had sprung up among the untouchables too, which sought to remove the social disabilities this segment of society suffered. Yet the purpose of the creation of the sects remained largely unfulfilled. The failure was not due to want of trying.

The social disabilities the untouchables were afflicted with operated like a spell that held them prisoners. They couldn't break the spell without some assistance from outside. This assistance was not forthcoming now. The *bhakti* movement had ceased to be a force of social rejuvenation. The sects gradually turned into castes with their own peculiar beliefs, practices and superstitions. They continued to exist like ugly ruins of once beautiful buildings, reminding future generations of the grand dreams some courageous men had dared to have.

NOTES

1. A.B. Keith, 1961, p.56 ff.
2. The Greek writers probably meant Śiva when they said that the worship of Dionysios was prevalent among the Indians. But D.D. Kosambi (1970:117) believes that Indra is meant.
3. K.A. Nilakanta Sastri, 1980, p.57.
4. D.D. Kosambi, 1970, pp 42-3.
5. T.M.P. Mahadevan, *Ten Saints of India*, Bombay, Bhartiya Vidya Bhawan, 1971, p.62 ff.
6. J.N. Farquhar, *The outlines of the Religious Literature of India*, Delhi, Motilal Banarasidas, 1967A, p.232.
7. *CHAU* 4:1:1.
8. Radhakrishnan, 1962, p.617.
9. *Ibid.*, p.616 (see footnote).
10. J.N. Farquhar, 1967 A, p.237.
11. Radhakrishnan, 1962, pp.606-7.
12. *Ibid.*, p.709.
13. Urmila Bhagowalia, *Vaiṣṇavism and Society in Northern India: 700-1200*, New

Delhi, Intellectual Publishing House, 1980, p.34.
14. *Ibid.*, p.70.
15. R. Thapar, 1978, p.133.
16. R.S. Sharma, *Indian Feudalism*, New Delhi, Macmillan India Ltd., (980B, p.136.
17. *HSL*, p.99.
18. S. Dhar, 1978, p.19.
19. G.S. Ghurye, 1969, p.99.
20. U. Bhagowalia, 1980, p.90.
21. *Ibid.*, p.78.
22. R.S. Sharma, 1980B, p.7.
23. *Ibid.*, p.29.
24. *Ibid.*, p.99.
25. *Ibid.*, p.35.
26. *Ibid.*, p.72.
27. *Ibid.*, p.172.
28. *Ibid.*, p.178.
29. J.N. Farquhar, *Modern Religious Movements in India*, Delhi, Oriental Publisher and Bookseller, 1967B, p.30.
30. V. Ramakrishna, *Social Reform in Andhra*. Delhi, Vikas Publishing House, 1983, pp.42-3.
31. *CHI*, IV, p.101.
32. *Ibid.*, p.379.
33, *Ibid.*, p.379.
34. *SWS*, p.15.
35. Parasanath Tiwari, *Kabir*, New Delhi, Sahitya Akademi, 1980, p.11
36. B. Nemade, *Tukaram*, New Delhi, Sahitya Akademi, 1980, p.11.
37. *CHI*, IV, p.356.
38. G.P. Deleury, *The Cult of Vithoba*, Poona, The Deccan College Post-Graduate and Research Institute, 1960, p.32.
39. *Ibid.*, p.103
40. B. Nemade, 1980, p.181 ff.
41. *Ibid.*, p.51.
42. M.G. Ranade, *The Rise of the Marathas*, New Delhi, Government of India, 1961, p.68.
43. *Ibid.*, p.68.
44. *HSL*, p.665.
45. U. Bhagowalia, 1980, p.99.
46. G.P. Deleury, 1960, p.5.
47. *SWS*, p.93.
48. *Ibid.*, p.125.
49. *Ibid.*, p.136.
50. *CHI*, IV, p.597.
51. Aziz Ahmed, *Studies in the Islamic Culture in the Indian Environment*, Oxford, Clarendon Press, 1960, p.85
52. *CHI*, II, p.632.
53. *Ibid.*, p.632

5

A NEW ERA DAWNS

THE COMING of the British marks a turning point in the history of Indian society. The Indian people have in the past interacted with various nationalities and groups, such as the Persians, Greeks, Huns, Scythians, Turks, Arabs, Mughals, French, Portuguese and the Dutch. But no group has exerted such far-reaching influences on Indian society as the British. The two-century long close association with them brought about changes not merely in externals but in the very value system of the Indians. The Mughals would come closest to the British in the extent of transformation brought about by the British presence in India. Barring the many monuments the Mughals have left as their legacy, much of the impact of their period has worn off. In contrast, the most momentous development of the British period was a serious self-examination Indian society was forced to undertake.

The Traders Who Built an Empire

The group of traders who established a trading post at Surat on the west coast of India in A.D. 1610 could not have known that they were the harbingers of a grand scheme for establishing political power which went far beyond financial gains or import and export of goods. The possibilities of realising such an objective dawned on the merchants gradually. They were quick to grab the chances that came their way. The future historians of India will find it a great enigma how a company of merchants succeeded in capturing political power in a land that boasts a host of martial races. Not only did they achieve this objective but retained their hold for two centuries. The East India Company turned into makers and breakers of kings and kingdoms, swallowing them up in its insatiable greed for power and fortune. The Company brought in tow adventurers, fortune-seekers, missionaries and scholars some of whom would uncover for the Indians the vast and invaluable treasures of their past. It was thus a love-hate relationship that developed between the people of India and the British Isles. It had its moments of greatness; it also left many wounds. The relationship was doomed from the outset, because it was founded on financial interest. The British never let themselves forget that fact of life. Profit must remain the over-riding concern of their presence in India. They were prepared to do some good within the narrow limits that policy imposed.

The British rulers introduced several measures and social legislations that had a salutary effect on the future of India. They unified the vast sub-continent under one yoke, inter-connecting the different regions. For the first time the various races inhabiting the land came to know one another, discovering their common heritage.

The educational system the British introduced in India in the 19th century was the most potent instrument of change for the country. Through the system they hoped to share their learning, their science and their philosophy of life. Many Indians themselves would become enthusiastic advocates of the British system of education or English education. Ram Mohan Roy was one of these enthusiasts.

Bombay Presidency was the first beneficiary of the educational effort of the British. Lord Elphinstone, first Governor of Bombay, took a keen interest in opening schools. Ram Mohan Roy himself was a pioneer in English education. Ram Mohan established an English school in Calcutta as early as 1822. He was so convinced of the value of English education that he opposed the proposal to open a Sanskrit college in Calcutta.[1] Moreover, he denounced any move by the government to give an Orientalist flavour to the planned programme of education.

In the late 1820s the controversy produced much heat. Acrimonious debates were carried on in the publications of the day which arrayed themselves on either side. The parties were known as the Orientalists and the Occidentalists. The Occidentalists were led by a group called DeRozians.

Henry DeRozio was born of European and Indian parents. He showed much poetic talent and became a teacher in the Hindu College, Calcutta. His radical ideas drew towards him some senior students. He inspired them with his bold thinking and magnetic personality. These students became very articulate and were the force behind the Occidentalists, vehemently advocating the introduction of English education. Though DeRozio died at the age of 22, he had sown the seeds of revolt in the minds of his students.

The English periodical, the *Enquirer*, and the Bengali weekly, *Inanveṣam*, were launched by two DeRozians – Kṛṣṇa Mohan Banerji and Dakṣinaranjan Mukherji – which carried on a campaign against the views of the orthodox.[2]

What tipped the scales in favour of English education was the coming of Lord William Bentinck as Governor-General to India in 1828. He strongly believed that the English language was the key to the progress of the country. His hands were greatly strengthened by the arrival in India of Thomas Babington Macaulay in 1834. The decision was taken in March 1835 that the objective of the British government ought to be imparting the knowledge of English literature and science through the medium of English. On the basis of this resolution, the government began to establish schools and colleges.[3]

No less important than the government's educational effort were the exertions of the missionaries in the same field. The first of such ventures was the establishment of a grammar school in Madras in 1836 by Bishop Corrie. Madras Presidency was the beneficiary of the Church's initial educational efforts. In 1844 it was decided that an English medium school be set up in Tirunelveli. As early as 1835 a proposal was made to establish an English school in Bombay for the native children to be named the Money School after a civil servant who had taken interest in education.[4] On the renewal of the East India Company's Charter in 1813 missionaries were permitted to operate in India. By the 1840s women missionaries also arrived who devoted themselves to girls' education especially in the Madras Presidency. By 1850 there were more than 2,000 girls attending school in the Presidency. In 1850, well-known missionary Sara Tucker opened a lady teachers' training school in Palayamkottai to meet the growing demand for teachers.[5] Good vernacular education was being provided through the schools.

The first girls' school in Andhra was founded by missionary, C.P. Heyer. Within a year, he had established seven schools in the district of Guntur.

Early Attempts at Social Reform

Raja Ram Mohan Roy is honoured as the first of the Indian social reformers in modern times. He was born in the orthodox brahmaṇa family which had long association with Muslim administration in

Bengal. At the age of 12, Ram Mohan was a much-married husband with two living wives. He was sent to Patna for studies where he came in contact with Muslim rationalist thought. Later, he studied Sanskrit and the Hindu scriptures in Varanasi. He also established contact with the Christian missionaries of Serampore.[6] The varied influences he came under moulded his thinking and produced the kind of man that he became. When he rejected idolatry, he had to leave his home and his own wives refused to live with him.

Ram Mohan Roy is best known for his views on Hindu society of his day. He had already denounced idolatry. He vehemently attacked such practices as *satī* and polygamy. The plight of women and the injustices heaped upon them moved him deeply. Lord Bentinck, then Governor-General, must have felt encouraged by Ram Mohan's denunciation of *satī* to adopt the measure against the inhuman practice. In 1928 Bentinck abolished *satī* through an executive order. Bentinck's own enthusiasm for measure can be gauged from the fact that he had assumed office only the previous year.

Ram Mohan was of the view that there was no justification for the observance of caste rules and they must be done away with. Yet he was not prepared to take an open stand against caste.[7] Moreover, he took care not to lose caste by mixing with members of other castes. He even retained his sacred thread. Thus, he displayed some ambivalence on the matter.

Ram Mohan also favoured marriage of widows. It is said that elderly widows of Bengal used to tease one another saying they would get married again when the Babuji returned from England. It was rumoured that he had gone to England to plead the cause of the widows.

In Ram Mohan Roy we detect the breath of fresh air that had begun to waft gently into Indian society. It would grow in force gradually to become a mighty storm sweeping away much dead wood in its path. Ram Mohan clearly indicated the breadth of vision many Indians were to gain by their contact with the liberal thought and ideals of the West. It was no easy task he had undertaken. He was clearing out a new path for himself. One should find it easy to excuse some of his hesitations.

He beqeathed much of his idealism to the Brahma Samaj for which he provided the inspiration. It had its beginning in the small group that met regularly in Calcutta. The group was at first called the 'Brahma Sabha'. The meeting held worship by chanting hymns from the *Upaniṣads*. Entry was limited to brāhmaṇas. Ram Mohan did not live to see the full flowering of the society that had come into being. He sailed for England in November 1830 never to return. He died at Bristol in August 1833.

Ram Mohan's purpose was never to undertake a reform of society, but rather to restore Hinduism to its original purity. It was under the leadership of Debendranath Tagore that Brahma Samaj became a well-knit organisation. He was endowed with leadership qualities. He drew up a formula of promises to be taken by every member of the Samaj. These promises included rejection of idolatry and worship of God. Most of the prayers and manuals used by the members of the Samaj were prepared by Debendranath.[8] The entry of Kesab Chandra Sen into the Brahma Samaj would bring about notable changes in it.

Kesab was born in an environment hardly calculated to produce social reformers. He belonged to the upper crust of society. Born on November 19, 1838, Kesab grew up amid comfort. His grandfather, Ram Kamal Sen, had risen from poverty to become the dewan of the Bank of Bengal. He had also a reputation of being a scholar. Hence Kesab had the benefit of a good education. English education had an unsettling effect on him. It left a void in him. He gave up idol worship and was virtually in a no-man's land, without a positive creed to follow. 'At last', says Kesab, 'it pleased Providence to reveal Himself unto me'.[9] At the age of 20 he came under the spell of Maharṣi Debendranath.

It was Kesab who laid before the Samaj a programme of action. He called for an overhaul of the system of education. He maintained that education should not be the monopoly of the well-to-do classes and that it should be thrown open to even the lowliest. Education was a pre-condition of the regeneration of society. In his scheme of things, the education of women formed an indispensable part.

Equality of all men and women was the mainstay of Kesab's programme. He took an uncompromising stand on it. Kesab declared war on caste distinctions and inequalities of all kinds which claimed patronage of established religion. Debendranath had been somewhat soft on the question of caste. Under Kesab's influence the Maharaṣi gave up his sacred thread, a mark of caste status.[10]

The Sangat Sabha was an association founded by Kesab in 1860. Every member of this group was required to abjure caste as well as every mark and expression of it. To Kesab the sacred thread was such a mark implying superiority of man over man. Kesab had to pay a price for his unorthodox views. On the day he was ordained to ministry, he was forbidden by his uncle to enter the family mansion in Calcutta.[11]

Brahma Samaj encouraged inter-caṣte marriage. Several such marriages were performed. But Kesab's emphasis on speedy social changes was to cause a rift in the Samaj. He differed on this issue with Debendranath who rather played down the need for social reform. The Maharṣi was in favour of letting time change matters in society. Kesab was not prepared to wait. So the break with the Maharṣi was inevitable.

The break came in February 1866. Kesab left the parent body. In November of the same year he established the new body called the 'Sadharana Brahma Samaj'. In a major departure from the practice in Brahma Samaj, the new Samaj accepted for it scriptures the sacred books of other religions.

Kesab was capable of dreaming great dreams. A universal church was one of his dreams. 'Instead of a hundred hostile churches', he declared, 'there shall be upraised, in the fulness of time, one vast cathedral where all mankind shall worship, with one heart, the Supreme Creator. Such brotherhood among all mankinds will be realised in the church of the future.'[12] The fulness of time Kesab visualised seems far off and the universal church must remain a mere dream for a long time to come. But this declaration shows forth a heart that was wide enough to embrace the whole world.

The torch that Ram Mohan Roy had lit burned brighter in the hands of Kesab, lighting up the path of many, not only in Bengal but in distant parts of the country. Few have surpassed the breadth of his vision, the universality of his goal. During his time Kesab guided the Brahma Samaj, it evolved a programme of its own and was transformed into a powerful instrument of social regeneration. One of the greatest sons of modern India, Kesab died on January 8, 1884.

Kesab had preached a new humanism to which the India had hitherto been unaccustomed. He had freed himself from superstitions and inhibitions of his age. That is why he was able to give expressions to the yearning of the human heart for freedom, dignity and equality of all human beings.

In Kesab the consciousness of the equality of all men and women reached the high point which will not be surpassed in many decades to come.

The Untouchables Dare to Hope

During the *bhakti* movement some members of the untouchable community had shaken off the spell that had been cast upon them by the Śāstras. As a group they were unable to improve their position in society. In the Muslim period some of them discovered a new opportunity to raise themselves socially through a change of religion.

The missionaries began to arrive in India after the renewal of the Company's Charter in 1813. Some of these missionaries launched their operations among the untouchables. The Pulayas of southern Travancore, then a princely state, was one such community. Inevitably conversions followed. With conversion they acquired a better self-image. These Pulayas (now christened Ceramar) had been denied the right to cover the upper part of their bodies. The prohibition applied to both sexes. In the late '40s of the last century, the new converts picked up enough courage to claim the right to cover their bodies fully and began to move about so clothed. The upper caste Hindus objected to the innovation. The missionary in residence there, Charles Mead, took up the matter and was able to secure an order from the magistrate exempting the converts from the dress restriction in force. But the upper caste Hindus pressurised the Maharaja of Travancore to cancel the exemption granted by the magistrate. The matter did not end there. The converts refused to give up. In 1858 they petitioned the Governor of Madras, Charles Trevelyan, claiming their birthright. He issued an order declaring the Christians free in the matter of dress. This was no small victory for the former untouchables. It was just the beginning of their long struggle for human rights.

The untouchables were not slow in realising that education would be a crucial factor in their quest for human rights. One of the untouchable groups to come in touch with the British were the Mahars of Maharashtra. They began to seek entry into schools established by the British government or local bodies and private citizens but supported by the government. In 1856 a Mahār boy was refused admission to a school in Dharwar. The matter was brought to the attention of the government of Bombay Presidency. The government was slow to come to a decision. Finally a press note issued in 1858 stated that the government did not wish to introduce students from low castes to those schools the expenses of which are partially shared by the government; but that the government reserved the right to refuse assistance to those schools which denied the benefits of education to the children of the depressed classes. It declared further that all schools maintained at the sole expense of the government shall be open to all classes.[13]

The British were sympathetic towards providing educational facilities for the untouchables. To do so, they had to break down the wall of the deep-seated prejudices of the upper castes. The government was not prepared to antagonise them. Yet there were individuals among the British who stood by their conviction and rose to the challenge. The Agra College affair bears this out.

The Anglican missionaries established St. John's College at Agra in 1851. A crisis occurred during the tenure of John Barton as principal from 1860-62. Barton admitted the son of a sweeper (*bhangi*) to the College. The upper caste students were furious. They sent a letter to Barton, threatening to leave College if the sweeper boy was not withdrawn. Barton stood his ground. No fewer than 160 students left the College, hoping to gain admission in the Government College at Agra. The principal of the Government College refused them admission, maintaining that they had left their College without submitting an explanation. The students petitioned the Director of Public Instruction against the stance of the principal of St. John's College. But the Director ratified his decision. The students set up a new college named Victoria College.[14]

The issue of Christians who were former untouchables caused a serious crisis in the Anglican Church. The śūdra Christians refused to treat the former untouchables as equals. They avoided sitting along with them in church. The problem had cropped up as early as the second decade of the 19th century. At this time the Anglican Churches of South India were under the jurisdiction of the Bishop of Calcutta. The caste problem had exercised the minds of several Bishops. But Bishop Daniel Wilson on assuming office in the early 30s decided to act decisively. In a pastoral letter issued on July 5, 1833, he declared that 'Distinction of caste must be abandoned decidedly, immediately and finally.' When the letter was read out in the Vepery Church in Madras, the śūdra Christians in the congregation walked out in protest. They even withdrew their children from the church-managed school. Later, wiser counsel prevailed and the śūdra Christians returned to the church. Gradually the crisis blew over.[15] The problem of caste consciousness has continued to plague all denominations of Christians in south India.

The Syrian Christian community of Kerala traces its origin to the preaching of St. Thomas Didymas, a disciple of Jesus. Until the arrival of the European missionaries the Syrian Christians did not welcome the lower classes such as the Pariahs and the Pulayas into their community. Even when the Pulayas were admitted with in recent times, they have occupied a lower status in the community. The Christians of Parava origin have traditionally been associated the communities founded by European missionaries.

Phule's Revolt

No one has demonstrated the spirit of revolt against the traditional social system as Jotirao Govindrao Phule of Maharashtra, a 19th century social activist. Though springing from a śūdra community, he would challenge the power centres in society. In doing this he drew much inspiration from his fellow Maharashtrian, Tukārām, and the great poet-saint of Varanasi, Kabīr.

Phule was born in a Mali family in 1827. He received only elementary education. In spite of this handicap he would one day challenge the learned in society. He made up for the lack of education through personal study and reflection.

Phule rejected outright the ancient *samhitās* and commentaries on them. He held that these *samhitās* had taken away the legitimate rights of the untouchables and women. The brāhmaṇas came in for severe criticism. In his work *Gulamgiri* (Slavery), Phule condemned the brāhmaṇas for their cunning and self-seeking.[16] To understand Phule's strong words, one must have some idea of the way the brāhmaṇas had managed to create a special niche for themselves in Maharashtra society.

During the time of the Peshwas, the brāhmaṇas had managed to make a comeback to power politics. Untouchability had a field-day during this time. The untouchables were forbidden to walk through the city streets of Pune in the afternoon, lest their lengthened shadow should fall on the high-brows of society.

When the Peshwa's kingdom was annexed by the British in the early part of the 19th century, the brāhmaṇas managed to hold their own. The British took care not to antagonise the brāhmaṇas, the leaders of the community, to prevent them from exploiting the disaffection that was bound to exist among the people over the annexation. With this view, the government extended grants to the brāhmaṇas for Sanskrit studies.

The brāhmaṇas of Maharashtra, like those of Bengal, looked upon all non-brāhmaṇas as śūdras. This was the condition in Maharashtra in which Phule was born and brought up.

In a great humane gesture, Phule befriended the untouchables. He opened a school for the boys and girls of this community in 1851. Missionaries had been till then the only people who would speak of education for the untouchables. Phule arranged for supply of water for them. He had opened a school for women in 1848.

In 1873 Phule founded the Satyasodhak Samaj. The Samaj taught that all men and women are God's children. God is one. One's greatness does not depend on one's birth. Every human being has direct access to God and is in need of no middlemen.[17] These were the principles on which reform of society was to be based. Phule wanted to found a new religion based on truth, reason and equality. He rejected in religion all that offended reason. He called the new religion 'The Sarvajanik Satya Dharma' or the Universal Religion of Truth.

Phule called for radical changes in society. He wanted all hereditary functions in the village communities abolished. He believed that education was the key to the emancipation of the untouchables. It was on this conviction that he set out to provide educational facilities for them. He asked the non-brāhmaṇa communities not to summon the brāhmaṇas to perform religious rites in their homes. Phule denounced caste as an importation of Aryans who are represented by the brāhmaṇas. They had imposed caste on the inhabitants on the land.[18]

Phule wanted to forge a united front of all backward classes, the tribals and the untouchables. His front would include such groups in the region as the Malis, the Kumbis, the Mahārs, the Dangars, the Mangs and the tribals. Even the kṣatriyas would have a place in it. He named the front 'Bahujana Samaj'.[19]

Phule faced vicious opposition from the orthodox sections of Maharashtrian society. He was even denounced as a stooge of the missionaries. V.K. Chiplunkar and B.G. Tilak were two of his most implacable adversaries. They carried on their attacks through the columns of the Marathi periodicals, *Nibandhamālā* and the *Kesarī*.

Justice for Women

The liberal ideas that had begun to percolate into Indian society caused rumblings in many quarters. The agitation against widow-burning had been an example of this new wave. But widow-burning was but one instance of the oppression of women. The plight of women was the subject of campaigns by thinkers and social reformers of the 19th century. Kesab Chandra Sen had already in the first half of the century pleaded for the universalisation of education. Few have done so signal a service in the cause of women as Iswar Chandra Vidyasagar.

Vidyasagar came from a family that was known for its orthodoxy. He was born on September 26, 1826, in the village of Birsingha in Midnapore district of West Bengal. His rural background with scant educational facilities was hardly designed to turn him into a great advocate of social reform and of women's emancipation. Vidyasagar received his early education in his native village. Future generations would never have heard of Vidyasagar but for an uncle of his who thought that times were on the move. One had to move with them. So the young Vidyasagar was taken to Calcutta. There he joined the Sanskrit College.[20]

The twin institutions of the Hindu College and the Sanskrit College were making a great contribution to the education of the youth of Calcutta. The Hindu College was founded by a group of Bengali citizens with the assistance of some Englishmen in 1817. The Sanskrit College was established in 1822 at a time when the government leaned towards an Orientalist policy in education. It was during Vidyasagar's stint at the Sanskrit College that the controversy between the Orientalists and the Occidentalists broke out. He could not have remained unaffected by the storm that was raging about him. He must have heard the arguments so vociferously aired by the two groups. He was thus in a position to see the relative merits of the arguments adduced by the opposing groups. The controversy undoubtedly played a part in shaping his attitudes towards modern education.

As principal of his almamater, the Sanskrit College, Vidyasagar proposed wide-ranging reforms of the syllabus. His proposals were approved. He abolished admission to College on caste basis. The brāhmaṇas had till then opposed the entry even of Kayasthas, not to speak of the śūdras.[21] He very pointedly asked how it was that the brāhmaṇas who were very eager to teach Englishmen Sanskrit were unprepared to teach their fellow Hindus the same language. He also was in favour of introducing the study of English into the syllabus. He realised the need for teaching Western sciences but insisted that the native language was the proper medium of instruction.

Vidyasagar's attention had now turned to the problem of women's education. He made common cause with others fired by the same ideals as his. Their efforts bore fruit in the establishment of the Bethune school in May 1849 in Calcutta. This was the first school for girls in the city. Lord Dalhousie in his circular of April 11, 1850, promised official support for the efforts of those who were promoting women's education. Vidyasagar's effort in this area was not confined to Calcutta. He looked for a field for fresh ventures. He was instrumental in establishing during 1857-58 no fewer than 35 girls' schools in the districts. These were all vernacular schools in conformity with his policy on the medium of instruction.[22] He is rightly regarded as a pioneer and a champion of women's emancipation.

Vidyasagar's greatest contribution lay in his work for one of the most oppressed groups in Hindu society, the widows. Vidyasagar first put forward his proposals on widow re-marriage in 1854 in an article. He followed this up with a pamphlet on the subject in January 1855, in which he quoted *Parāśara Samhitā* which permits the remarriage of a woman in the event of her husband becoming a *sanyasi*, being found impotent or becoming degraded (*patita*) or insane or if he dies.[23] In October of the same year he sent a petition carrying hundreds of signatures to the government asking for legislation to permit re-marriage of widows. The orthodox Hindus also started a campaign against the move to legalise widow re-marriage. They sent several petitions to the government against the move.

The Widow Re-marriage Bill was introduced in Central Legislative Council and read for the third time, and passed on July 19, 1856. It received the assent of the Governor-General on July 26 and became law.[24] The first marriage under the new Act was performed on December 7, 1866, in Calcutta under tight security.

Vidyasagar had already in December 1855 submitted a petition to the government, which was signed by 25,000 persons, urging the government to prohibit polygamy. Before the government could take any action, it faced the serious crisis of the armed revolt of 1857. On account of the revolt, the government became more wary and fought shy of any measure that might antagonise a section of the people. It decided to shelve the matter. In February 1866 Vidyasagar submitted a new petition signed by 21,000 persons, asking the government to act on polygamy.

The Bengal government on its own planned to bring forward legislation to prohibit polygamy. On August 6, 1866 the Governor-General wrote to the Bengal government, directing it to postpone the legislation and to make further inquiries into the matter. The Bengal government then appointed a committee to study afresh the prevalence of polygamy in the Presidency. The committee submitted its report in February 3, 1867. The report exposed the shocking conditions of the widows. The evil was widespread among the *kulīna* (blue-blooded) brāhmaṇas. Some brāhmaṇas had dozens of wives. The largest number of wives any one person had was 82. As in the 20th century, marriage was used as a means of enriching oneself. There was a double benefit in this form of polygamy. A husband received substantial cash dowry at the time of marriage. The wife continued to live with her parents. It would of course have been impossible for a husband to bring to home all his wives. Instead the husband made a round of the homes of his numerous fathers-in-law. He received valuable presents at this visit. After spending a few days there, he would move on to the next.[25] In their anxiety to secure a *kulīna* husband for their daughter, a father gave his daughter's hand to a man who already had dozens of wives.

Another issue relating to women on which social reformers were campaigning was the age of consent. Child marriage inevitably led to the evil of a man having sex relations with a minor girl. But as the *śāstras* permitted, even enjoined, early marriage, they were up against a mighty wall of resistance. Vidyasagar had the satisfaction of reading on his death-bed a copy of the Age of Consent Bill introduced in the Central Legislative Council. He died on July 29, 1891.

Ever since Vidyasagar sponsored the campaign for widow remarriage, virulent attack was mounted against him. He was subjected to abuse, harassment and physical assault. The campaign had forced him into a virtual retirement. But the great warrior had fought his great battles, run his great race. He had won his place among the men and women of all ages who had fought courageously for human rights. Future generations of Indian women will remember him with gratitude. Many of them would still be living a life without hope but for Vidyasagar.

A New Wave in Andhra

As in other parts of India, English education brought on a new wave of fervour for regeneration of society. It was during the tenure of Lord Munro as Governor of Madras Presidency that a start was made in this area. In June, 1822, he issued a note enquiring into the state of education in the Presidency. The response elicited by the enquiry drew a bleak picture of education in the districts. To remedy the state of affairs, a Board of Public Instruction was formed in 1826. The Board was authorised to open two schools in each district. The first such school was founded at Rajahmundry.[26]

The school was apparently a success. The people began clamouring for English schools. The missionaries made a valuable contribution by opening the first-ever girls' school at Guntur in 1842. They went on to open six other schools in the district within the span of a year. It was also at Rajahmundry that one of the first-grade colleges to be established in 1877 in the Madras Presidency was located.

Even before the English education was introduced into the region, social criticism had been voiced by those who had come in contact with the British. Enugula Veeraswamiah (b. 1780) was an interpreter at the high court in Madras. He appears to have made a tour of India. In his memoirs, he has passed severe judgement on such social evils as caste and untouchability. According to him there is no warrant for untouchability in the Vedas and the *smriṭis*. Ill-treatment of the lower classes led to their mass conversions, he argued.

Kandukuri Viresalingam (b. 1847), a younger contemporary of Iswar Chandra Vidyasagar, played much the same role in Andhra as that of the Bengal reformer in the cause of women. Viresalingam came of a rural and orthodox family and received his early education in the traditional method. But later he attended the government school at Rajahmundry. He was at first very faithful in the observance of the traditions of his caste. What brought about a change in his attitude was the chance reading of a collections of the speeches of Kesab Chandra Sen. The Brahma Samaj had already made a beginning in Andhra. Viresalingam was always a great admirer of the British and greatly appreciated the benefits they brought to India. He thought that if the British withdrew from India, it would result in lawlessness and would halt the social reform movement.[27]

Yet Viresalingam was one of the first who gave a call for adoption of *swadesī* or use of locally produced goods. He bemoaned the craze for foreign cloth both among the rich and the poor.[28] This was long before B.G. Tilak talked about a *swadesī* movement. Viresalingam wished to see a greater sense of self-reliance among the people of his country.

In 1874 Viresalingam launched the journal, *Vivekavardhini*, to create awareness of the need for special change. Along with others holding similar ideas he founded the Rajahmundry Social Reform Association in 1878. The orthodox section of Andhra society was still opposed to the education of women. Education was good enough for prostitutes and *devadāsis* only. The protagonists of girls' education opened a school for them at Dewaleswaram in 1874. A campaign for women's education and for dissemination of Western knowledge was launched in the columns of the *Vivekavardhini*. Viresalingam himself opened a school for girls at Rajahmundry in 1881.[29]

Early marriages and the practice of accepting *śulka* were two of the evils prevalent in the region. The Rajahmundry Social Reform Association started a movement against early marriages. The reformists' group agitated for legislation to bring about a change. Those who did not marry off their daughters early were regarded as irreligious. The practice was more common among the brāhmaṇas. Poverty was a factor in the custom of accepting *śulka* or *kanyāśulka* as it was called. The fear of the parents that they might not find for their daughter suitable mate if the marriage was delayed, also went to strengthen the custom. Young girls were frequently given to elderly males in return for *śulka*. Those who had the means, even though senile, could buy girls for *śulka*.[30] This was the state of affairs at this time. Viresalingam mercilessly attacked the practice in *Vivekavardhini*. Women's education had brought to the forefront of the reform movement a number of women leaders.

Viresalingam took up the cause of widow remarriage in the late 70s of the century. He delivered several lectures on the subject in 1879. The first ever widow remarriage in Andhra was performed on December 11, 1881, while Madras had to wait till June 1883 to witness a widow remarriage.[31] During his stay in Madras, Viresalingam founded a home of widows there. Later, he founded a similar home at Rajahmundry.

After Viresalingam launched his campaign for the remarriage of widows, the ultra-conservatives unleashed their fury on him. It became necessary for him to deliver lectures under police guard. A batch of his students guarded the approaches to his residence. He was even expelled from his caste.[32] But nothing could daunt or deter him from the task he had undertaken.

Besides Viresalingam, there were others who made valuable contributions to the regeneration of society. One such reformer was Venkataratna Naidu. He agitated against *devadāsi* system. The agitation bore fruit when a Bill was brought to the Central Legislative Council on protection of minor girls.

Maharashtra Social Reformers and Revivalists

Lord Elphinstone opened a school in Pune in 1821. This school grew into the Poona College in 1851, which was renamed the Deccan College in 1861. This institution was destined to play a crucial role in the life of Maharashtra society by turning out a host of young men infected by modern liberal ideas. Some of these young men would become reputed leaders of the country and aid in shaping her destiny.

Meanwhile the process of change and renewal had set in Bombay. A few intellectuals of the city led by Dadoba Pandurang and Bhau Mahajan established a secret anti-caste society. Branches were established in several towns of Maharashtra with a total membership of more than 1000. In 1861 someone managed to secure a copy of the list of members and had it published. There was a hue and cry over it. Most of the members preferred to withdraw from the society, rather than face censure and persecution from their castemen.[33]

The visit by Kesab Chandra Sen to Bombay in 1864 put new heart into the advocates social change. The founders of the erstwhile anti-caste society were only lying low. They were determined to revive the spirit of the society and with this aim they founded the Prarthana Samaj on March 31, 1867 in Bombay. The Samaj drew much inspiration from the Brahma Samaj of Bengal. Absolute equality of all human beings was one of its cardinal tenets, and social reform one of its avowed aims. Eminent men like R.G. Bhandarkar and M.G. Ranade were members of the Samaj. An innovation in those days was that the men brought along their wives to weekly gathering and worship. The scene of action now shifts to Pune.

In the second half of the 19th century the controversial figure of Visnuśastri Kṛṣṇasastri Chiplunkar broke in upon the Maharashtra scene. Ciplunkar was born in 1850 in a Citpawan family. His father was an employee of the Bombay government. After his matriculation, he joined the Deccan College.[34]

What drew the attention of the public were his essays in the *Nibandhamālā* which he had launched. On the one hand he favoured some change in society and on the other he defended caste. Chiplunkar denounced both Dayananda Saraswati's Arya Samaj and the Prarthana Samaj. He gave it out that the large attendance at the prayer meetings of the Prarthana Samaj was due to the presence of ladies.[35]

Chiplunkar joined hands with B.G. Tilak to open the New English School in Pune in January 1880. But his tenure as principal of the school was a near disaster. He made the mistake of telling his students that juvenile exuberance would not be mistaken for deliberate insolence. The students made full use of the latitude thus promised so openly. The result was that a riotous atmosphere prevailed in the school. He had to give up the post in August of that year.[36]

Chiplunkar was not opposed to caste. He thought, as did B.G. Tilak, that caste would disappear in time with the advance in education. Yet he let loose his fury on anyone who set out to destroy caste. He carried on a venomous attack on the missionaries, Phule and the British (in that order). He could not see anything good in the missionaries or Phule. But Chiplunkar grudgingly admitted that there were qualities in the British which his countrymen could emulate with profit. Another person on whom he spewed his venom was Hari Deshmukh, better known to Maharashtrians as 'Lokhitavadi'. Unlike Chiplunkar, Deshmukh was a great admirer of the British. He went so far as to say that the coming of the British to India was an act of providence. Even as close a collaborator of Chiplunkar as G.G. Agarkar had to admit that Chiplunkar was frequently unfair in his criticism of Phule, Lokhitavadi and the missionaries.[37] Chiplunkar died at the early age of 32.

The spirit behind the New English School provided the inspiration for the Deccan Education Society which came into being in October 1884. This society established the Ferguson College in 1885 which has rendered commendable service to higher education in Pune.

The latter half of the 19th century was the age of giants, especially in Maharashtra. The greatest of them were G.K. Gokhale, B.G. Tilak, M.G. Ranade and R.C. Bhandarkar. They were in the thick of the controversies on social reform. Tilak differed from the others in his approach to the reform of society. But he understood the value of modern education, and believed in the power of the written word. This was a period which saw the rise of nationalism. Unfortunately much obscurantism masqueraded as nationalism. Tilak would clash with Ranade, Gokhale and Bhandarkar on the nature of reforms to be introduced in society.

Bal Gangadhar Tilak was born at Ratnagiri on July 26, 1856. He studied at the Deccan College, securing a Bachelor's degree. He went on to take a law degree. Even as a college student he displayed a flair for oratory.

The Tilak-Chiplunkar-Agarkar team launched two periodicals. The *Mahratta* the English periodical, first appeared on January 2, 1881, and the Marathi journal *Kesari* on January 4, 1881. The *Mahratta* was edited by Tilak and the *Kesari* by G.G. Agarkar. Both journals were plunged into the furious controversy that erupted over the issue of social reform.

Tilak shared Chiplunkar's views on social reform. While conceding the need for it, they opposed practically every measure brought forward by the government. The Age of Consent Bill clearly demonstrated where Tilak's sympathy lay. He termed the Bill an interference in religous affairs by the government.[38] In theory he was in favour of raising the age of marriage, but was opposed to any legislation. In the face of opposition from the conservative Hindus the Bill was passed in the Central Legislative Council in 1891 to become a law.

During the Congress session of 1895 in Pune, the reformist group in the Bombay Congress led by M.G. Ranade wanted to hold a social conference. The anti-reformist group led by Tilak violently objected to the conference at the same venue. They even threatened to burn down the *pandal* (tent). In a bid to avert a confrontation, the Congress president, Surendranath Banerji, intervened and succeeded in persuading the Ranade group to hold the social conference elsewhere.[39]

Tilak played a questionable role in the establishment of revivalist festivals. Certain Muslim festivals were at the time attracting crowds in Maharashtra. Large numbers of Hindus were drawn to them. To counter-act this, Tilak instituted the Ganesh festival and the Shivaji festival. The aim was mostly diversionary. Tilak has been charged with inciting communal sentiments. In the years following the institution of the festivals, several communal clashes occurred. It is indeed a great irony that communal discord should be associated with the name of Shivaji, the great secularist that he was. But as elsewhere, anything is grist to the communalist mill.

Tilak possessed great courage and was capable of great sacrifices for a cause. He gave a call for the use of Indian goods and the spirit of self-reliance. Unfortunately Tilak frequently chose to be the spokesman of the conservative opinion, and assumed unreasonable postures on social reform measures. In so doing he at times strengthened reactionary forces.

Mahadeva Govinda Ranade is a study in contrast. Though Tilak and Ranade had an identical background, they differed widely in their views on most things. Ranade (b. 1842) received his education at the Elphinstone High School, Bombay, and its sister institution Elphinstone College. R.G. Bhandarkar was his fellow student there. Later both became teachers of the Elphinstone College.[40] It was then that they joined the Prarthana Samaj.

Widow remarriage was a hotly debated issue in Maharashtra. Visnusastri Pandit had translated Vidyasagar's articles into Marathi. He was also one of the founders of the Widow Remarriage Association which came into being in 1861. Yet the first marriage under the new Widow Remarriage Act was performed in Maharashtra only in June 1869. Ranade supported and campaigned in support of the measure.

Dayanand Saraswati was making waves at this time. The reformist group in Pune and Dayanand were both convinced of the urgent need for social change but from entirely different standpoints. Hoping that Dayanand would strengthen the cause of reform, Ranade invited him to Pune. Dayanand stayed a month in the city. His admirers wished to give him a grand farewell. A procession was to be taken through the streets of Pune on the eve of his departure. On the morning of the day of procession, the orthodox group also took out procession to give vent to their anger over Dayanand's views especially on caste and idolatry. The morning procession was headed by 'Swami Gardabhananda', a donkey with a red scarf wrapped around its head and a brightly coloured cloth draped over its back. Behind the donkey there followed a group of people jeering and yelling and generally making a large volume of noise. The procession made its cacophonous round through the city streets. In the evening the procession in honour of Dayanand started from the home of Ranade. Dayanand was seated on a caparisoned elephant. Immediately the processionists were met by another group of people who showered abuses on them. They also threw filth picked from the gutter at the processionists. Those accompanying Dayanand kept their cool and did not react to the abuses.[41] That was the way a section of Pune's orthodox brāhmaṇas treated a reformer in 1874.

Ranade and Bhandarkar were in the forefront of the reform movement. Women's education was a major item on their programme. This took concrete shape in 1882 when the Poona Female High School was opened. The guardians of orthodoxy vigorously opposed the effort of the reformers to educate the women. A Marathi periodical of the day, *Pune Vaibhava*, made the charge that the sponsors of the school were bent on destroying the character of the Indian woman.[42]

Ranade was mainly responsible for organising the social conference along with the yearly Congress session. The purpose of the conference was to focus the attention of the delegates to the Congress session on the reform movement. The first social conference was held in Madras immediately after the Congress session in 1887. The social conference in 1889 passed a resolution recommending that the age of consent be raised through legislation. A law was actually enacted in 1891 as mentioned earlier. The resolution was opposed by B.G. Tilak.[43] A crisis arose at the Pune session of the Congress in 1895 over the issue of the holding of the social conference, as has been noted above.

About this time, an incident occurred involving Ranade, Tilak and many others which reveals the preoccupations of the period. The United States has its Boston Tea party. So has India its very own Pune Tea party. The Panch Howd Christian Mission organised a lecture at the mission. About 50 persons were invited to the lecture which was to be followed by a tea party. Now drinking tea at a Christian residence was a serious breach of caste rules. A brāhmaṇa could lose his caste. Some of the invitees merely pretended to drink without actually tasting the brew. The more adventurous ones drank it. The *Pune Vaibhava*, the Marathi journal and the mouthpiece of the extreme right, published names of the guests at the tea party. Predictably a storm followed. The Shankaracharya was requested to look into the affair. He appointed a committee to investigate 'the crime'. The committee found the guests in the tea party guilty of violating caste rules. They were asked to do penance. Some including Tilak acquiesced. Ranade with a few others refused to comply and was ostracised. Tremendous pressure was brought to bear even on the in-laws of the daughters of the recalcitrant. Some buckled under pressure and meakly submitted.[44]

Ranade was endowed with a great breadth of vision. His nationalism embraced those who did not profess his own religion. He assumed an enlightened attitude towards the Muslims and Muslim culture. Ranade believed that the benign Providence had arranged a fusion of ideas and thoughts through the coming of Islam to India which benefited both the Hindus and Muslims.[45] He refused to take an alarmist view of the presence of the Muslims that was common to many of his contemporaries.

Women of western India owe much to Ranade. On their behalf he battled on many fronts such as widow remarriage, the age of consent and their right to education. He scored impressive achievements together with his collaborators, while carrying on the duties of a judge with great devotion and integrity. When a full history of the struggles for human rights in India is written, Ranade's name will appear prominently. He will be remembered for his dauntless courage, great humanity, his broad vision and sense of justice.

Gopal Kṛṣṇa Gokhale (b. 1866) stood out among the leaders of 19th century India with his nobility of character, his love of humanity, his ability to rise above narrow interests and his total commitment to the people. Mahatma Gandhi would describe Gokhale as the most perfect in the political field. Gokhale firmly believed that mobilisation of the people was imperative if the country was ever to attain political freedom.[46] He stood for the abolition of all distinctions in society and was very sensitive to the issues of justice, which evoked a ready response from him.

Gokhale was very active in the Sarvajanik Sabha founded in 1870 by some citizens of Pune to create public awareness of matters of public interest. When the orthodox lobby led by B.G. Tilak gained control of the Sabha, Gokhale along with Ranade left it and founded the Deccan Sabha. He became editor of *Sudharak*, the mouthpiece of the latter body.

On more than one occasion Gokhale was chosen by the Congress party to present India's views before the British public, which mission he carried out with great distinction.

Gokhale had risen from dire poverty to achieve brilliant academic results, as well as play a leading role in the country's life. He could thus sympathise with the socially and economically under-privileged.

He condemned untouchability in no uncertain terms. He actively sympathised with the aspirations of the lower classes.

Gokhale's concern for equality may be grasped from the fact that one of the vows the members of the Servants of India Society were to take touched on this matter. They pledged themselves to treat all Indians as their equals and to work for the good of all.[47] He will be remembered for his unswerving faith in the untapped strength of the masses. Gokhale died in 1915 before he could realise his dream of forming a band of dedicated men who would sacrifice everything in the service of the country.

Pandita Ramabai (b. 1858) did much in Pune to promote the education of girls. She was the daughter of a brāhmaṇa Sanskrit scholar. He was ostracised by his neighbours for teaching Sanskrit to his wife. It is given to few people to pass through so many tragedies and emerge triumphant as Ramabai did. She came through them all to play a sterling role in the liberation of her oppressed sisters of India.

Ramabai's father, Anantasastri, took up a life of a pilgrim, visiting the holy places all over India, together with his wife and three children. Terrible times came upon them during the famine of 1877. Ramabai's both parents and her sister died, she and her brother continued the wandering life and arrived in Calcutta. There she attracted the learned of the city with her calm dignity and mastery over Sanskrit. She could hold her own in a discussion and speak to a large audience with complete self-possession. It was here that she was invested with the title of 'Pandita', a rare honour, now her brother died. Within a short time she married an educated Bengali, a *śūdra* by caste. Ramabai's cup of suffering was not filled yet. A year and a half after the marriage, her husband died, leaving behind a baby girl in her care. Now she made a momentous decision in her life. Tracing her roots, she returned to Pune in 1882.

The idea of working for the liberation of her sisters of India had come to her during her Calcutta days. She had come in contact with the Brahma Samaj as well as many Christians. Her search for a new ideal took her to England. There Ramabai had occasion to observe the work of some dedicated women for the rehabilitation of fallen women. She had now embraced Christianity. On her visit to the United States, she impressed many with her charm. She told her audiences about the plan that was now forming in her mind. Her American friends promised her assistance in her future work.

Ramabai returned to India in 1889. With the assistance of M.G. Ranade and G.K. Gokhale she established a school for widows called Widows Home in Bombay. As the number of students increased, the institution was moved to Pune. Two of the young widows decided to follow Ramabai into Christianity, drawn by her deep commitment, her personality and love that she radiated. This created a furore in Pune. Many of her friends in Pune severed all links with her. The trial further tested her inner strength and her resolve to uplift her sisters. Ramabai acquired a farm outside Pune and shifted the Home there and now renamed it Mukti (liberation). She sheltered at one time several hundred girls. It was no longer a home for widows of the upper castes as was originally planned. The girls were taught various skills and they began to manufacture articles like baskets, garments, caps and buttons. Ramabai was assisted by a team of dedicated women both Indian and European. She died in April 1922 and left behind a flourishing institution.[48]

Till Ramabai's day the work of emancipation of Indian women was undertaken mostly by committed menfolk. Ramabai set a new tradition by launching her great enterprise. Hers was a rare personality. Even when left in the lurch over the matter of the conversion of young women under her charge, she followed her star.

Social Change through Religious Regeneration

The diffusion of Western ideas through modern education left its mark on the religious environment of the country. As never before, those who professed the Hindu religion were compelled to take a look at the practices and many ancient institutions. Some were thus led to a conviction that accretions of the centuries had clouded authentic religion. Many religious reforms were undertaken which were confined to particular regions of the country. One such reformer was Swami Narayana of Gujarat.

Sahajananda was born in 1780 in a village near Ayodhya. Early in life he displayed an intense interest in matters spiritual. He became a mendicant and wandered all over north India. On being initiated into the sect of Ramananda, he assumed the new name Narayana. Eventually he became the head of the sect and settled in Gujarat. In the course of time Swami Narayana developed a doctrine of his own. Though a professed Vaiṣṇava, he moved away from the sect and finally founded a sect, which came to be known as the Satsang.[49] A brāhmaṇa by birth, he worked for the uplift of the Dheds (untouchables) and Kolis, a backward community of Gujarat. He denounced the brand of monasticism that had established itself in the region, especially of the Vallabhacaria, (not related to the Vallabhas of the Souths). He also berated the princes for their habits of heavy drinking, gambling and other excesses.

Among founders of monastic orders Swami Narayana was unique in this that he made physical labour obligatory for the monks. They performed hard tasks such as digging and hoeing. He also founded an order of women. His ethical teachings are contained in his work, *Śikṣāpatrikā*, originally written in Gujarati but later translated into Sanskrit. Swami Narayana condemned such practices as *satī* and female infanticide and other forms of oppression of women. Infanticide was widely resorted to by the Rajputs and the Kathis of the region.[50]

Swami Narayana sincerely aimed at a regeneration of society on the foundation of human equality. The ideals of the great medieval saints were reasserted by him. Moreover, he seems to have been influenced by the new currents that were flowing through the country. The followers of Swami Narayana seem to have fallen much short of the ideal he set before them.

Though a revivalist, Swami Dayanand Saraswati carried on a campaign against caste. He strove to restore Hinduism to its ancient glory and purity. The Vedas were the only scriptures he recognised. Caste and idolatry can find no justification in the Vedas, Dayanand maintained.

The formative incident in the life of Dayanand (b. 1824) took place when he was yet a boy. He was keeping vigil on the *śivrātri* with his father in the *śiva* temple. Overcome with sleep and exhaustion, his father drowsed. As the boy watched, he saw to his shock a mouse crawling on the idol of *śiva*. How could *śiva* allow this indignity if he was really a god, the young boy asked himself. His belief in idol worship was shaken to its foundation. Later, he voiced his doubts to his father who asked him to dismiss these unholy thoughts. But the temple scene remained etched in his memory and was to determine the stance he assumed later towards idolatry.

The Arya Samaj founded by Swami Dayananda has made a notable contribution to women's education. As part of its programme, the Samaj established a chain of girls' schools which promoted education of this neglected section of society. In fact education has been the most positive contribution the Samaj has made.

But it can hardly be denied that inroads Christian missionaries were making into the communities in the lower rungs of Hindu society played no small part in the policies of the Samaj. Providing a counter-force does not make for a sound ideology. Some of the vehemence Dayananda expended on non-Hindu religions would prove an embarrassment in time to come.

The orthodox Hindus were alarmed at attacks by the Ārya Samaj on idolatry and caste. The alarm resulted in a counter-movement that first appeared in Punjab. The counter-movement found its expression in the founding of Sanatana Dharma Sabha in 1895. The Sanatanists came to the fore in the first quarter of the 20th century. Mahatma Gandhi was fiercely attacked by them on his views on untouchability.

The revival movement in the latter half of the 19th century received encouragement with the arrival in India of Madame Blavatsky and party in 1879. The party later established themselves at Madras.

Blavatsky posed as a defender of the Indian religions. She declared herself a Buddhist. Blavatsky's notion of defending the Indian religions was a blind espousal of everything in them, both rational and irrational, and the most dubious practices. To the guardians of orthodoxy which was under siege, Blavatsky appeared as a heaven-sent relief army. Those who took an alarmist view of social reform movement that was gaining ground in several parts of India, Blavatsky was a great morale booster. The Theosophist Society founded by her defended the sacredness of even the caste system.

Madame Blavatsky made an inglorious exit from the Indian scene in April 1885.

Mrs. Annie Besant, Blavatsky's heir, tried to carry forward the Theosophical movement. At a time when the movement was facing evil days, she had even recourse to the gimmicks of launching a social reform programme. This was no small change in the stand of the Theosophists in earlier days.[51] But Besant has contributed to the education of women. She played an important part in the establishment of the Banaras Hindu University. At the opening ceremony of the University, M.K. Gandhi (not yet a Mahatma) disconcerted many dignitaries with his forthright speech.

A Messiah for the Ezhavas

In the latter half of the 19th century the backward communities were throwing up leaders and reformers. One of the most articulate leaders was undoubtedly Jotirao Phule. Less well known, there arose among the Ezhavas of Kerala, a leader who strove to raise his community from stagnation, illiteracy and superstition. He is Sri Narayana Guru.

Nanu Asan was born in a village near Trivandrum in the late 50s of the last century. Like Phule, he succeeded in acquiring only a rudimentary education. Yet he would rise above this handicap. Like Swami Narayana of Gujarat, Nanu yearned for a more intense religious experience. He left home in search of light and teachers. He received his initiation at the hands of a Tamil guru and took the new name Sri Narayana. He then set out towards the forest where he lived for some time. Emerging from this life of solitude, he sought to share the religious experience of other religious groups such as the Muslims and Christians.

Once an ascetic advised Sri Narayana to devote his life to the good of the poor. The advice gave a new orientation to his life.[52]

His religious ideas began to take shape. He believed in God and the oneness of mankind. He rebelled against the domination of society by brāhmaṇas. Determined to end the total control by the brāhmaṇas on the whole area of worship, Sri Narayana built temples in different parts of Kerala and consecrated them himself. The first of these temples was constructed at Aruvipuram where he had settled down. He also appointed priests of his own Ezhava community to these temples. The revolt against the authority of the brāhmaṇas predictably aroused their anger. They began to persecute him.[53]

Sri Narayana founded an order of monks called Sri Narayana Guru Sangham, which drew many non-Ezhavas to its ranks. He denounced brahmanic practices the Ezhavas had adopted in the course of time. Many in the upper castes supported Sri Narayana's reform efforts. Sri Narayana tried to promote education among the Ezhavas. The Sri Narayana Dharma Paripalana Yogam which came into existence in the early years of the 20th century succeeded in instilling a sense of unity into the community. This society has functioned as the representative body of the Ezhava community.

Modern times have provided several illustrations of how communities managed to move up socially. One of the more striking instances is of the Nadars of Tamil Nadu.

The Nadars were traditionally toddy tappers of the region. Ethnically they appear to be closely related to the Ezhavas of Kerala. They are also known by the alternative name of *Sanars*. Tapping of toddy has never been regarded as respectable occupation. Hence the Nadars stood low on the social ladder. Suddenly a change seemed to have come over them in the early 70s of the last century. The change, however, was not inexplicable.

The district of Tirunelveli was one of the areas where the missionaries established schools. These schools existed already in the 40s of the century. The Nadars appear to have responded to the lure of education with enthusiasm. Education invariably resulted in self-awareness and rising aspirations. The changing mood among the Nadars exhibited itself in a new aggressiveness.

In 1874 the Nadars attempted to force an entry into the Minakṣi temple at Madurai but were foiled. Again they tried to enter the temple at Tirutangal in Srivilliputtur but were unsuccessful in the attempt. In 1885 trouble arose at Sattur when the Nadars wanted to hold a rally in the upper caste quarters of the town.[54] In 1895 the Nadars asked the Tirunelveli temple committee to appoint a Nadar on the temple Trust. The request was turned down. The Tirunelveli temple had to be closed down when the Nadars continued their attempts to enter the temple.[55] The Nadars resorted to conversions as a means of social protest. Social aspirations have been inextricably linked to conversion by lower classes in modern times. The Nadars were now using it as a weapon. Many instances of the same use of conversions by other communities would be witnessed in the decades to come.

It was in 1895 too that the serious communal riot brokeout at Kalugumali in Tirunelveli district. In all nine persons were killed and hundreds of houses were destroyed. Once again the Nadars were one of the feuding groups.

In the beginning of the present century, the Nadars launched a movement aimed at gaining social upgradation. Now they prohibited their women from carrying headloads, wearing lead ornaments and going to market.

The Decline of the Brahma Samaj Movement

The Brahma Samaj arose as a response to the need of the times. Its sister societies such as the Sadharan Brahma Samaj founded by Kesab Chandra Sen and the Prarthana Samaj of Bombay further broadened its vision. All these bodies worked among the educated classes of the day. They were unable to create a mass movement but restricted themselves to the upper crust of society. Towards the last decades of the 19th century strong forces arose to counter the influence of the Brahma Samaj movement.

One of the counter-forces to the Brahma Samaj movement was the new wave of nationalism. Nationalists played down the importance of social changes while at the same time emphasising the urgency of political change. Many nationalists tended to defend existing institutions of society and viewed all criticism of these institutions with suspicion. This attitude resulted in the defence of patently anachronistic practices and customs. Much obscurantism passed under the guise of nationalism. The revivalist spirit that animated a certain brand of natioalism was not conducive to bringing about social change.

The new upsurge of animation which many caste groups displayed towards the end of the last century and in the early decades of the 20th century ran counter to the spirit of brotherhood that the Brahma movement was promoting. Many of these caste groups were now trying to establish a new identity for themselves. This was the centrifugal force operating then in Indian society. Several castes were straining to upgrade themselves vis-a-vis other groups. These attempts at upgradation generally accentuated caste consciousness and case loyalty. The negative aspect of upgradation attempts was heightened, unwittingly though, by the British themselves.

The census operations carried out by the British government were partly responsible for mounting caste consciousness. The 1901 census attempted to classify the multiplicity of castes.[56] Here the census officials were faced with a gigantic task. Some lower castes viewed the census as an unlooked-for opportunity to secure a higher caste standing. An instance of a caste seeking a new status is that of the caṇḍālas of Bengal. They wanted to be referred to as Namasudras in the census. Several groups seemed to have woken up to status and began to assume elitist postures. Even some depressed classes adopted the use of the sacred thread and the food fads of higher castes. The Dusadhs of eastern India are a depressed class community, yet they wear the sacred thread, the symbol of upper caste status.

The changed situation saw a widening of gaps between lower castes. The lowest classes, such as the untouchables, suffered in the bargain. They sank lower; they had no castes below them towards whom they might behave superciliously.

It was indeed ironic that at a time when education seemed to offer an antidote to caste, the very aspirations generated by this education should have strengthened the distinctive identities of caste groups.

It would however be a gross misrepresentation of history to hold the British responsible for the grip caste had on the Indian mind. Caste had become the overriding value long before the British established their hegemony over India. We have the testimony of Abbe Dubois, a French missionary who studied the social organisation of the Hindus about the time the British were tightening their hold on the country. Dubois made his investigations mainly in Mysore in the latter half of the 18th century. He has a story to tell.

Four brāhmaṇas were travelling through a war-torn country. They could find no food in the devastated land. They had some rice with them but no pot to cook it in. Looking about for some utensil, they came upon a pot which, as unluck would have it, had belonged to a washerman. How could the brāhmaṇas use the washerman's pot? But hunger overcame caste considerations. They had the rice cooked in it. One of the brāhmaṇas refused to partake of a meal, as it was polluted. Returning to their village, the abstainer denounced his three companions to the caste pancāyat. The three were summoned to the pancāyat to answer charges. Forewarned about the accusation, they had their defence ready. They turned the tables on their accuser by charging him with the crime of having cooked a meal in a washerman's cooking pot, while they had gone hungry. The testimony of one against the word of three was of no avail. The accuser was convicted of the charge and was expelled from the caste.[57] The caste law transcended all moral laws. To save one's caste, one could resort to fraud, trickery or perjury.

The brāhmaṇas in the story, of course, did not know their *śāstras* very well. Else they could have appealed to Manu, who permits some latitude in emergencies. Manu cites with approval the example of Viśwamitra who accepted a dog's leg from a caṇḍāla when he was revenously hungry, and, we may presume, ate it with much relish.

Besides nationalism and a strengthening of caste loyalties, a new force entered the Indian political scene. Such was the non-brāhmaṇa movement that made its appearance in the second decade of the century. This force would prove further obstacle to the growth of the Brahma movement, which was viewed as a movement inspired by the brāhmaṇas. Of the non-brāhmaṇa movement, more to be said later.

NOTES

1. Binoy Ghose, *Ishwar Chandra Vidyasagar*, New Delhi, Govt. of India, 1965, p.21.
2. Ibid., p.40
3. Percival Speer, *A History of India*, Vol. 2, Harmondsworth, Penguin Books Ltd, 1981, p.126 ff.
4. M.E. Gibbs, *Anglican Churches in India* : 1600-1970, Delhi, SPCK, 1972, p.251.
5. Ibid., p.271.
6. J.N. Farquhar, 1967 B, p.33.
7. Ibid., p.43.
8. Ibid., p.35.
9. P.K. Sen, *Keshub Chunder Sen*, Calcutta. The Centenary Committee, 1938, p.13.
10. Ibid., p.37.
11. Ibid., p.48.
12. Quoted by P.K. Sen, 1938, p.71.
13. G.S. Ghurye, 1969, p.272.
14. M.E. Gibbs, 1972, p.228.
15. Ibid.,p.228.
16. Ibid., p.226.
17. W.N. Kuber, *B.R. Ambedkar*, New Delhi, Govt. of India, 1978, p.20.
18. A.D. Pant & Shiv K. Gupta (ed). *Multi-Ethnicity and National Integration*, New Delhi, Vohra Publishers and Book Sellers India, 1985, p.250 ff.
19. Ibid., p.255 ff.
20. Binoy Ghose, 1965, p.20 ff.
21. Ibid., p.44.
22. Ibid., p.66 ff.
23. Ibid., p.83.
24. Ibid., p.84.
25. Ibid., p.119.
26. V. Ramakrishna, 1983, p.17.
27. Ibid., p.80.
28. Ibid., p.81.
29. Ibid., p.94.
30. Ibid., p.107.
31. Ibid., p.126.
32. Ibid., p.120.
33. Y.D. Phadke, *V.K. Chiploonkar*. National Book Trust India, 1983, p.6.
34. Ibid., pp.11-13.
35. Ibid., p.51.
36. Ibid., p.20 ff.
37. Ibid., p.80.
38. N.G. Jog, *Lokmanya Bal Gangadhar Tilak*, New Delhi, Govt. of India, 1965, p.32
39. Ibid., p.44.
40. P.J. Jagirdar, *Mahadeo Govind Ranade*, New Delhi, Govt. of India, 1971, p.34.

41. Ibid., p.74.
42. Ibid., p.110.
43. Ibid., p.155.
44. Ibid., pp.168-69.
45. P.J. Jagirdar, op cit., p.133.
46. D.G. Karve & D.V. Ambekar (ed.), *Speeches and Writings of Gopal Krishna Gokhale*, Bombay, Asia Publishing House, 1966, p.ix.
47. Ibid., p.219.
48. I owe many of the details of Ramabai's life to Stephen Neill, *Builders of the Indian Church*, London, Edinburg House Press, 1934, p.134 ff.
49. Stephen Fuchs, *Rebellious Prophets: A study of messianic Movements in Indian Religions*, Bombay, Asia Publishing House, 1965, p.210 ff.
50. Ibid., pp.214-5.
51. J.N. Farquhar, 1967 B, p.289.
52. Stephen Fuchs, 1965, p.269 ff.
53. Ibid., p.268.
54. G.S. Ghurye, 1969, p.383.
55. Ibid., p.384.
56. Ibid., p.281.
57. Abbe Dubois, *Hindu Manners, Customs and Ceremonies*, tr. by Henry Beauchamp, Oxford, The Clarendon Press, 1983, p.40.

6

THE BATTLE HOTS UP

AS INDIA stepped into the 20th century, the struggles within Indian society took on a new complexion. The pre-occupation no longer was with mere social reform. The Indian National Congress, the foremost body agitating for self-government, was finding its voice. Guided by such stalwarts as Dadabhai Naoroji and Pherozshah Mehta, the Congress was growing more articulate and gaining in confidence. The century that witnessed so much turbulence would also see vast changes in Indian society. While the struggle for political freedom grew more intense, so did the struggle for social equality. Yet the course of true freedom, as of true love, never did run smooth. While on the one hand the lower classes deprived of human rights for millennia were clamouring for dignity and a rightful place in society, the privileged groups on the other girded up their loins to defend even such execrable practices as untouchability. It is within the context of the determination of the disadvantaged groups that we must view the newly emerging forces such as the depressed classes movement and the non-brāhmana movement.

Stirrings among the Depressed Classes

There were clear signs of a changed mood in the growing self-assertion of the depressed classes. Their voices were growing more strident. A landmark in the struggles of the depressed classes was the establishment of the Depressed Classes Mission on October 18, 1906, under the presidentship of Justice N.G. Candravarkar.[1] Candravarkar, sensitive to the aspirations of the lower classes, toured western India extensively, speaking of the need to render justice to them. His lectures succeeded in creating some public awareness of the conditions of the deprived sections of society.

Among the depressed class communities, it was the Mahars who fired the first salvo, demanding the attention of the rest of society. The Mahars' new posture was reminiscent of the protest of the

Pulayas of Tranvancore in the mid-19th century as discussed in the previous chapter. There was, of course, this difference that whereas Pulayas only demanded the right to clothe themselves fully, the Mahars demanded a lot more.

A Mahar conference was held in Pune in November 1910, where a memorandum to the secretary for India was drawn up.

'As British subjects', said the memorandum, 'we cannot, we should not submit to ordinances which are entirely foreign to British ideas of public justice and public honour. We are sick of the bondage which the barbarism of Hindu customs imposes upon us; we long to enjoy the perfect freedom which the British nation and the British Government desire to offer impartially to all those who are connected with them as British subjects.'

'We would, therefore, earnestly appeal', the memorandum went on to say, 'to the Imperial Government to move on our behalf. We have long submitted to the Jagannath of caste. We have for ages been crushed under its ponderous wheels. But we can now no longer submit to the tyranny.'[2]

It had been the practice of the British to recruit the Mahars into the army. This recruitment went on till 1892 when recruitment of the untouchables was stopped. Ramji Ambedkar, B.R. Ambedkar's father, petitioned the Bombay Government to restore the recruitment right of the Mahars. G.K. Gokhale also intervened on their behalf. On February 6, 1917, the Bombay Government withdrew the order banning the recruitment of the untouchables. A Mahar battalion was raised during World War I.[3]

A depressed classes conference was held in Bombay on November 11, 1917, under the presidentship of N.G. Candravarkar. The conference placed before the government the demands of the untouchables. These demands were also submitted to the Congress at its annual session in Calcutta in 1917.[4]

The growing sensitivity towards the rights of the depressed classes could be clearly seen in a discussion that took place in the Bombay Legislative Council on July 8, 1919. Two resolutions were moved in the Council. The first of these recommended that persons from depressed classes be included among the nominated members to municipalities and other local bodies. The government accepted the recommendation, provided there were suitable candidates. The second resolution recommended that wells and *dharmaśālas* (lodges) owned by the government be thrown open to the untouchables or that these be maintained separately for them. The chief secretary to the government replied that the local bodies themselves had the power to take appropriate action on the matter.[5]

The Non-Brāhmaṇa Movement

The birth and growth of the non-brāhmaṇa movement is a significant development on the Indian social scene. The movement proved to be a powerful force for the attainment of social justice. Like the depressed classes movement, this too was the outcome of the growth in self-awareness of the people. A mild surge of power seemed to course through the people. Both the depressed classes movement and the non-brāhmaṇa movement arose much before Mahatma Gandhi ever appeared on the Indian political stage.

Jotirao Phule was undoubtedly the father of the non-brāhmaṇa movement in modern times. He wanted to forge a front of all non-brāhmaṇa communities of Maharashtra which would be called Bahujana Samaj. The 20th century resurgence of the movement was not a conscious revival of Phule's dream. The brāhmaṇas were partly responsible for the outburst of hostility towards them. It all began in Madras Presidency in the second decade of this century.

Proportionate representation of communities on government posts has always been a bone of contention. The tussle between the brāhmaṇas had the non-brāhmaṇas arose precisely over this issue. With the tremendous advantages the brāhmaṇas held in their hands, they found it easy enough to grab the lion's share of the higher-grade posts as well as a substantial portion of the subordinate posts. When the non-brāhmaṇas began to put forward claims for a share of these posts, the brāhmaṇas resented the intrusion into their territory.

As a consequence of the armed revolt of 1857 the British rulers realised that over-dependence on the brāhmaṇas for the administration of the Colony was harmful to British interests. Suspicion of the brāhmaṇas had begun to burgeon in the British mind. They wanted to reduce their influence on the administration. This was one of the reasons why the British wished to bring other communities also into the administrative service. The betterment of other communities was not their sole motive.

As early as 1854 the Revenue Board, Madras, through its standing order asked the district collectors to see to it that the subordinate appointments were not monopolised by a few families. It stipulated that every effort should be made to distribute appointments among the principal castes in the districts.[6] There were difficulties in the implementation of the order. The sudra castes had long been deprived of the opportunity to acquire education. There had been heavy odds against the lower classes till then. Many of these communities were unable to enter the services. They were in no position to enter into a competition with the elite classes.

In 1871 the Census Superintendent, Madras, W.R. Cornish, pointed out in his report the domination of the brāhmaṇas in the services. 'Politically,' he observed, 'it is not to the advantage of the government that every question connected with the progress of the country should be viewed through the medium of Brahmin spectacles. 'The true policy of the State,' Cornish added, 'would be to limit their numbers in official positions and to encourage a large proportion of non-Brahmin Hindus and Muslims to enter official service so as to allow no special pre-eminence or preponderance of a particular caste.'[7]

What brought the cleavage between the brahmaṇas and the non-brāhmaṇas to the fore was the enquiry conducted by the Royal Commission of Public Services appointed in 1912. It interviewed many prominent citizens, both brahmaṇas and non-brāhmaṇas, to ascertain their views on the desirability of distributing appointments to the public services on the basis of the numerical strength of the various communities. The brāhmaṇas to a man insisted on merit as the only safe criterion for selection of candidates for appointments. They feared that proportionate representation would jeopardise the prestige of the services. The non-brāhmaṇas interviewed by the Commission supported the principle of proportionate representation.[8]

The Madras Government realised that in order to end the hold of a particular community on the civil services, there was no other way but to adopt the policy of setting apart certain percentages of appointments to other communities. The cleavage between the brāhmaṇas and non-brāhmaṇas became more apparent in the election of members from Madras to the Central Legislative Council.

Two seats in the Central Legislative Council fell to Madras and these were to be filled by the votes of non-official members in the Provincial Legislative Council. Among candidates seeking election was a reputed non-brāhmaṇa leader, Dr. T. Madhavan Nair. Six other candidates were also in the fray. Nair was defeated and two brāhmaṇas elected. The disappointment of the non-brāhmaṇas was acute and palpable. They were now convinced that they would never obtain justice at the hands of the brāhmaṇas. The groundwork of a non-brāhmaṇa movement began to be laid now.[9]

The brāhmaṇas saw the threat to their long-enjoyed monopoly of jobs. They dubbed those demanding a just share of the appointments as short-sighted and communal. In their anxiety to ward off any threat to their security, some of them even resorted to unreason ableness.

The non-brāhmaṇas formed the South Indian Liberal Federation in 1916. This party would be popularly known as the Justice Party. The formation of the Party marks a new phase in the struggles of the non-brāhmaṇas for social equality. The non-brāhmaṇa leaders met at Madras on November 20, 1916, and issued a manifesto. It called upon all enlightened members of the non-brahmaṇa community to be 'up and doing'. 'Their future,' the manifesto reminded them, 'lies in their own hands.' It further asked them to give high priority to the education of boys and girls.

The South Indian Liberal Federation feared that self-government, f attained by India, would inevitably mean brāhmaṇa domination in place of the British domination and that in consequence the plight of the lower classes could be far worse than under the British. The federation issued its constitution in 1917.[10]

Proportional representation was a major issue in the campaign of the non-brāhmaṇas in the Madras Presidency. The movement won a major victory when the Government of India Act, 1919, provided for the reservation of constituencies for non-brāhmaṇas as was done for the Muslims. Later, it was declared that 24 out of the total 65 constituencies would be reserved for the non-brāhmanas and that there would be open contests in the remaining constituencies.

The non-brāhmaṇas' movement had emerged so strong that it threatened the unity of the Congress Party. The Nagpur session of the Congress in 1920 took note of the tussle between the two groups. A resolution of the session appealed to the Hindu leaders to settle all disputes between brāhmanas and non-brahmanas wherever they existed.[11]

In view of the growing demand for proportional representation of non-brāhmana communities on government posts, the government of Madras in 1922 prescribed specific quotas of posts for various communities. In the same year the Madras Legislative Council decided that out of every 12 posts, five should be allocated to non-brahmaṇa Hindus, two to Muslims, two to brāhmaṇas, two to Anglo-Indians and Christians including Europeans, one to other communities including the depressed classes.[12] This decision was a landmark in the struggles of the non-brahmaṇas. The allocation of quotas was to apply not only at the point of recruitment but also at promotion. There was understandably a great deal of alarm in brahmaṇa circles over the measure adopted by the Council.

The princely state of Mysore also witnessed a strong non-brāhmaṇas' movement in the early part of the present century. The state had been introduced to modern education already in the first half of the 19th century. The conservative sections of Mysore society continued to oppose the education of women. Yet a ferment was plainly discernible. The proof of the changed attitude was a resolution passed in the Legislative Assembly in 1894 that banned marriage of girls before the age of eight. The new law can hardly be called revolutionary, yet it can be regarded as a beginning of a new wave of changes in the offing.

In 1916, a resolution was moved in the Assembly for a grant of Rs. 1 lakh for the education of backward classes. The Dewan disallowed a discussion on it. There was resentment among the backward class members. However, the Maharaja intervened to sanction the grant. The backward classes hailed this as a victory for them.

The non-brahmaṇa communities, which accounted for 96 per cent of the population, now joined hands to form the Praja Mitra Mandali, a united front of all non-brāhmaṇa groups, to press their claims. The Mandali pleaded for the appointment of a committee to study the problems of the non-brāhmaṇas. Visweswarayya, the then brāhmaṇa Dewan of the State, opposed the proposal, fearing that reservation of posts, an inevitable result of the committee, would endanger the efficiency of the administration. He resigned on this issue.[13] Kantaraj Urs, the first ever non-brāhmaṇa Dewan of the State, assumed office in 1919.

The Miller Committee, headed by Justice Leslie Miller, a high court judge, appointed to study the problems of the backward classes, submitted its report in 1919. It rejected the contention of the brāhmaṇas that special provisions for backward classes in appointments would seriously mar the efficiency of the administration. The committee did not specify job quotas for different communities, but it stipulated that not more than half of the gazetted officials' posts should be held by the brāhmaṇas. Most of the top officials who were brāhmaṇas opposed the recommendations of the committee.[14] The orthodox sections were especially enraged over the recommendation that all public schools be thrown open to the pancamas or the depressed classes.

As a result of the implementation of the Miller Committee's recommendations, the share of the non-brāhmaṇas in the total number of appointments rose from 32 to 42 per cent by 1926.

What has come to be known as the 'Sringeri Order' created a furore in the state in 1925. In that year the education department asked the headmaster of a government school at Sringeri to admit untouchables to the school. The brāhmaṇas were incensed. Even the Muslims opposed the order and withdrew their wards from the school.[15] But the education department stuck to its order. An ardent supporter of the non-brāhmaṇa movement, C.K. Reddy, was the inspector-general of schools at that time. Separate schools for the untouchables had been established in the last decade of the 19th century. As the government schools were thrown open to the untouchables, the practice of establishing separate schools for them was discontinued.

The irony of the situation was that two of the main non-brāhmaṇa communities – the Lingayats and Vokkaligas – were not happy at including the untouchables among the non-brāhmaṇas. Now the brāhmaṇas posed as the defenders of the untouchables who were made up chiefly of the Holeyas and the Madigas. They made an effort to organise them. C.K. Reddy too lent his support to the cause of the depressed classes.

In 1927 a resolution was moved in the Assembly to abolish untouchability but it failed to receive adequate support. A similar move was made in the Assembly in 1931 and received the support even from those who had opposed it the first time. The first ever Hindu-Muslim riot in Mysore, known as the Sultanpet riot, took place in Bangalore in 1928 and was closely linked to the non-brāhmaṇa movement. It so happened that a Muslim was leading the non-brāhmaṇa movement. Moreover, the implementation of the Miller Committee's recommendations was to come up for review in 1928 when the specified seven-year period ended. The discontented sections of the population were bent on ending the special concessions to the non-brāhmaṇas. Visweswarayya, who was asked to investigate the causes of the riot, put the blame on those who were unhappy with the Miller Committee. The British Resident openly blamed the brāhmaṇas for engineering the riot.[16]

Gandhi makes His Entry

Nothing like the phenomenon of Mahatma Gandhi has ever been seen in India. A few have left such a deep impression on the country as Gandhi did. He was to transform Indian politics and the Congress Party he guided for more than a quarter of a century. Gandhi was far more than a politician. He was deeply involved in the struggles of the masses for freedom from their century-old slavery.

Gandhi returned to India early in 1915 with the prolonged struggle in South Africa behind him. Though a veteran in political action, he was virtually unknown in India. G.K. Gokhale, Gandhi's mentor, told him to travel and study the Indian situation for two years. The Champaran *satyagraha* of 1917 was Gandhi's first major political action. But it was at the Nagpur session of the Congress in 1920 that Gandhi emerged as a national leader. Both Gokhale and Tilak were dead. Gandhi now stepped in as the foremost leader of the Congress.

As a child, Gandhi was introduced to the rules of untouchability. An untouchable sweeper named Uka used to serve the Gandhi household. Gandhi's mother warned him to be very careful not to touch the sweeper. If he ever accidentally touched an untouchable, his mother had instructed him, he could undo the touch by the counter-touch of a Muslim. Gandhi the child treated these maternal injunctions lightly as he did not understand how a human being was unfit for human contact.

Gandhi felt the full force of the power and irrationality behind caste observance when he was preparing to go to England for his studies. Such a thing wasn't done in his caste. Strangely enough, it was a brāhmaṇa friend of the family who had advised Gandhi's mother to send him to England. Now it was his fellow castemen who showed themselves more zealous for the observance of caste. When Gandhi persisted in his decision to go abroad, he was summoned by the *pancayat* at his community, the Modh Banias. There he was ordered to abandon his project. Gandhi nevertheless told the elders that he would go ahead. He was then declared a renegade, and all members of the community were forbidden even to see him off at the pier.

His castemen had not done with him yet. During the days before his departure, he stayed in Bombay. One day as he was walking by, he was surrounded by his castemen and jeered at. That was their way of punishing him for his disregard of caste rules.[17]

Soon after his arrival in Durban (South Africa) in May 1893, on a request by a client, Gandhi had a painful experience of the type of treatment meted out to his fellow Indians by the white masters. Gandhi called the episode one of the formative incidents of his life.

Gandhi himself had told us the story. He was on a business trip to Johannesburg. He had to travel part of the way by train for which he held a first class ticket. Yet he was forcibly ejected from the train at Meritzburg station along with his suitcase. Gandhi spent the night in the waiting room shivering, as he had only a light coat on. The station staff had retrieved the luggage from the platform where it had been thrown out, but he was afraid to ask for it for fear of being snubbed again. Gandhi was being treated as an untouchable much as an upper caste Hindu would treat a pariah. But Gandhi's humiliation was not yet complete. The last stretch of the journey was by stage-coach. Here he was belaboured by a white passenger. It was an ominous beginning for his South African sojourn.

Since barbers refused to serve Gandhi, he bought himself a pair of clippers and, using a mirror, tried his hand at clipping his own hair. The effect was a near disaster. 'Whatever has happened to your hair?' asked his fellow barristers next day. 'Have the rats been ate it?' He had to fight caste distinctions in the Indian community in South Africa. Kasturba, Gandhi's wife, was very orthodox in observance of caste rules, so he had to fight untouchability in his own home. 'It was in 1897,' Gandhi once wrote, 'that I was prepared to turn Mrs. Gandhi away from the house because she would not treat on a footing of equality Lawrence who, she knew, belonged to the pariah class and whom I had invited to stay with me.'[18] Gandhi had an excellent chance to observe Congressmen practise untouchability during the Congress session in Calcutta in 1901. He had taken time off from South Africa. 'Even here', he writes, 'I was face to face with untouchability in a fair measure. The Tamilian kitchen was far away from the rest. To the Tamil delegates, even the sight of others whilst they were dining, meant pollution. So a special kitchen had to be made in the college compound walled in by wicker work.'[19]

Gandhi had been treated like a pariah in South Africa. He was similarly treated in his own native land. After the Congress session in 1917 in Calcutta, Gandhi set out for Champaran. He passed through Patna chiefly to obtain information on the legal position of peasants of Champaran. With a farmer from Champaran, Gandhi called at the residence of Rajendra Prasad, then a well-known lawyer and later the President of India, but Prasad happened to be away at the time. Prasad's domestic staff would not permit Gandhi to use the lavatory inside the house nor to stay indoor. Gandhi spent the night with his friend on the verandah. He must have been reminded of the night at Meritzburg station in May 1893. True, the night at Patna was not as chilly as at Meritzburg. He speaks of the incident in his autobiography. He had plenty of occasions to see the foul face of untouchability later on in his political career.

It is mentioned at the beginning of this chapter that the issue of the untouchables was coming to the fore. Gandhi had espoused several causes – some of them lost causes – during his career. The Khilafat, Hindu-Muslim unity and untouchability were among these. The problem of untouchability came up at the Nagpur session. But Gandhi had taken up the problem of untouchability in earnest even before the Nagpur session. He had begun to write and speak on the evil.

Starting with the Khilafat conference in Delhi in November 1919, the Khilafat issue occupied Gandhi's attention. The Khilafat agitation was to add a new element to the Indian political movement. The issue centred on the temporal power of the Caliph, the spiritual head of the Muslims. At the end of World War I the British had divested the Caliph of his vast dominions. The Indian Muslims were greatly agitated over the matter. Gandhi argued that as a grave injustice had been done to Islam, it was the duty of Hindus to express solidarity with the Muslims. Gandhi, going far beyond the mere expression of sympathy, led the agitation to restore the Caliph to his lost throne.

If the Muslims wanted to settle the Khilafat question, Gandhi told a Muslim audience at Lahore in July 1920, they must stop weeping. They were fighting, not against one empire (British), but against Christendom itself, Gandhi told them.[20]

Gandhi toured India to address meetings, accompanied by one or other of the Ali Brothers – Maulana Saukat Ali and Maulana Muhamad Ali. Gandhi had told the Hindus at the Khilafat conference at Delhi that they should not regard the support to Muslims as a bargaining point to extract the Muslims' support on the cow issue. By this time in his career, Gandhi had declared war on the British. From an admirer of the British Government, he had turned into an adversary. He called it satanic. While Gandhi was bent on pulling down the British empire, he was agitating to shore up another. His position was not without some irony. To some people who thought that the British presence in India was beneficial to the Hindus as it protected them from the Muslims, Gandhi retorted: 'I would prefer that the Hindus and the Muslims settled their accounts by means of the sword than that the British Government maintained artificial peace between them.'[21] Gandhi's words eerily came true in the Hindu-Muslim riots at the dawn of India's freedom from Britain. Gandhi went so far as to say that in the event of an Afghan invasion he would not support the British.[22]

In the early 1920s Kamal Pasha Ataturk was the new star rising on the Turkish horizon. Gandhi wrote in *Young India* on April 2, 1922, that the cause of the Caliphate was safe in the hands of Kamal Pasha.[23] But alas, Kamal Pasha took the wind out of the sails of Gandhi and the Khilafat agitators when he abolished the caliphate in November of that year. Thus ended the Khilafat movement.

Gandhi has sometimes been blamed for the Khilafat movement. He had made an extraneous issue the subject of a nation-wide movement. With the collapse of the agitation, the cause of the Hindu-Muslim unity suffered a severe setback. The agitation had unnecessarily aroused much religious emotion. Some of the communal incidents in the mid 1920s have been traced to the vacuum created by the sudden death of the Khilafat movement.

Though Gandhi had told the Hindus not to put a price of their support to the Muslims on the Khilafat question, he himself was not without some hope on the outcome. Gandhi told a meeting of the AICC at Bombay on August 8, 1942, explaining his reason for lending support to the Khilafat agitation: 'I did in my heart of hearts cherish a hope that it might enable me to save the cow.'[24]

Despite the disappointing outcome of the Khilafat agitation, Gandhi had a chance to forge, temper and sharpen a powerful weapon during its course. That was the non co-operation strategy which proved to be so effective in the struggle for freedom. The idea of non-co-operation first came to Gandhi at the Khilafat conference in Delhi. The birth of this inspiration may be termed one of the most decisive moments in the freedom struggle.

Gandhi launches His Crusade

The great humanist that Gandhi was, he revulsed at the practice of untouchability. He called it a sin, a heinous crime and a satanic practice. 'Hasn't just Nemesis overtaken us,' he asked, 'for the crime of untouchability? Have we not reaped as we have sown?' The chief reason why the Indians became the Bhangis (scavengers) of the British Government was that the Vaiṣṇavas and the Śaivas who called themselves genuine Sanatanis behave like beasts towards the *antyajas*,' he said.[25] Gandhi undertook an untouchability tour of India in 1920. At Kalol in Gujarat the *mahajans* (traders) mingled with the untouchables. Gandhi wrote glowingly on the change in the *mahajans*. Later, he learned to his chagrin that the *mahajans* had been very angry with him and that they had purified themselves by bathing.

Gandhi had an untouchable family staying in the *āsram* at Sabarmati and he adopted as his own daughter a little girl of this family called Lakṣmi. The presence of the family infuriated the elite members of society and they stopped coming to the *āśram*. Some benefactors of the *asram* stopped their contributions. For Gandhi, removal of untouchability was a condition for attaining *swaraj*. But by January of 1920 he began to say that it was quite possible that India would gain freedom before she freed herself from the curse of untouchability.

On a visit to Kalighat in Calcutta he saw goats being sacrificed there. The sight moved him even more deeply than the untouchables did. 'I sometimes writhe with agony,' he wrote to C.F. Andrews, 'when I think of it. All the same I am qualifying myself for the service of these fellow creatures of mine who are slaughtered in the name of my faith.'[26] Gandhi returned to the subject of Kalighat goats in another letter to C.F. Andrews of March 2, 1921.

Gandhi hoped to attain *mokṣa* at the end of his life. That was the reason why he undertook in so earnest a manner the non-cooperation movement. But if his aspiration was not fulfilled and if untouchability had not disappeared by the end of his life, then he wished to be born in an *antyaja* family so that he could suffer like them and mitigate their sufferings.[27] Gandhi received angry letters from his correspondents on his unorthodox views on untouchability. Some of them thought him plain mad, others held out threats. Gandhi pointed out on the treatment of the *antyajas* by the Hindus that the British did not treat the Indians with such scorn.[28]

When correspondents adduced proofs from the *śāstras* in support of untouchability, Gandhi dismissed these texts supporting the practice as interpolations, because untouchability outraged reason.

For Gandhi the protection of the weak and oppressed was not the central fact of Hinduism. That place was occupied by cow protection. So he said in the *Young India* of October 5, 1921.[29] But he hastened to add that it was a denial of Hinduism to kill a human being to protect a cow. An *antyaja* friend of Gandhi wrote to him saying that the worst form of untouchability was in force in Gandhi's homeland, Kathiawar. The correspondent noted that nowhere in Gujarat was so much contempt shown to the *antyajas*.

Gandhi has his own explanation of the origin of the practice. He refused to believe that it had been handed down from immemorial times. The practice must have been adopted when the people were at one of their lowest ebbs in the cycle of their lives. And as long as that curse remains, so long we are bound to hold that every affliction we labour under is a fit and proper punishment for the great crime.[30]

In 1925 the merchants of Bombay organised a meeting at which the speakers denounced Gandhi's campaign against untouchability and declared that the Hindu religion was in peril at the hands of Gandhi.[31]

Gandhi, Caste and Varṇas

Gandhi's view of untouchability was shaped by his understanding of caste and *varṇa*. It would seem that he wanted to build a bridge between the orthodox view and the reformist view of society. Gandhi was deeply influenced by the *Bhagavadgītā* in his thinking. He wrote a commentary on this work.

Gandhi was an ardent believer in the institution of *varṇa*. He had of course his own interpretation of it. He raised *varṇa* to the status of an eternal law. 'It is not a human invention,' Gandhi wrote in *Young India* of November 24, 1927, 'but an immutable law of nature – the statement of tendency that is ever present at work like Newton's law of gravitation.' Gandhi says further that just as the people of the West by their discoveries and application of laws of nature increased their material welfare, in the same way the people of India by their discovery of the social tendency were able to achieve in the spiritual plane what no other nation in the world has been able to achieve.

'*Varṇa*,' Gandhi asserts, 'has nothing to do with caste. Down with the monster of caste that masquerades in the guise of *varṇa*. Our failure to follow the law of *varṇa* is largely responsible for both our economic and spiritual ruin. It is one cause of our unemployment and impoverishment and it is responsible for untouchability and defections from our faith.' Gandhi went on to affirm that *varṇa* is the best insurance for happiness and for real religious pursuit. And what does *varṇa* consist of? It is essentially following the occupation of one's father. But what if the son exhibits a different tendency from his father's? Gandhi has the answer. 'If my father,' said he, 'is a trader and I exhibit the qualities of a soldier, I may without reward serve my country as a soldier but must be content to earn my bread by trade.'[32]

There can be no doubt about Gandhi's view of the gravity of the obligation to follow one's ancestral occupation. The so-called natural law of *varṇa* permits no freedom to follow one's natural bent. The reference to *varṇa* is of course to *cāturvarṇya*. The duty of the fourth *varṇa* is to serve the first three *varṇas*. That can hardly be called an occupation. The fourth *varṇa* thus is thought of as a class of servants and slaves. In primitive societies no class of slaves or servants existed. It is comparatively advanced societies that have come in contact with other primitive societies that possess slave classes. Hence, it is only a *traivarṇya* (three-fold division) that can be shown to be a natural institution. There is no clear evidence to demonstrate that at any time in the Vedic period a *traivarṇya* was in force. Gandhi could not thus be alluding to any period of which we possess any reliable information.

Gandhi makes the obligation to follow one's ancestral profession the constitutive element of *varṇa*. His concept of *varṇa* is a blueprint for an ever static society. In fact Gandhi was promoting a highly dubious interpretation of *varṇa*. Enlightened individuals throughout history have repudiated the concept of social determinism. Gandhi was not a historian nor a scholar. He has merely projected into the past his conception of an ideal society.

Gandhi's understanding of *varṇa* influenced his thinking on untouchability. He maintained that the untouchables should not seek to embrace other professions but must be content to serve society in their ancestral occupation of scavenging. In other words, in his scheme of things, there would always be a class of people who would from generation to generation perform the scavenging task, whatever be their innate desires and attitudes. Scavenging is both their God-given right and duty. To abandon this duty is to disrupt the natural order of things.

By holding an occupational theory of the *varṇa* system, Gandhi has landed himself unwittingly in the position of having to defend a five-fold division of society, that is, not *cāturvarṇya*, but a *pāñcavarṇya*. He had in the first place set out to defend the *cāturvarṇya*. Now not even Manu recognises a fifth *varṇa*. Manu regarded a certain group of people who later came to be classified as *antyaja*, *pancạma*, depressed classes, or Scheduled Castes, as unfit to be included in the larger community. So he thought it best to leave them to their own devices. But Gandhi was not prepared to do so in his anxiety to rope them into the Hindu community. This concern of Gandhi was the rationale behind his well known Yeravda fast.

What Gandhi in effect appeared to promote was a class of untouchables. He frowned upon the efforts of the depressed classes to assert themselves. Their deliverance had to come from the Hindu reformers. He counselled the upper castes Hindus to show goodwill towards the unfortunate scavengers, to open schools, to dig wells for them and help them to keep their surroundings clean. But they had to remain content with their present occupation.

Just as Gandhi extolled the beauty of the *varṇa* system, so did he on the caste system. His views on the subject are no less intriguing.

On the one hand Gandhi condemned the caste system as monstrous and a travesty of the *varṇa* system, and on the other he did not find it intrinsically evil. At this point we must bear in mind that one belonged to a *varṇa* by birth, which was linked to an occupation. With the scope of *varṇa* so restricted, he had little room for manoeuvring in explaining his stand on caste.

'We in India,' says Gandhi, 'have evolved caste; they in Europe have organised classes. If caste has produced certain evils, class has not been productive of anything less.'

'If class,' continues Gandhi, 'helps to conserve certain social virtues, castes does the same in equal, if not greater degree.'

'The beauty of the caste system,' Gandhi goes on to say, 'is that it does not base itself upon distinctions of wealth, possessions. Caste is but an extension of the principle of the family.'[33]

It is difficult to maintain that Gandhi was using the word, 'caste' in the same meaning throughout. While caste has produced certain evil, he nevertheless describes its beauty. Caste is an extension of the family. Gandhi seems to shift from caste as *jāti* to caste as *varṇa*. 'The spirit,' said Gandhi, 'behind caste is not arrogant superiority; it is the classification of different systems of self-culture. It is the best adjustment of social stability and progress. Just as the spirit of the family is inclusive of all those who love each other and are wedded to each other by ties of blood and relation, caste tries to include families of a particular way of purity of life (not standard of life, meaning by this term economic standard of life).'[34] Gandhi here reverts to caste understood as *varṇa*.

Gandhi concedes that though caste does not imply superiority, a certain hierarchy has come into the system. But one may ask, if caste means purity of life and self-culture, how does *varṇa* differ from it? Gandhi is obviously guilty of a careless use of both the terms, considering that all the foregoing four quotations come from the same issue of *Young India*.

If Gandhi was actually using the term caste in the sense of *jāti*, one is somewhat mystified by his following statement in which he condemns 'modern castes': 'I have frequently said that I do not believe in the caste system in the modern sense. It is an excrescence and a handicap on progress. Assumption of superiority by any person over any other is a sin against God and man. Thus caste, as far as it connotes distinctions in status, is an evil.'[35]

It seems that Gandhi thought of castes as sub-divisions of the *varṇas*, confusing the issue further. Castes are innumerable and are a drag on Hinduism. Gandhi has repeatedly stated that *varṇa* means profession. It has nothing to do with inter-dining and inter-marriage, he said. A man falls from his *varṇa* when he abandons his hereditary profession. Gandhi, however, was opposed to both inter-dining and inter-marriage. When J.B. Kripalani wanted to marry Sucheta, a Bengali girl, Gandhi opposed the move. With his paternal authority, Gandhi at first vetoed the proposed marriage of his son, Devadas, and Rajagopalachari's daughter, Lakṣmi, on the ground that it was an inter-caste alliance. Eventually he consented to both marriages.

But it is unfair to regard Gandhi as a blind follower of laws. He had too keen a sense of justice to be that. He disregarded and advised others to disregard all unjust laws. Gandhi could at times be even iconoclastic. Minoo Masani in his autobiography, *Bliss Was It In That Dawn*, narrates an episode which brings out the above-mentioned trait in Gandhi. A member of Gandhi's *āśram*, a social worker, became enamoured of a fellow member of the *āśram*, who had been abandoned by her husband. But the man would turn up after long intervals. They could not marry as the woman's husband made his presence known occasionally. The lovers brought the problem to Gandhi, who unhesitatingly told them to marry. When told that the step was against the existing law of the country, he replied that it was an unjust law fit only to be broken. The couple followed Gandhi's advice and were duly married. Fortunately the woman's first husband never returned. The couple were very greateful to Gandhi for his advice.[36]

Gandhi weighed everything on the scales of reason. That is why he rejected so much of the *Dharmaśāstras* as irrational. In weighing the value of things, authority did not count for anything. He felt completely free to follow his own counsel. He was led to what may appear to many as an incomprehensible stand on *varṇa* and caste by his historical *naivete*. He once confessed that he had not read the *Dharmaśāstras* even once carefully. He assumed far too much about the evolution of social institutions. Consistency was not a virtue he prided himself on. 'Consistency,' he said,' is the virtue of an ass.'

A Struggle for Basic Rights

In 1924 the non-brāhmaṇas of the princely state of Travancore in the deep South launched an agitation to secure the rights of the lower classes. The venue of the historic struggle was a little town called Vaikom in the picturesque land of stately coconut palms and lagoons in the coastal region of the State. At issue was the right of the lower classes to use the roads on the perimeter of the temple in the town. Not only were the untouchables and some śūdra communities barred from the temple, they were not even permitted to use the roads around it. If a member of these communities wished to pass from one part of the town to another, he had to take a circuitous route. To secure access to these roads for the untouchables and śūdras the struggle was started at the end of March 1924. Leading the struggle were such non-brāhmaṇa leaders as K.P. Kesava Menon, T.K. Madhavan and George Joseph. Gandhi closely followed the agitation from the outset, supported and encouraged it.

As the agitation got underway, the Maharaja of Travancore tried to suppress it with a violent hand, clamping the leaders in prison. A frantic message was then sent to E.V. Ramasami Naicker, a noted non-brāhmaṇa leader of the Madras Presidency. Naicker lost no time in making his way to Vaikom and took matters in hand. When he violated prohibitory orders, he too was imprisoned. Now more volunteers joined the struggle. The repressive measures adopted by the government had failed to intimidate the volunteers or their supporters. The volunteers drew much public sympathy which found expression in contributions for their care.

Gandhi objected to the presence of non-Hindus in the agitation. He held that untouchability was a purely religious matter and that non-Hindus had no place in it as it concerned the Hindu religion. George Joseph was not impressed by Gandhi's argument and refused to withdraw. Meanwhile, a group of Sikhs arrived at Vaikom to lend a muscular hand and opened a free kitchen for the volunteers. Gandhi opposed their participation too.[37] But that did not deter the Sikhs.

The agitation dragged on for a whole year. The queen, who now held the reins of the government, was prepared to negotiate with the agitators. Gandhi was prevailed upon to intervene in the matter. According to E.V. Naicker, it was Rajagopalachari who persuaded Gandhi to negotiate with the royal house of Travancore.[38] Following Gandhi's talks with her, the queen agreed to declare the roads in question open to the untouchables and śūdras. The struggle ended in April 1925.

A Man of Destiny

On the Indian socio-political scene, nothing makes us more forcefully aware of the changing times as the entry of Bhimrao Ambedkar (b. 1891). He was to emerge as the most articulate leader of the depressed class community and an indefatigable champion of their cause. Never before had a member of the community been able to present their case before the Indian public so convincingly as did Ambedkar.

Born at Mhow in Central India where his farther Ramji was stationed at the cantonment, Ambedkar was educated in Maharashtra. As a student of the Government High School at Satara, he had to sit apart from other boys. The Sanskrit teacher refused to teach him Sanskrit. While still a boy, Ambedkar had an experience which was one of the formative incidents of his life. It was his Meritzburg. Ambedkar and his elder brother were on their way from the Masur railway station to Goregaon. At the station they succeeded in hiring a bullock-cart. On the journey the cartman discovered that the boys were untouchables. He now refused to share the same cart with them. Alighting from the cart in a fury, he walked along. The boys themselves piloted the cart. At the journey's end the cartman extracted from them a double fare, penalising them for their low status. Ambedkar could never forget the incident.[39]

Ambedkar studied at Elphinstone College, Bombay, on a scholarship from Maharaja Sayaji of Baroda. After his graduation in 1912, he joined the Baroda State administrative service. Here he saw the evil face of untouchability. Even the upper caste clerks would throw the files at him rather than place them on the table. In 1913 Ambedkar entered the University of Columbia in the United States, assisted by a scholarship from the Maharaja of Baroda. Returning to India, he joined the Sydenham College, Bombay, as professors of political economy. His fellow upper caste professors would not permit him to drink from the water pot kept for the exclusive use of the professors.[40]

The first ever Depressed Classes Conference was held in Bombay in March 1918 and presided over by the Maharaja of Baroda. Ambedkar played a prominent role in its organisation. Ambedkar shot into prominence with the Mahad agitation for securing access for the depressed classes to public water supply sources. A resolution had been passed in the Bombay Legislative Council in July 1919 which asked the government to make public wells and water-tanks accessible to the untouchables. The Bombay Government on September 11, 1923, had issued instructions in accordance with the earlier resolution of the Council. A mass meeting of the untouchables was held at Mahad on March 19-20, 1927, over which Ambedkar presided. It was decided that the untouchables would march to the public tanks. Fearing a breach of peace the authorities promulgated prohibitory orders. Thus the proposed march had to be abandoned. The *Manusmṛti* was publicly burned on December 25, 1927, at Mahad. Ambedkar demanded that the *sastras* be proscribed as they lowered the dignity of the whole people in sanctioning untouchability.[41]

The next major agitation in which the untouchables were involved was the temple entry movement launched in 1930. It began with the *satyagraha* demanding entry for the untouchables into the Kala Ram temple at Nasik in Maharashtra, which was opposed by the upper caste Hindus. Finally, to appease the agitators they agreed to include a few untouchables in the select group that carried the idol in the annual procession. But at the last moment they backed out of the agreement. The temple was closed for a year when the untouchables continued to agitate for the right of entry.[42]

It was the controversial issue of separate electorate that thrust Ambedkar forward as the foremost spokesman of the depressed classes. The controversy generated considerable heat in political circles. It hot up at the Round Table Conference held in London which opened in December 1931 and was attended by 112 delegates of whom 64 were from the British territories and 23 from the princely states. Of the remaining 25 delegates, 21 represented the British Government, while Gandhi and party accounted for the rest.[43]

At the conference most religious and minority groups, such as Muslims, Christians, Sikhs, Anglo-Indians and depressed classes, demanded separate electorates. Gandhi vehemently opposed this dismemberment of India. He maintained that freedom would be meaningless if all the demands for separate electorate were conceded. Ambedkar was convinced that for the deliverance of the depressed classes from slavery and oppression, it was necessary for them to establish an identity of their own, apart from the larger Hindu community. He flatly refused to have the depressed classes included among the Hindus for the purpose of sharing political power. Hence, he demanded a separate electorate which would elect their own representatives in constituencies set apart for them, besides voting with the general electorate. This was unacceptable to Gandhi. He, however, conceded a separate electorate for the Muslims. The conference ended without a consensus having been arrived at. Gandhi returned to India sorely disappointed with the outcome of the conference. On August 12, 1923, the British Prime Minister Ramsay McDonald announced the decision of the British Government to grant separate electorate. In his letter of August 18 Gandhi opposed the decision of the government. He also informed McDonald of his decision to undertake a fast unto death in protest. He was doing so to maintain the unity of the country, and he was prepared to sacrifice his life for this cause, he said. McDonald, in his reply of September 8, defended the government's decision on the separate electorate. 'Under the government scheme,' the Prime Minister wrote, 'the depressed classes will remain part of the Hindu community and will vote with the Hindu electorate on an equal footing. But for the first 20 years, while still remaining part of the

Hindu community, they will receive through a limited number of special constituencies a means of safeguarding their rights and interests.'

'You propose,' McDonald told Gandhi pointedly, 'to adopt the extreme course of starving yourself to death, not in order to secure that the Depressed Classes should have joint electorates with other Hindus, because that is already provided, nor to maintain the unity of Hindus, which is also provided, but solely to prevent the Depressed Classes, who admittedly suffer from terrible disabilities today, from being able to secure a limited number of representatives of their own choosing to speak in their behalf in the legislatures.'[44]

'Without arguing,' Gandhi wrote to McDonald on September 9 from Yeravda jail, 'I affirm that to me this matter is one of pure religion. The mere fact of the Depressed Classes having double votes does not protect them or Hindu society, in general, from being disrupted. You will please permit me to say that no matter how sympathetic you may be, you cannot come to a correct decision on a matter of vital religious importance.'

'I should not be,' continued Gandhi, 'against even over-representation of the Depressed Classes. What I am against is their statutory separation, *even in a limited form*, from the Hindu fold, so long as they choose to belong to it. Do you realise that if your decision stands and the constitution comes into being, you arrest the marvellous growth of the work of the Hindu reformers who have dedicated themselves to their suppressed brethren in every walk of life?'[45] (emphasis added)

But did Gandhi grant the depressed classes the freedom to choose to remain in the Hindu fold? He was treading on perilously thin ground when he said that the matter of separate electorate was one of pure religion.

Gandhi began his Yeravda fast on September 20. When the fast was announced, a campaign was let loose against Ambedkar. The responsibility for Gandhi's fast was now being laid on Ambedkar's shoulders. But Ambedkar did not wilt under the blitz.

Gandhi's decision to fast was not quite consistent with his principles. He had shown himself opposed to any compulsion. His fast was worse than compulsion. It was tantamount to imposing his view on those who did not share it and, worse still, it was foisting his view of religion on others.

Even before the fast began, intense parleys between the Congress leaders and Ambedkar along with his colleagues also commenced. A meeting of Hindu leaders was held in Bombay. Pandit Madan Mohan Malaviya, who played a major role in the parleys, was the leader of the Hindus.

The fast undoubtedly directed public attention to the problems of the depressed classes. Announcing the fast Gandhi had said that unless untouchability was banished root and branch from Hinduism, it would have to sacrifice him. There was widespread, positive response to this call to purify Hinduism of the curse of untouchability. Many temples hitherto closed to the untouchables were thrown open. Notable among these were the temple at Kalighat and the Ram Mandir at Varanasi; several other temples in Allahabad and in the princely states of Baroda and Kolhapur were also opened to the untouchables.

Meanwhile, unceasing parleys were carried on to hammer out a formula acceptable to Gandhi and leaders of the depressed classes. Ambedkar was keenly aware that if Gandhi were to die, the blame would be laid on his head. This awareness failed to make him abandon his position which was backed by his many colleagues.

An agreement between Gandhi and Ambedkar was reached as a result of the tireless efforts of those who were determined to save Gandhi's life. The agreement, known as the Yeravda Pact, was signed on September 24 and Gandhi ended his fast. The Pact was ratified by the Hindu leaders at their meeting in Bombay on September 25, 1932. According to the agreement, the double voting was done away with, which in any case was not a major issue. Ambedkar never regarded it as of great importance. The depressed classes would now remain part of the Hindu community and vote with it. The number of reserved constituencies was enhanced. This was the crucial point on which Ambedkar had refused to compromise.

The Hindu leaders conference, presided over by Pandit Madan Mohan Malaviya, held on September 25 to ratify the Yeravda Pact took the following pledge:

> This Conference resolves that henceforth amongst Hindus no one shall be regarded as untouchable by reason of his birth, and that those who have been so regarded hitherto shall have the same right as other Hindus in regard to the use of public wells, public schools, public roads and all other public institutions. This right shall have statutory recognition at the first opportunity and shall

> be one of the first Acts of the Swaraj Parliament, if it shall not have received such recognition before that time.
> It is further agreed that it shall be the duty of all Hindu leaders to secure by every legitimate and peaceful means an early removal of all social disabilities now imposed by custom upon the so-called untouchable class, including the bar in respect of admission to temples.[46]

The Yeravda Pact has been the subject of controversy ever since. The depressed classes have thought of the Pact as a betrayal of their cause. Ambedkar has expressed his unhappiness over it. And he remained unconvinced by the arguments against separate electorates.

'My only regret is,' Ambedkar told the leaders' conference, 'Why did not Mahatmaji take this attitude at the Round Table Conference? If he had shown the same consideration to my point of view then, it would not have been necessary for him to go through this ordeal....'[47] The formula to which Gandhi had assented was virtually the same as Ambedkar's proposal on the representation of the depressed classes placed before the Round Table Conference.

Gandhi, however, maintained that he had merely responded to the voice within him when he undertook the fast. 'Suffice it to say,' he told a correspondent who doubted the propriety of his fast, 'that it was at God's call that I embarked on the fast.'[48]

The Yeravda fast moreover projected Gandhi as the spokesman of Hindu orthodoxy. In contrast, Ambedkar emerged as the spokesman of the depressed classes and he rose in stature as a result. The Yeravda fast had a parallel in the Khilafat agitation. Gandhi had chosen to espouse an issue peripheral to the great task of freeing India from the British Yoke. He had now turned the separate electorate into a religious matter, thus giving it a new complexion that would not substantially affect the fortunes of the depressed classes.

Gandhi came in for attack from the orthodox Hindus. A mass meeting held in Calcutta on January 11, 1933, denounced the Yeravda Pact. The resolution adopted by the meeting declared that the reservation of seats for the depressed classes was out of proportion and need.

The all-party meeting held in Calcutta on January 23 asked the British Prime Minister to revoke the Pact.

The Sanatanists maintained that untouchability was of the essence of Hinduism. They wanted a statutory guarantee of non-interference by the state in matters of religion.

A New Phase in the Crusade against Untouchability

The determined stand taken by Ambedkar and other depressed class leaders evoked a response in the leaders' conference. The voices of the depressed classes were growing more insistent. The urgency of action to end the oppression of a section of the population was unmistakably brought home to the leaders. Though the leaders echoed Gandhi's convictions in the resolution adopted by the conference, the experience of participating in the momentous decisions of the Yeravda Pact and parleying on an equal footing with the depressed classes must have been educative for them. Their exertions on Gandhi's behalf made them more receptive when he gave the new call for the uplift of the depressed class.

To give a fresh momentum to the work of uplift of the untouchables, Gandhi inaugurated the Anti-Untouchability League in Bombay on September 30, 1932, within a week of the Yeravda Pact. The league was later re-christened the Harijan Seva Sangha. Provincial and regional units of the League were established. Ambedkar suggested that the scope of the activities of the League should be enlarged to include, besides removal of untouchability, the educational economic and social improvement of the untouchables as well as temple entry and inter-dining. He further proposed that members of the depressed classes should be inducted into the League.[49] As the latter suggestion of Ambedkar was not accepted, he dissociated himself from the league.

To further the cause of the anti-untouchability movement, Gandhi founded the journal, *Harijan*. Its first issue appeared on February 11, 1933. The term, 'harijan' was not of Gandhi's coinage. A reader of the Gujarati journal, *Navajīvan*, to which Gandhi contributed regularly, complained to Gandhi on his use of the word '*asprśya*', meaning untouchable, as the word carried a note of opprobrium. Gandhi asked for suggestions in selecting a better term. Someone proposed the word 'harijan' and it was accepted. Though the word means 'Children of Hari', it was exclusively used to designate the untouchables and it became synonymous with 'untouchable'. Hence, the majority of the Indian people would take violent objection to being called 'Children of Hari'. In the early 1980s the Government of independent India relinquished the term 'Harijan', as the members of the Scheduled Castes themselves disowned it.

Gandhi asked Ambedkar for a message that the first issue of *Harijan* was to carry. 'The outcastes,' Ambedkar wrote, 'are a by-product of the caste system. There will be outcastes as long as there are castes. And nothing can emancipate outcastes except the destruction of the caste system.' He termed caste 'an odious and vacious dogma.'

Gandhi took exception to Ambedkar's statement on caste. 'And I do not,' Gandhi wrote in *Harijan*, 'believe the caste system, even as distinguished from the *Varnāśrama*, to the an odious and vicious dogma. It has its limitations and defects. But there is nothing sinful about it as there is about untouchability.'[50] Here Gandhi has clearly distinguished the 'caste system' from *Varnāśrama* and he is thus speaking about what he calls 'modern castes'. Yet he writing in the *Young India* of March 5 of the same year, would call 'modern castes' an excrescence and a handicap on progress.

On May 8, 1933, Gandhi began a three-week fast in the cause of the harijan movement. He was released from the Yeravda jail on the eve of his fast. The five-year period of waiting Gandhi had imposed on his son Devadas and Lakṣmi, C. Rajagopalachari's daughter, now ended and they were married on June 16, 1933.

On November 7 of that year Gandhi embarked on an anti-untouchability tour of India. He set out from Wardha where he had moved in September from Sabarmati *āśram*. Several temples opened their doors to the depressed classes in the course of his tour. 'I hold it a blasphemy,' he said at Selu village near Wardha, 'to say that the Creator resides in a temple from which a particular class of His devotees sharing the faith in it are excluded.'[51]

Though Gandhi opposed legislation as a means of bringing about changes in society, he defended the anti-untouchability Bill that had recently been introduced in the Central Legislative Council. The Sanatanists had denounced the Bill as an interference by the state in religious matters.[52] From the very beginning of his harijan tour, Gandhi was harassed by the Sanatanists. Their volunteers would lie prostrate across the path of his car or shout slogans, making themselves a nuisance.

Gandhi began the tour of South India at Bezwada (now Vijayawada) on December 16, 1933. He told the audience at a meeting at Masulipatnam that unless they purified themselves of the curse of untouchability, they would pay with bitter tears.

Gandhi's tour of Malabar which began at Palghat on January 10, 1934, was to prove a new experience for him. He observed that the Kerala country had developed such vicious forms of untouchability as unapproachability and unseeability. At Palghat while he was conferring with Congressmen, he was called out to watch an untouchable walking through the fields as he was not permitted to use the public road. Gandhi called out to the man. When he approached Gandhi, he told the bewildered man that he had a right to walk on the public road. But the man stared at Gandhi in disbelief and blurted out. 'It cannot be.'[53] Referring to the practice of untouchability in Kerala, Gandhi remarked, 'It is the vilest thing on earth.' He also found the greenery that envelops the landscape equally unmatched by anything elsewhere in India.

When Gandhi reached the temple town, Guruvayur, on the evening of the first day of the Kerala tour, he received a grand welcome. But the Sanatanists, who had followed him from North India, staged a black flag demonstration. Though an opinion poll held earlier had shown that the majority of the people favoured the opening of the ancient temple to the untouchables, the temple authorities had held out for a time but had finally relented to admit them. Gandhi's visit was intended to express his happiness at the change in the attitude.

Gandhi continued to propound his thesis that removal of untouchability was purely a religious matter. Untouchability, according to him, was something specifically Hindu and hence non-Hindus could not participate in the movement for its abolition. He asked the non-Hindus to dissociate themselves from it. Gandhi of course did not explain how it was that those who had disowned Hinduism held tenaciously to untouchability.

Beginning on April 10, 1934, Gandhi visited Assam, continuing his untouchability tour. Removal of untouchability, he said, meant abolition of all grades of high and lower. We are guilty of untouchability as soon as we make distinctions between man and man. Gandhi entered Bihar on April 20. The Sanatanists were hot on his heels. Leaflets had been circulated denouncing his efforts on behalf of the harijans. There was a black flag demonstration when Gandhi visited Deoghar.[54]

Gandhi was convinced that untouchability was on its last leg. His optimism was quite misplaced as later events would show. While he was trying to persuade the upper caste Hindus to purify Hinduism of the curse, Ambedkar was marking out a trail for the depressed classes.

To Ambedkar, Gandhi spoke with the voice of the upper caste Hindus. Though Ambedkar never repudiated the Yeravda Pact, he was unhappy over it. To him the temple entry agitation had become irrelevant, as far as the depressed classes were concerned. At a meeting of the depressed classes at Yeola in Maharashtra on October 13, 1935, he asked them to suspend the temple entry movement and conserve their energy to fight for their rights. It would seem that by this time Ambedkar had resolved to lead the depressed classes out of Hinduism. For him it was the only way to their deliverance. The Nagpur depressed classes conference of April 19, 1936, affirmed its faith in the leadership of Ambedkar. Ambedkar had already told the depressed classes to embrace any religion they chose. He invited representatives of non-Hindu religions to explain their stand on the untouchables to enable the depressed class leaders to judge for themselves the comparative merit of each religion. To provide such an opportunity to the various religious groups, an all-religion conference was held at Lucknow on May 22 to 24, 1936. Leaders of non-Hindu religions descended on Lucknow to woo the depressed classes. Gandhi dubbed the conference a religious bazaar. The decision on which religion the depressed classes would embrace was deferred to the next conference. Ambedkar, addressing the Mahar conference in Bombay on May 31, 1936, declared that the only course open to the Mahar community was conversion.

Less than four years after the controversial Yeravda Pact, Ambedkar entered into an intriguing agreement with a Hindu Mahasabha leader, Dr. B.S. Munje, on August 19, 1936. The agreement was the outcome of prolonged discussion between Ambedkar and the Mahasabha leader, who was obviously trying to salvage something from the situation, since the depressed class leaders seemed bent on conversion. According to the terms of the new Pact, the Mahasabha pledged not to oppose the conversion of the depressed class to Sikhism. The neo-Sikhs would be classified as Scheduled Caste and would thus enjoy all the political rights granted to the Scheduled Castes by the Yeravda Pact.

M.C. Raja, a depressed class leader and follower of Gandhi, rejected the Ambedkar-Munje agreement. His views were endorsed by such eminent leaders as Gandhi, Pandit Madan Mohan Malaviya and C. Rajagopalachari.[55] The Congressmen frequently used M.C. Raja as counter-weight to Ambedkar.

In the mid-1930s the talk of conversion was much in the air. On May 29, 1936, Harilal, Gandhi's son, became a Muslim, taking the name of Abdulla. Thereafter he toured Kerala to promote his new-found faith. Many conversions that took place at that time have been attributed to the impact of Harilal Gandhi's conversion. It is against the background of these developments that the Travancore temple entry proclamation must be seen.

On November 12, 1936, the Maharaja of Travancore issued the historic edict throwing open to the untouchable communities the temples administered by the Government, which had hitherto been barred to them. The step was widely acclaimed all over the country. 'The Travancore Durbar,' wrote Gandhi, 'has earned congratulations of the whole Hindu world and all thoughtful men by issuing the proclamation about temple entry for all Harijans.'

'The action,' he added, 'has been long overdue. But better late than never.'[56]

At a meeting held in Bombay on November 29, 1936, the Sanatanists viewed with alarm the action of the Maharaja of Travancore and declared it a serious violation of the rights of upper caste Hindus. There was also protest from the Sanatanists of Madras against the proclamation.

Gandhi congratulated C.P. Ramaswami Aiyer, Dewan of Travancore, for advising the Maharaja to issue the proclamation. What actually motivated the proclamation may have been the fear of mass conversions from depressed class communities.

The scene of action now shifts to the princely state of Cochin, the northern neighbour of Travancore. The little kingdom found itself in the vortex of a controversy, which was closely linked to the Travancore temple entry proclamation.

On April 15, 1937, the Cochin Government issued an order which declared that the priests who had officiated in Travancore temples after the temple entry proclamation came into force and had then participated in ceremonies at the temple at Kudalmanickem, near Irinjalakuda in Cochin, had polluted that temple. The Raja of Cochin had issued the order, it appears, against the advice of his Dewan but under pressure from the Nambūdiri brāhmaṇas. The order carried a strong disapproval of the Travancore proclamation. The Nambudiri brahmaṇas were fighting a last ditch battle. The priests who were judged to have polluted themselves were barred from entering temples. Commenting on the Cochin order, Gandhi said it clearly interfered with the right of the Maharaja of Travancore.[57]

Strongly reạcting to the Cochin order, the Travancore Government declared that only those who dissociated themselves from the ideas contained in the Cochin order would be entitled to gifts and grants from the Government.[58]

Taoudeva Kaimal, the administrator of Kudalmanickem temple, now represented to the British agent, O.P. Skrine, that he was the only competent authority on matters relating to administration of the temple. He declared that the priests, who had been judged to be polluted, were not polluted and they were entitled to perform ceremonies in the temples. The Sanatana Dharma, he stated, permitted such changes in customs as modern times demanded.[59]

Gandhi makes his Retreat

As far back as 1921 Gandhi said that untouchability was on its last legs. He repeated this assertion in the early 1930s. While he termed untouchability an excrescence, a curse, a sin and an evil, the Sanatanists were proclaiming it an essential element of Hinduism. Gandhi had to bear the full brunt of their opposition. Fortunately for Gandhi, he did not live to see the hold of untouchability on society even after statutory prohibition was imposed against it in the Constitution of Independent India.

In 1920, Gandhi had declared that unless untouchability was rooted out from the Indian society, India could not free herself from foreign yoke. By 1921 he abandoned this position. Now he began to assert that a slave nation could not grant freedom to its own slaves. It was a tacit admission that he had been over optimistic about rooting out untouchability.

Gandhi at first ruled out legislation as a means of abolishing it. He believed in the power of persuasion to achieve this end. His idealism was mercilessly battered on the rock of the Indian social reality.

Gandhi's incurable idealism showed through in his attitude towards the *Zamindars* or the class of landlords. He was against the abolition of the institution of *Zamindari*. He had hopes of reforming them. Gandhi counselled them to devote their income to the welfare of their tenants. He asked them to open schools, dispensaries and night schools for adults. They should look to the sanitation of the villages. He saw Santa Claus Indian garb emerge from the grasping, avaricious and cruel landlord that India had so far known. In the late 1930s Gandhi began to put forward the thesis that the land belonged to the man who worked on it. He was abandoning the dream of the benign landlord and was set to transfer the right over the land to the peasant-farmer.

Gandhi at first found no merit in inter-dining and inter-marriage. He disapproved of both. He appears to be advocating some form of untouchability in his opposition to inter-dining.

'Hinduism', wrote Gandhi in 1921, 'does most emphatically discourage inter-dining and inter-marriage is essential for the rapid evolution of the soul'.[60] But by mid 1940s he had abandoned this position. He went so far as to stipulate that if a marriage was to be performed in Sevagram, Wardha, one of the parties had to be a harijan.[61] Gandhi had come a long way from 1921.

Gandhi's views on caste and *varṇa* continued to bristle with contradictions. The position he had assumed was clearly untenable. The only course open to him was retreat. Gandhi did retreat, though not with perfect grace.

A Bombay writer, J.E. Sanjana, published a series of articles in a Bombay journal, *Rast-Rahbar*, which attempted to set forth Gandhi's views of *varṇa* and caste. The articles appearing during 1944-45 exposed inconsistencies in Gandhi's stand on the subject. The writer quoted extensively not only from Gandhi's contributions to *Harijan* and *Young India* but also from his Gujarati contributions to *Navajīvan*. These articles were later brought out in a book under the title, *Caste and Outcaste*. But Bombay's Congressmen would not permit the open sale of the book. Hence it had to be sold clandestinely.

When Sanjana's articles were being serialised, the Editor of *Rast-Rahbar* received a courteous note from Sevagram asking him to meet Gandhi at Sevagram. The note gave the Editor the option of meeting Gandhi when he visited Bombay. The Editor preferred to meet him at Bombay. He was also asked to submit a list of questions he might wish to ask Gandhi. Among the questions submitted were:

> 'Do you still believe that the caste system is the best possible system and that you want the whole world to adopt it?'

'Is caste system compatible with democracy?'

Gandhi did not keep the appointment. On the eve of the interview, he sent a note to the Editor, regretting his inability to meet him. Gandhi wrote:

> 'Instead of undertaking the thankless task of going through the forest of my writings to find out what I have or have not said you have rightly handed me the following questions for me to answer. Here then is my answer.
>
> 'I do not need to refer to my past writings to say what I believe today and what is apposite is my present belief. I wish to say that the caste in Hinduism as we know it is an anachronism, must hinder the growth of true religion and must go if both Hinduism and India must live and grow from day-to-day. The way to do it is that all Hindus should become their own Bhangis and treat the so-called hereditary scavengers as their own brothers. . .'[62]

It is a great credit to Gandhi that he did not find it necessary to defend his earlier views at all cost. What was important was that he thought on a particular subject at a given time. He modified his stand guided by the inspiration of the moment and as the need of the hour dictated. This was quite a sensible approach. But his abandoned positions had frequently imposed unnecessary burdens on others. His decisions at times seemed wholly arbitrary, as for instance, when he forbade Harilal to remarry when his wife died. From then on Harilal was an embittered and unhappy man. His conversion to Islam was a revolt against his father.

Gandhi, one must remember, was a child of the 19th century. This fact explains some of his preoccupations. He displayed almost till the end of his life a mild form of social intolerance, which was in sharp contrast to his religious tolerance and cosmopolitanism. The only Indian who surpassed him in his cosmopolitanism was Kesab Chandra Sen. We are today separated by a century from the formative years of Gandhi's life. He must be judged not from our standpoint, but by the concerns of his time. The subtle influences of his time were later overlaid with other values.

Despite Gandhi's somewhat outmoded social thinking, he stands absolutely alone and unsurpassed in several other qualities. One of these qualities was faith in the people's power. To win freedom, Gandhi realised, the dammed up power of the masses had to be released. Firmly grounded in this faith, he worked towards making the Indian National Congress a people's movement. The Indian people vindicated Gandhi's faith in them by the way they responded to his call for non-cooperation. But to the latter-day Congressmen, people are merely a pawn in the political game. What they ask from the people is their vote. In the cut-throat game of politics people's interests are forgotten. People's rights are gradually being chipped away on various pretexts. When a leader has recourse to political gimmicks, with no sign of accountability to the people, he has already fallen in his own eyes, thus forgetting his right to be a representative of the people.

One of the conditions Gandhi laid for his joining the Congress was that there should be complete openness in politics. He never subscribed to the dictum that everything is fair in politics. Politics was not amoral. Duplicity was distasteful to him. Openness is a great casualty in modern Indian politics. This happens when one's intention is to retain power at any cost. Gandhi did not suffer from such anxieties.

One supreme quality of Gandhi which raised him high above other Indian leaders was his ability to transcend all personal, regional, sectarian and clannish considerations. He did not display signs of personal insecurity which ordinarily makes a man resort to narrow loyalties.

It is not those bent on making a demi-god of Gandhi who pay the greatest tribute to him. To make him so is to declare him irrelevant. But Gandhi remains very much relevant for our time. He challenges our cultivation of narrow loyalties, our duplicity, our recourse to all forms of untruth.

The 20th Century Indian Woman

The 20th century witnessed new gains in the emancipation of Indian women. Educational opportunities now available to women were bearing fruit. Unlike the previous centuries, women themselves were coming forward to take a hand in their own destiny. In the 1920s, annual conferences of women began to be held. The first ever such conference was convened in 1919.

The freedom movement brought many women to the fore. Gandhi called upon women to lead the hand-spinning campaign. One of his devoted followers was Maniben Patel, who was instrumental in popularising the movement. Gandhi said that Indian men had enslaved their womenfolk, keeping them ignorant. Women had become willing slaves. Yet Gandhi did not want women to take up jobs outside their homes; their place was in the home. But he insisted that women had to fight shoulder to shoulder with men in liberating India from her yoke. Gandhi was overjoyed when Sarojini Naidu became president of the Congress in 1925. Vijay Lakṣmi Pandit was another woman of great stature thrown up by the freedom movement.

Woman leaders, no longer prepared to accept the lot of Indian women as God-ordained, began to demand legislation to improve their status in society. The traditional Hindu law pertaining to property rights was heavily weighted against them. There was opposition to the move even from orthodox Congressmen. Another custom that victimised the female sex was the child marriage. Women wanted an end to child marriages. The Child Marriage Restraint Act, also known as the Sharda Act, came into force in 1930. It was named after its mover, Rai Saheb Harbilas Sharda. The old charge of interference in religion was also brought against the new law. The bogey of religion had been raised in the previous century against the legislation on abolition of widow-burning, widow remarriage and the age of consent. The Sanatanists denounced the Sharda Act as an interference in religious matters. This Act fixed the minimum age of marriage as 14 for girls and 18 for boys. The practice of child marriage, however, continued unabated in spite of the Act even half a century after its promulgation.

A series of laws enacted since the late 1920s beginning with the Hindu Law of Inheritance (Amendment Act) of 1929, gave women equality with men in matters of inheritance, rights to marriage, adoption, divorce and rights to property. These laws are an index of the consciousness of the need to remove the millennia-old disabilities imposed on women by custom and law. The new laws meant that discrimination against women had no longer any legal sanction. To secure their rightful place in society they still had to battle deep-rooted prejudice, superstition and resistance to change. Nonetheless, the laws were a powerful weapon to be used in the battle. Women had suffered from the handicap of being barred from acquiring education and being segregated. Some obstacles in the way of their emancipation had been overcome.

The Star of Freedom Rises

Malcom Muggeridge, who lived in India in the World War I period and in the early 1920s, says in his autobiography, *The Chronicles of Wasted Time*, that, had anyone hinted then that the sun would ever set on the British empire in India, the British would have laughed at him in derision. Yet the sun did set on the British empire to the utter disbelief and dismay of many Britons. By the end of World War II many of them had begun to think of the end of the empire as inevitable. So it was that the Labour Party somewhat unexpectedly was voted to power in the first post-war British elections. Clement Attlee, the new Prime Minister, set about giving India its freedom. Attlee appointed Lord Mountbatten to preside over the dismantling of the eastern empire. The heroic struggle for freedom in which the people of the vast sub-continent had participated came to an end when the British transferred power to the Indian people on the midnight of August 14, 1947. 'A new star rises,' Jawaharlal Nehru said in his inimitable way, 'the star of freedom in the East, a new hope comes into being, a vision long cherished materialises. May that star never set and that hope never betrayed. . .'[63]

Even before the transfer of power to the Indians, the interim Cabinet headed by Jawaharlal Nehru had initiated the process of Constitution-making and had set up the Constituent Assembly.

Long before the star of freedom rose, the lower classes had begun to ask what their position would be in an Independent India. The British had given them a respite from the tyranny of ancient laws. They wanted statutory guarantees against recurrence of oppression. The non-brāhmaṇas of South India had asked the British once not to transfer power to the Congress as it was dominated by the brāhmaṇas.

How did the new rulers go about meeting these demands? How did they live up to these hopes, remove haunting fears of the lower classes? The Constitution and its aftermath tell that story.

NOTES

1. W.N. Kuber, 1978, p.8.
2. Quoted by J.N. Farquhar, 1967 B, p.369.
3. W.N. Kuber, 1978, p.9.
4. *Ibid.*, p.8.
5. *The Indian Annual Register*, 1920, p.169.

6. K. Veeramuni, *The History of the Struggle for Social and Communal Justice*, Madras, Madras Dravida Kazhagam Publications, 1981, p.4.
7. Quoted by K. Veeramuni, 1981, p.5.
8. *Ibid.*, pp.7-8.
9. *Ibid.*, p.9.
10. *Ibid.*, p.20 ff.
11. *CW*, XIX, Appendix I, p.378.
12. K. Veeramuni, 1981, pp.27-8.
13. S. Chandrasekhar, *Dimensions of Socio-Political Change in Mysore*, New Delhi, Ashish Publications, 1985, p.55.
14. *Ibid.*, p.55.
15. *Ibid.*, p.85.
16. *Ibid.*, p.95.
17. *CW*, I, p.58 ff.
18. *Ibid.*, p.289.
19. *SW*, I, p.334.
20. *CW*, XVIII, p.53.
21. *Ibid.*, p.190.
22. *CW*, XX, p.59.
23. *CW*, XXI, p.492.
24. *SW*, VI, p.57.
25. *CW*, XIX, p.289.
26. *Ibid.*, p.290.
27. *CW*, XX, p.53.
28. *Ibid.*, p.319.
29. *CW*, XXI, p.248.
30. *SW*, VI, p.139.
31. G.S. Ghurye, 1969, p.284.
32. For this passage as well as the three preceding quotations from *Young India*, see M.K. Gandhi, *My Religion*, compiled and edited by Bharatan Kumarappa, Ahmedabad, Navajivan Publishing House, 1958, pp.139-43.
33. *SW*, VI, p.426.
34. *Ibid.*, p.478.
35. *Young India*, March 25, 1933, see M.K. Gandhi, 1958, p.144.
36. Minoo Masani, *Bliss Was It In That Dawn*, New Delhi, Arnold Heinemann, 1977, p.192.
37. *CW*, XXIV, p.67.
38. E.V. Ramasami Naicker, *Untouchability*, Madras, Periyar Self Respect Propaganda Institution, 1983, p.17.
39. W.N. Kuber, 1978, pp.10-11.
40. *Ibid.*, p.17.
41. *Ibid.*, p.24 ff.
42. *Ibid.*, p.25.
43. Louis Ficher, *The Life of Mahatma Gandhi*, New York, Collier Books, 1962, p.290.
44. *Ibid.*, p.310.
45. *Ibid.*, pp.311-12.
46. *DC*, p.548.
47. Quoted by Louis Ficher, 1962, p.321.
48. G.G. Tendulkar, *Mahatma*, III, New Delhi, Govt. of India, 1961, p.179.
49. W.N. Kuber, 1978, p.46.
50. G.G. Tendulkar, III, 1961, pp.192-93.
51. *Ibid.*, p.222.

52. G.G. Tendulkar, op cit, p.222.
53. *Ibid.*, p.239.
54. *Ibid.*, p.367.
55. *DC*, p.146.
56. *Ibid.*, p.261.
57. *Ibid.*, p.397.
58. *Ibid.*, p.389.
59. *Ibid.*, p.400.
60. *CW*, XXI, p.247.
61. Louis Ficher, 1961, p.338.
62. J.S. Sanjana, *Caste and Outcaste*, Bombay Thacker & Co., 1946, p.199.
63. G.G. Tendulkar, VIII, p.79.

7

THE CONSTITUTION AND AFTER

THE INDIA the British were leaving behind was not the India they had conquered centuries before. All the various parts of the country had been knit together. The country had been introduced to modern parliamentary democracy. The process of transition from a caste-based hierarchical society to a modern society that recognised the principles of equality of all citizens before the law had been set afoot.

The most momentous change had come over the lowest rungs of Indian society. Large sections of them had ceased to believe that their poverty and their degraded state were God-ordained and immutable. They wanted to break free of their bonds that had fettered them for the past millennia. They saw visions of an apocalyptic age of deliverance from slavery and segregation from fellow humans. God's own earth was for them too. Now no one would be able to hoodwink them. But the battle was only half won yet.

No less revolutionary was the change brought about in the condition of another oppressed group in society. Segregated, condemned to life-long dependence on menfolk, regarded unfit for learning, treated like a moron and no more than a baby-producing machine – such had been the Indian woman. The law now forbade her, if widowed, to immolate herself with her dead husband. She could now marry again, just as a widower did. Child marriage was banned by law, the law recognised her rights. She had emerged into the bright light of freedom of a real human being. For her too the battle was only half won.

In spite of the many gains the oppressed groups could take pride on, it was a stupendous task that was set before the Constituent Assembly. It not only had to consolidate these gains but to actualise the hopes and dreams of a genuinely egalitarian society in which all men and women walk God's earth in freedom and dignity. India had still a great deal of the dead-wood of the centuries to shed before it could march courageously and freely into the dawn of equality of all the people of the vast country.

The Constituent Assembly had first met on December 9, 1946. Jawaharlal Nehru set the tone for the new Constitution in the objective resolution he moved in the Assembly on January 22, 1947. Of the Constitution India needed and the spirit that was to animate it, he said:

> 'WHEREIN shall be guaranteed and secured to all the people of India justice, social, economic and political; equality of status, of opportunity and before the law; freedom of thought, expression, belief, faith, worship, vocation, association, subject to law and public morality and
>
> 'WHEREIN adequate safeguards shall be provided for minorities, backward and tribal areas and depressed and other backward classes . . . .'[1]

The drafting committee was appointed on August 29, 1947, under the chairmanship of B.R. Ambedkar, and the draft Constitution was published in February 1948. The sessions of the Assembly from November of that year debated and voted on each of the articles of the Constitution. The whole Constitution was approved by the Assembly on November 26, 1949.

The spirit of the object resolution was embodied in the preamble to the Constitution. The framers of the Constitution had been guided by that spirit, regarding the resolution as a pledge to be fulfilled. India was now constituted a sovereign, socialist, secular and democratic republic.[2] The new law of the land contained many remarkable features to thrill the hearts of those who awaited the dawn of equality.

The Constitution of the Republic of India does not recognise caste. A citizen's rights are not determined by his caste status. The Constitution makers could hardly have been ignorant of the existence of caste considerations among the people. Else they could not have made provisions for the protection of the Scheduled Castes. Article 14 guarantees to all citizens equality before the law and equal protection of the laws. No privileges are any longer attached to any social group. Further, article 15 prohibits the state from discriminating against any citizen on the ground only of religion, race, caste, sex, place of birth; nor shall a citizen be subject to any disability on any of the above grounds. Article 16 provides for equal opportunities to all citizens and guarantees protection from all forms of discrimination.

What may be regarded as a revolutionary departure from the past was the statutory abolition of untouchability. Article 17 abolished untouchability in all its forms and prohibits its enforcement in any of its forms. It declares the enforcement of any disability arising from it to be an offence punishable by law. According to article 17(2), no citizen shall on the ground only of religion, race, caste, sex, descent or place of birth, shall be subject to any disability, liability or restriction, with regard to access to shops or restaurants, hotels, wells, tanks, bathing *ghats* places of entertainments, roads, or places of public resorts, maintained wholly or partly at the state expense.

The ground of discrimination against women has been abolished. In the past, different norms were enforced for the sexes. Once the principle of equality was accepted, all forms of discrimination or disabilities imposed on any group by law or custom ceased to have any legitimacy. The Constitution left no one in doubt over its concern for equality of all citizens.

The concern for equality did not stand in the way of the founding fathers authorising the state to make special provisions for the representation of groups inadequately represented in public services. The fathers considered it the duty of the state to assist such backward groups as the Scheduled Castes and Scheduled Tribes. They thought these special provisions indispensable to enable the deprived classes to enjoy the fruits of freedom and equality granted to all citizens.

The Herculean Task Ahead

The immense difficulty of forgoing a secular, democratic nation out of the old feudal, caste-based society became immediately evident. It seemed like asking for the impossible to integrate large masses of people hitherto deprived of basic human rights into the general body of citizens. The difficulty did not lie solely with the deprived masses. The classes that had enjoyed the privileges could not relish the prospect of abandoning the master-slave relationship with the deprived classes to welcome an era of full partnership with them. The administration that was entrusted with the task of implementing the Constitution was largely controlled by the privileged classes.

The Indian population lived at various levels of democratic

consciousness. Some did not believe in democracy and accepted it only in the absence of other options. At independence the princes were left free by the British to join the Indian Union or to retain separate existence. Joining the Union meant loss of absolute power, which now they could hope to command, and the use of unlimited wealth. Democracy would mean an end to all that, Hundreds of brāhmaṅa families of Travancore State publicly opted for a monarchical State in which they could wield great power. This was before the Constitution was still in the making. They would have been even more alarmed, had they learned of its provisions.

There were other groups in society that were wholly untouched by any sympathy for the aspirations of the lower classes. Naturally they could not be expected to assist in the process of building up a truly democratic society. They were prepared to accept democracy on their own terms and as long as it did not interfere with their prerogatives. There were others still who were rapidly hostile to the newly emerging groups. This group of people was not averse to employing brute force, money power, its prestige and influence to achieve its objective.

Nor were there lacking people who continued to believe in the sanctity of the *varṅa* system. This was not surprising since Gandhi himself stoutly defended it. True, it was no easy matter to determine what he meant by the term. This group awaited the return of a mythical golden age in which social democracy had no place. The law governing that society of the golden age would of course be the *dharmaśāstras* of old, which were thought capable of ushering in prosperity and happiness of the populace.

The Constitution was the expression of the new humanism that was the creed of the enlightened sections of the Indian people. The founding fathers had made a forceful assertion of the tenets of this new humanism. But what was there to nourish the roots of that humanism when those who inspired it were no more? What would happen when the charisma was no longer present to guide the generations to come? Will the foundations of the structure of social democracy be undermined?

The Congress party that guided the destiny of independent India uninterruptedly for nearly three decades was a moving menagerie of diverse elements. Some would devoutly mouth the socialist and democratic cant but were at heart obstructionists and obscurantists. Yet they could assume a very convincing from to pose as champions of democracy, socialism and secularism.

Gandhi had said in the early '20s that a slave nation that India was could not emancipate its own slaves. He was referring to the prospect of the deliverance of the untouchables from the age-old bondage. He could have said, with better logic, that unless India freed her slaves, she had no right to demand freedom from her masters. Gandhi did voice such a view when he launched his anti-Untouchability movement. Daunted by the immensity of the task he had undertaken, he had backed away. Now that India had her freedom, how could she go about emancipating her won slaves. The Constitutional provisions were a wonderful beginning.

To give effect to article 17 of the Constitution, the Indian Parliament passed the Untouchability (Offences) Act in 1955. In 1965 a commission was appointed to inquire into the actual working of the 1955 Act. The 1955 Act was then amended in 1976 in the context of the findings and recommendation of the commission. It is now known as the Protection of Civil Rights Act, 1955. The Act prescribed penalties against enforcement of disabilities springing from untouchability or related matters. The Act moreover makes every offence committed on the ground of untouchability a cognizable offence.

The New Alliances

Independent India brought all its citizens into the democratic process. The right of adult franchise imparted a measure of self-respect to even the most poverty-ridden and illiterate segments of the population. This was no small matter to a group of people who counted for nothing either in the eyes of others or in their own. The privileged minority now had to reckon with numbers. Numerical strength was a new factor in society as never seen before.

The princes and the land-owning elite had stood by the British in the Pre-Independence days. This was not surprising, since their interests lay in maintaining the *status quo*. Thus they found themselves outside the struggle for freedom. When freedom dawned for India, they had no share in political power.

This was precisely the situation the Rajputs of Gujarat faced at the dawn of Independence. The political area was dominated by the Patels, one of the land-owning classes of the region. Nor did the Rajputs possess the strength of numbers as they constituted a small minority, no more than five per cent of the total population. The way the Rajputs solved the problem was both novel and ingenious.

The Rajputs decided to make an alliance with the lower castes. This they did by conferring kṣatriyahood on them. History was repeating itself. They themselves had attained kṣatriyahood in the past through a sheer historical accident.

The Kolis were one of the lower castes on whom kṣatriyahood was conferred. It was the unmaking of the past. The British in the 19th century considered them one of the most intractable criminal tribes of India. The British arch trouble shooter of that century, James Outram, once besieged them in their hideout in conjuntion with the Gaekwad of Baroda, and dispersed them. In the times of Ferista, the chronicler of the Delhi Sultanate period, the Kolis were regarded as an aboriginal tribe. Twice in the space of six centuries the Kolis had acquired new identities.

The Rajputs found all those castes worthy of kṣatriyahood which displayed the martial spirit or those that were prepared to die for the country. The Bhils were also now reckoned among the martial races. The Kolis assumed such Rajput surnames as Mahiḍa and Solanki, and married into Rajput families.[3]

This Rajput fraternisation with lower castes did not take place in the Saurashtra and Kutch regions of Gujarat state. There they owned much of the land and hence had an interest in maintaining the status quo in social relations, since they drew their labour force from the lower castes. Thus the new policy was selectively applied.

In the late '60s Mrs Indira Gandhi was engaged in desperate struggle with the veteran leaders for the control of the Congress party. Morarji Desai could call the shots in the Gujarat Congress organisation. Mrs Gandhi needed some new allies. Here the Rajputs saw their chance and offered their support to her. Eventually they dislodged the deeply entrenched Patels from the Congress.[4]

The tussle between the Rajputs and the Patels continues unabated. The issue is not merely political power, but is no less economic supremacy. Open conflicts have broken out between them, resulting in massacres by both communities.

Great changes were taking place in the status and prestige of upper castes. As the Constitution did not recognise the sanctity of caste status, the upper castes could no longer enforce their will on those below them. There was no royal patron to assist them in keeping up their pretensions. A decline in their prestige was thus inevitable.

The authority of caste *pancāyats* had disappeared, which had in the past enforced a code of behaviour for the members of caste groups. Caste membership had also ceased to be linked to a profession. This was true of both honourable and less honourable professions. Tyagis and Pandeys now figured among the leaders of notorious dacoit gangs. The levelling of society had reached this extent.

An even more dramatic change was taking place in the state of Kerala in the South. With the reservation of jobs now available in all categories of government posts, the former untouchables were drawing high salaries. The Nairs of southern Kerala, who would not have permitted the untouchables to step into the front yard of their houses in the pre-Independence days, were now only too happy to hire themselves out as domestic servants of the former untouchables. History, for these Nairs, had come a full circle.

A notable change had come over the work ethic of the Nairs. In former times, the Nairs, in imitation of the elitist habits of the Brāhmaṇas, had spurned Physical labour. With the zamīndārī rights they held, they could live on the toil of their tenants. All this had changed. Now they did not regard wielding the hoe as injurious to their sense of dignity. Though only śūdras in *vaṇṇa* status, they had adopted the pretensions of the brāhmaṇas. Yet it is to their credit that the Nairs read correctly the signs of the times.

Many brahmaṇas of Kerala fared even worse than the Nairs. When zamīndārī was abolished, they had nothing to lean back on. To dig, they were unaccustomed and unwilling; to beg or something close to it, they were now reduced by a cruel trick of fate.

In the Andhra Pradesh it was the śūdra communities that had emerged dominant. The Kammas and Reddis, between them, owned a large chunk of the cultivable land in this region. There was intense tussle between the two communities for supremacy. In the post-Independence period, Andhra remained a strong bastion of the Congress Party. The Reddis dominated Congress politics in the State.

The Reddis had extended their economic dominance farther afield into the Tamil-speaking regions of South India. They were the large land-holders of Pondicherry and some districts of Tamil Nadu.

Unlike in the former times the balance of rural power now shifted in favour of the economically dominant agricultural communities. No doubt, in the past too, caste status was frequently determined by the economic base of a community. The change in the rural sector was partly brought about by an extraneous factor.

The Indian agriculture had a re-birth in the 1960s and the 1970s. The use of new techniques had put new life into an occupation that was associated with extreme conservatism marked by resistance to change and fresh ideas. The new high-yielding varieties of seeds, use of fertilisers and of modern machinery brought in an era of comparative prosperity to farmers with large holdings. Agriculture was now a paying proposition. Agricultural farmers found a new confidence. The farm lobby was at the zenith of its influence when a champion of the farmers, Charan Singh, became Prime Minister of India, though his tenure was short lived.

Some of the prominent leaders of the non-brāhamaṇa movement in Madras Presidency were śūdras. The South India Liberal Federation which spearheaded the movement later came to be known as the Justice Party. The non-brāhmaṇas had succeeded in forming a government as early as 1920, since the Congress Party stayed away from the provincial elections. The Justice Party continued to be in power till 1934 with a break between 1926-1930. In 1938 the Congress fought the elections and the Justice Party was routed and disappeared from the political stage.

It was on the issue of communal representation that the non-brāhmaṇa leader, E.V. Ramaswami Naicker, left the Congress Party. He had first raised the matter at the Congress meeting in 1920, but a discussion was disallowed by the president. Naicker brought up the subject again at the provincial session of the Congress in 1923. He was shouted down and manhandled by Congress toughs. He left the meeting, vowing to destroy the Congress. Along with some colleagues, Naicker founded the Self Respect Party in 1925. In the late 1930s, the party converted itself into Drāviḍa Kazhagam. C. Annadurai then was a prominent leader of the party. Differences cropped up in the party at its Tiruchirapalli session in 1945 over Naicker's decision to marry a 28-year old woman. In 1949 C. Annadurai led the dissidents out of the party to form the Drāviḍa Munnetra Kazhagam (DMK).[5]

The accession to the office of chief minister in 1945 by K. Kamaraj, a Śūdra leader belonging to the Nadar community, was hailed as a victory for the non-brāhmaṇas. Kamaraj was to emerge later as a national leader when he become president of the Indian

National Congress.

The DMK-Opposition alliance was voted to power in 1967. With the formation of a DMK ministry there was much unease among brāhmaṇas in the state, resulting in an exodus, of brāhmaṇas, as the Party was known for its anti-brāhmaṇa stand. On the death of C. Annadurai in 1969, he was succeeded in office by M. Karunanidhi. The DMK split into two factions and the newly formed Anna-DMK, led by film-star-politician M.G. Ramachandran, captured power in the State in 1977. The trend of brāhmaṇa exodus was now reversed. The brāhmaṇas were able to retrieve much of their lost prestige and positions.

New Social Climbers

Though the Constitution did not recognise caste in determining a citizen's rights, it was too deep-rooted to wither away quickly. A believer in caste could console himself by pointing out that the Constitution after all did not expressly condemn caste.

Caste mobility was not a rare phenomenon in the Indian society. The process had continued in contemporary times. Some lower castes made an attempt to move up giving themselves, what they thought were. more respectable names. This was not a novel idea either. The pariahs of the Tamil country became Adi Dravidas. Idayar became Yādhavas. The Pulayas of Kerala were now called Ceramar.

Tracing the community's origin to a well-known historical person was a way of acquiring some respectability. There have been groups who claim poet Vālmīki for their own. Even the Bhils of western India have claimed that Vālmīki was an ancestor of theirs. Some untouchables of Punjab have been also calling themselves after the revered poet.

The Gadulya Lohar community of Rajasthan, a nomadic group, has taken a bold approach to ancestry. They trace their descent from no less than the heroes of Chittor. They wander from place to place and live in the open with the sky as their only roof. They make a living by dealing in agricultural implements and doing repair jobs of iron tools. They are also cartwrights. According to one of their stories, their ancestors fought alongside Rānā Pratāp during the siege of Chittor by Akbar. After the fall of Chittor, they vowed not to live in a permanent place. It is difficult to ascertain the truth of this story.

But several other nomadic groups tell similar stories about themselves.

The Mangs of Maharashtra are another group who have assumed a new name. They are a nomadic group on the lowest rungs of the social ladder. They now prefer to call themselves Matangs, tracing their origin to the *ṛṣis* named Mātang of old. Whatever be the truth in this particular claim, it is perhaps not wholly unhistorical to ascribe ancestory to *ṛṣis*. Like Viswamitra of yore, other *ṛṣis* too had their weak moments. While Viśwāmitra of course surrendered to the heavenly nymph Menaka, other *ṛṣis* may have surrendered to less ravishing beauties. Be that as it may, the Mangs have succeeded in having themselves classified as Scheduled Tribe. Interestingly enough, there are several claimants to Scheduled Tribe classification.

The search for new identities by the lower castes was to leave its mark on social relations. It would help them to shed their old inhibitions and fears and fatalism regarding their status. The new mood was a factor in the growth of caste feuds that characterised the '70s and '80s. We have already discussed the outbreak of the Nadar-Maravan feud in the last quarter of the 19th century. The agitations by the untouchables of Maharashtra in the late '20s were another expression of changed attitudes. Social tension came to be a part of the Indian scene.

One of the regions where virulent antagonism between communities has persisted for years is Tamil Nadu. This is no less due to the confidence the Adi Draviḍas gained in recent times. They no longer cower before the higher castes. Their confidence is sustained by a notable change in their educational levels which had paved the way for the improvement in the economic condition.

In some villages of South Arcot district a state of war existed between the Adi Draviḍas and the Vanniars, a backward class community of Tamil Nadu. The latter would not tolerate the new militancy of the Adi Draviḍas.

Another expression of revolt by the members of the former untouchable communities was conversion to non-Hindu religions. Ramanathapuram shot into limelight in 1980 with the mass conversion of Scheduled Caste families to Islam. Threats and allurements failed to bring the converts back into the Hindu fold.

The predictable at these times happened. There was a sudden eruption of fraternisation of the Scheduled Castes. This had been enacted twice before. During Gandhi's anti-untouchability exertions in the early '20s there was much befriending of the untouchables. There were many expressions of goodwill towards them coupled with some inter-dining. But the fervour was shortlived. The round of fraternisation, expressions of goodwill and inter-dining were repeated in the wake of Gandhi's fast and the Yeravda Pact of 1932. More vigorous and vociferous protestations of goodwill were heard then. After the Ramanathapuram conversions the fraternisation seemed to be a mere formality. It had become a meaningless ritual. Conversions, however, have continued in Tamil Nadu in spite of these gestures.

The Ramanathapuram conversions and the resulting emotional reactions and alarm in orthodox circles focused attention on the prevalence of untouchability. The problem of untouchability was something that both the Government and religious leaders preferred to ignore. Everyone knew it was there like the dirt under the table. No one wanted to talk about it. Some vicious forms of the practice have continued to exist in many Tamil Nadu villages where the upper castes dominated. Members of Scheduled Caste communities could not ride bicycles through the quarters of the upper caste Hindus. They could not wear clean clothes or wear shoes. It was not comforting to realise that in 40 years of freedom the nation had made little headway in efforts to eradicate the evil of untouchability.

Elsewhere in the country the situation is no better. There are localities where Scheduled Caste communities are barred from public wells even today. In tea stalls they must drink from different cups than those used by others. The aboriginals are at times treated like the Scheduled Castes. Scheduled Caste children are so harassed that they would rather stay home than face the ordeal at school. The harassment does not always come from the upper castes alone. Backward class communities are as much guilty in this matter as the upper castes. Scheduled Castes children face heavy odds in acquiring even elementary education, unless separate schools are maintained for them. But then separate schools for the Scheduled Castes are nobody's baby and no worthwhile education is imparted through them.

Depriving the Scheduled Caste children of proper education is one way of perpetuating their slavery. The privileged classes cannot be expected to be very enthusiastic about the education of those whom the Constitution had freed from statutory slavery. They will not willingly let go of their slaves who till now have provided cheap labour for them. There is little doubt that they consider the education of the lower classes a threat to their genuine interests. One should not be surprised that sections of the traditionally privileged communities attempt to thwart schemes for the advancement of hitherto deprived communities.

In 1986 the Rajasthan High Court appointed a commission to enquire into the prevalence of untouchability in the town of Badi Sadri in Chittorgarh district of the State. The commission in its report has pointed out some crude forms of the inhuman practice. What is of special interest for us are the remarks the report made about the municipal council of the town, an elected body of people's own representatives, how it discriminates against the Scheduled Caste employees in the matter of access to drinking water, minimum wage and other basic rights. In a town which practises discrimination and untouchability officially, one can well imagine the extent of the evil among its inhabitants. Broken cups are used by the members of Scheduled Castes to take tea in the tea stalls. These cups are kept in a separate place and washed by the users themselves.[6]

The custom of employing Scheduled Castes to carry human excreta has not yet been abandoned. It is a dehumanising practice and those who perform this type of work are robbed of self-esteem. Municipalities and other elected bodies display scant sensitivity and unconcern in the abolition of the custom. The Rajasthan report makes references to the revolting form of the disposal of excreta.

It was in Rajasthan too that a prolonged temple entry agitation was witnessed in June 1987. The agitation, led by the Harijan Seva Sangha, sought entry for member of Scheduled Caste communities into the well-known temple at Nathdwara in Udaipur district. It led to violence as the upper caste Hindu tried to prevent the entry of the so-called untouchables into the temple. The agitation continued unabated. Now Swami Agnivesh, the well-known social activist, took up the cause of the dalits, leading their rallies, but he was prevented from entering Nathdwara by the police. In September 1988, the Rajasthan High Court directed the State government to ensure that all discrimination against dalits on temple entry was removed. But the dalits who attempted to enter the temple, after the directive was issued, were beaten up.[7]

The conviction has been growing on the Scheduled Caste leaders that the deliverance of the Scheduled Castes will come about only through the efforts of the communities themselves. They have rejected the Gandhian theory that this deliverance will be effected though the efforts of Hindu reformers. They have not only rejected Gandhian theory but also the very designation 'Harijan' which he bestowed on them and have adopted the nomenclature 'dalit'. Significantly, it is Ambedkar who has emerged as a symbol of hope for the dalits. Ambedkar has inspired renewed efforts to emancipate themselves. In Tamil Nadu every dalit village has an Ambedkar Sabha, an association to further the advancement of dalits. These Sabhas have instilled a new sense of solidarity into the members of the dalit community. The solidarity has brought a new militancy. It was the Dalit Panthers of Maharashtra who first assumed a militant stance. They demanded a Dalitsthan, or a separate state comprising areas where dalits constituted a substantial part of the population. Another issue they agitated for was the renaming of the Marathwada University of Maharashtra as Ambedkar University. But there was also opposition to these demands from sections of the population. The agitation continued for more than a decade and gradually died out.

Ordeal by Reservation

The issue of reservation of posts in public service and educational institution was to dominate and determine the political scene in Independent India. The issue would lead to prolonged bouts of violence and agitations in several states of the country.

The concept of equality is susceptible of two distinct and divergent interpretations. Equality can be understood in a formal sense in which all members of society are treated equally without regard for their specific conditions. If understood thus, equality leaves little room for making distinction between various categories of people; it does not take into account their needs or actual situation. As opposed to formal equality, proportional equality regards all citizens as enjoying equal rights but does not apply identical standards to all in determining the amount of assistance required by various members. It makes allowance for preferential treatment of the weaker members of society, as their needs are special. If formal equality were to be applied, there would be no scope for preferential treatment of weaker citizens by the state.

If absolute standards were applied to all citizens, it would benefit only the privileged groups of citizens. Thus it defeats the very purpose behind the Constitutional provision of equality. Preferential treatment or 'protective discrimination' of the weak is not only desirable but becomes an obligation on the part of the state. If all citizens are to come to a level where they can enjoy the fruits of freedom and development, the disavantaged sections must be enabled to rise to that level through special assistance. The reservation of posts for certain disadvantaged groups is based on this understanding of equality.[8]

Preferential treatment of backward class communities as an indispensable element of real equality has not always been understood. In the decades following the enactment of the Constitution the concept has been further clarified.

The Constitution-makers had not been unconscious of the advisability of authorising the state to make special provisions for backward classes. A proposal was actually made by B.R. Ambedkar in the Constituent Assembly regarding such a provision. He had suggested that the following be added to article 8(2) of the draft Constitution, now article 13 (2):

> 'Provided that nothing in this clause shall prevent the State from making any law for the removal of inequality, disparity, disadvantage or discrimination arising out of any existing law.'[9]

The Assembly, however, did not incorporate the proviso. Articles 330 and 332 provide for the reservation of seats in the House of People or the Lower House of Parliament, and State Legislatures for the Scheduled Castes and Scheduled Tribes. They are to receive reserved representation proportionate to their strength in the total population. According to article 335 the claims of the members of the Scheduled Castes and Scheduled Tribes are to be taken into account in making appointments to services and posts, consistent with the maintenance of efficiency in conducting the affairs of the state.

Article 341(1) authorised the President to specify in consultation with the state governments the castes and groups to be classified as Scheduled Castes and Scheduled Tribes.

Article 16(4) moreover authorises the state to make any provision for the reservation of appointments or posts to any backwards class which in the opinion of the state is inadequately represented.

Exercising the powers conferred upon him by article 341, on August 10, 1950, the President issued the notification which carried the list of castes and groups that are classified under the term of Scheduled Castes and Scheduled Tribes. The Presidential order expressly states in paragraph 3 that no person who professes a religion different from the Hindu religion shall be deemed to be a member of a Scheduled Caste.

It was the Madras Government that first set apart fixed quotas of the posts in services for various communities such as the minorities and backward classes including the Scheduled Castes and Tribes. In 1951 the Supreme Court in its verdict in *the State of Madras* v. *Champakam Dorairajan* held that such fixed quotas are unconstitutional.[10] To overcome the hurdle created by the Supreme Court verdict, there was no way out but to amend the Constitution. Accordingly in 1951, in the first ever amendment of the Constitution, clause (4) was added to article 15, which read:

> 'Nothing in this article or in clause (2) of article 29 shall prevent the State from making any special provision for the advancement of any socially or educationally backward classes of citizens or for the Scheduled Castes and Scheduled Tribes.'

The way was now cleared for reservation of posts for any group judged to be socially or educationally backward.

On January 29, 1953, the President appointed a commission under the chairmanship of Kaka Kalelkar to enquire into condition of backward groups of people not covered by the term Scheduled Caste and to lay down criteria for determining the socially and educationally backward classes.

The report of the Kalelkar Commission was presented to the Parliament in September 1956. The Government unequivocally rejected the report and refused to accept caste as a criterion of backwardness as the commission had suggested. The Central Government has consistently refused to draw up a list of backward classes (OBCs) and instead asked the State Governments to draw up their own lists using economic and educational criteria.[11]

When the Janata Government was installed in 1977 the states of Utter Pradesh and Bihar extended reservation to certain backward communities. There was widespread protest over the measure. Following these developments, the Central Government appointed a Commission under the chairmanship of B.P. Mandal to determine criterion of backwardness.

The Commission in its report, submitted in 1980, recommended that 27 per cent of posts in Central services be reserved for the backwards classes (OBCs). The principle of proportional representation could not be applied in making this recommendation. The Scheduled Castes and Scheduled Tribes had already been allotted 22.5 per cent of the posts in government services. The Supreme Court had laid down the rule that total reservation could not exceed 50 per cent. Hence the commission was under constraint to restrict the reservation for the backward classes to 27 per cent. It also recommended the setting up of a ministry or department both at the Centre and the states to look after the affairs of the OBC.[12] The Mandal Commission applied social and educational criteria in determining backwardness. Specifically, caste and literacy were the criteria applied by the Commission in its field surveys. It consistently refused to consider economic backwardness as one of the criteria.

It was to Congress (I) Government that Mandal Commission report was presented. Though the Government accepted the report, it never implemented its recommendation.

Though the Central Government has repeatedly rejected the demand to allot quotas of posts in the Central services to the backward classes (OBCs), the state Governments have reserved varying percentages of posts in government service and seats in educational institutions for them. This reservation has sparked off violence and bloodshed in several states. No state has lived through such a paroxysm of violence as has Gujarat on this issue.

If caste criterion is to be applied, even somewhat well-off communities would be entitled to reservations. This anomaly would have introduced new conflicts and give a further fillip to the evil of caste that the Constitution had tried to remedy. Many communities have attempted to grab benefits of reservation on the sole ground of caste, even though they were not qualified for benefits on the basis of economic criteria. Caste thus becomes a tool for advancement.

When it came to appropriating the benefits of reservation, most castes were not averse to being classified as backward. Caste hierarchy could be bent a little for financial gains. There is nothing surprising or shocking in all this a deteriorating moral environment.

When a large part of the population demands reservations, it is understandable that it evokes strong reaction from those who are denied such special benefits. According to the criteria adopted by the Mandal Commission, as much as 50 per cent of the Indian population comes under the category of backward class. Considering that 20 per cent of all posts in public services and educational institutions have already been reserved for the Scheduled Castes and Tribes, the prospect of further reservation for the backward classes creates alarm in the minds of those who do not come under any of these categories. The backward class demand for reservation has heightened the sense of insecurity of the minority upper castes. They regard the resurgence among the backward classes a threat to their position and are prepared to stem the tide of new confidence in the lower classes with violence, if necessary.

The 70s and 80s saw much caste conflict all over the country. Diverse groups were involved in these conflicts. In Bihar, for instance, in some areas two upper castes, the Rajputs and Bhumihars were locked in a tussle. In Munger and Patna districts of the State the tussle was between the Bhumihars and the Yadavas and between Yadavas and the Kurmis, who are both backward classes. Elsewhere in Patna district the feuding parties were the Kurmis and the Scheduled Castes, on the one hand, and Rajputs and the Scheduled Castes on the other. Castse wars in Bihar recur with benumbing frequency and have attracted national attention. Such names as Belcchi, Parasbigha and Pipra once brought home to the nation the horrors of caste wars. But these wars have been dwarfed by later horrors, each of which surpassed the previous incident in brutality. The ceaseless tales of bloody reprisals wreaked often on the innocents deadened the people.

But all the horror tales coming from Bihar had not prepared the nation for the savagery witnessed in two villages of Aurangabad district of Bihar. On May 29, 1987, a 500-strong mob surrounded two villages, Dalelcak and Bhagaura, and murdered and burned members of seven Rajput families. Nearly 42 persons were done to death in this fashion. This was not an isolated incident. In an earlier massacre, the Rajputs had killed seven persons belonging to the Yadava caste. The massacre of May 29 was in retaliation to the killing of the Yadavas. In a first reaction to the massacre, the administration branded it as the doing of the extremist group. Later independent investigation rejected the theory of extremist involvement.[13]

There was long-standing feud between the land-owning Rajputs and the Yadavas. The massacre was but the climax of a series of killings and reprisals. A distressing phenomenon in Bihar has been the formation of *senās* (militias). At times these *senas* replace the local administration. They protect the interests of the particular caste groups which has inspired it. They have marked out territories for themselves. Little is known to the outside world of the scope of the activities of the militias.

The *senas* come in all colours. Some are caste-based while others are extremist-inspired. Aurangabad district had often witnessed struggles among the extremist *senas* themselves. The presence of the *senas* proves not only the breakdown of the rule of law but the deterioration in social relations. The desperate attempts on the part of upper castes to enforce traditional social relations have not succeeded. Desperate times call for desperate measures, they seem to say, and they are in dead earnest about it.

The transition from a hierarchical society into a democratic one is bound to be accompanied by tension. But what we observe in a state like Bihar, is not mere tension but open warfare between communities which appear to be bent on eliminating the rivals.

The entry of the Naxalite movement into the rural scene has even further heightened the conflict that rages there. The movement which first erupted in West Bengal has now established strong bases in Bihar and Andhra Pradesh. The Naxalites drawing inspiration from the Maoist ideology do not believe in a peaceful transition from a feudal society to an eqalitarian society. It has won many adherents from the lowest class of untouchables of Bihar such as the Camars and Musahars. It has befriended the peasants too.

The Naxalite movement has provided a grand excuse for the administration. Even the legitimate and peaceful protests are branded as extremist and Naxalite-inspired. It then justifies police high-handedness, which is no better than lawlessness by other groups of people, but far worse, since it is being committed by the guardians of law.

The way the police deal with protest which they regard as Naxalite-inspired is best exemplified by the police firing on a crowd of villagers at Arwal in Gaya district of Bihar. The unprovoked firing on April 19, 1986, took an unusually heavy toll of more than 40 lives, besides disabling many others. It appears that a backward class family had taken possession of a plot of land belonging to a Scheduled Caste family. The villagers had gathered in protest. The police were, it would seem, acting in the interest of the family that had illegally occupied the land. The only difference in the Arwal massacre by the police was that it was less brutal in execution than the massacre at Dalelcak and Bhagaura.

Like Bihar, Uttar Pradesh has been the scene of intense caste conflict. As in Bihar, dacoit gangs are organised on caste lines, Uttar Pradesh is a state where the upper castes hold the upper hand. These dacoit gangs are employed to get even with rival caste groups. This state has not lagged far behind Bihar in caste-inspired massacres. The Kurmis are pitted against the brāhmaṇas, Rajputs against the Scheduled Castes.

Similar conflicts raged in Andhra Pradesh, where usually one of the land-owning communities of the Kammas or the Reddis was pitted against one of the Scheduled Caste communities of Malls or Madigas, and the Rajputs and the Scheduled Caste in Gujarat and Madhya Pradesh were increasingly in conflict.

In North India, the upper caste themselves were in conflict with one another. The rivalry between the Rajputs and brāhmaṇas came into the open in the mid 1980s. The ruling Congress (I) party itself was divided on these lines. The brāhmaṇas have made considerable gains in recent years in the appointments made by the Central Government.

A significant development in the socio-political scene in India was the birth and growth of a new force inspired by a Scheduled Caste leader, Kansi Ram. He set out to forge a new front of all the under-privileged segments of society, comprising the dalits, aboriginals and the backward classes. This new front has been named Bahujan Samaj. The idea was first mooted by Jotirao Phule in the last century. Kansi Ram does not want to cling to the apron string of the major political parties of the country but wants to establish a separate force of the under-privileged classes. Though founded in 1983, Bahujan Samaj has made remarkable headway. This is demonstrated by the alarm the new front has caused in some political circles, especially the ruling part. Kansi Ram could no longer be ignored.

The Bahujan Samaj was launched in the very stronghold of upper castes. Among all the states of India, the under-privileged classes have made least headway in Uttar Pradesh. This state was, therefore, the most unlikely place for an experiment so ambitious as Bahujan Samaj. For that reason the state provides the supreme test of the viability of the grand scheme behind the new venture.

For the first time perhaps the emphasis has been laid on a political solution of the problem of the under-privileged segments of society. It must have dawned on the leaders of these sections that the reservation can at best be a temporary measure and can offer no lasting solution. Reliance on reservation must ultimately hamper the emancipation of the under-privileged.

Women in Free India

Like the other oppressed groups of India, the women were weighted down by the burden of centuries of prejudice, ignorance and superstition. As Gandhi once said, women had become willing slaves. Sections of women have made impressive gains through education. The Constitution had lifted all the statutory discriminations against them.

The Constitutional provision did not alter radically the condition of Indian women. The pitifully low literacy rates among the women is an eloquent proof of this. Prejudice cannot be eradicated through laws. Prejudice against female education was an accepted belief of the masses. It has to be shown up for what it is. Hence progress in this area of education has been painfully slow. Lack of education is not the only problem faced by women.

The dream of equality that the Constitution-makers presented to all the citizens can only remain a utopia as long as women are regarded as weaklings and liabilities. The grinding poverty and ignorance in which millions of them lived offer little scope for leading a satisfying human life, not to speak of securing justice for themselves.

Women of the lowest classes are also vulnerable to sexual exploitation by the upper caste men. Understandably enough, sex does not strictly adhere to the rules of caste. One might argue that it is not legitimate sex. But the *Dharmaśāstras* do not permit any latitude even in sex. The high brow Rajputs at times are not averse to philandering with Scheduled Caste women.

The Bhilala caste was the product of the liaison between the Rajput males and Bhil females. The tradition of claiming right over the women of the lower castes by higher caste males has continued to the present. Like the Rajputs, some upper castes of Kerala were never squeamish about clandestine intimacy with the Pulaya women. For that matter, even Syrian Christians of Kerala, who have elitist pretensions, show the same absence of squeamishness towards Pulaya women. It need hardly be pointed out that the backward classes suffer even less from squeamishness in the matter. Sex, like time, is a great leveller.

The view of woman as a liability is demonstrated by the prevalence of the practice of dowry in many communities. Though law makes taking or giving of dowry an offence, it has had little impact on the practice. Dowry has been the cause of horrendous crimes against young women. Newspapers have been carrying reports of the heinous crime of bride-burning. The 1980s saw a spurt in bride-burning incidents. Most of these crimes are committed against middle class women. In the middle class families, marriage is a means of economic advancement for the bridegroom's family. Naturally, young brides are expected to bring substantial wealth into the husband's family. Harassment of the young women begins soon after the marriage. The horror of the murder of hapless young women is re-enacted again and again. To the crime against the innocent butchered in cold blood in caste wars are added the cries of many dying young women who fall victims to the insatiable greed for dowry. It is in terror not merely tears that many urban young women count their days drained of every happiness.

Age-old inhuman practices such as female infanticide have still their advocates. Some Rajputs of Jaisalmer district of Rajasthan still practise female infanticide. The rustic midwife is entrusted with the horrible business. She stuffs some sand into the mouth of the new-born baby. The custom prevails among the Bhati Rajputs.[14]

A somewhat more 'refined' way of eliminating female babies is replacing the older method of female infanticide. The urban middle class has discovered in recent years sex determination as an effective way of preventing the birth of female babies. The medical profession has been very accommodating to the wishes of the middle class. Some feeble voices have been raised by certain women's organisations against the new practice.

In early September 1987, an unpretentious village in Sikar district of Rajasthan earned much notoriety and international publicity when Rup Kanwar, an 18-year old young widow performed *satī* on her husband's funeral pyre. The gruesome rite took place at the village of Deorala on September 4 in the presence of hundreds of people. But even greater shock was in store for the Indian public.

On a petition filed by a women's organisation, the Rajasthan High Court issued orders prohibiting the '*chunri*' ceremony scheduled for September 16, the 13th day of *satī*. Despite the court orders, the ceremony was performed with much religious ardour in the presence of lakhs of people. The people of Deorala had not yet done away with the affair. They now announced that a temple was to be built to commemorate the young woman's self-immolation. Rup Kanwar was now elevated to the status of a goddess. As the *satī* incident caused protest in many parts of the country, the Rajputs held rallies in Jaipur, the state capital, and other cities of the state, such as Jodhpur, Bikaner and Barmer, in support of *satī*. A large contingent of police was posted at Deorala to prevent the construction of the temple. On October 1 the Governor of Rajasthan promulgated the Rajasthan Satī (Prevention) Ordinance, 1987, which laid down death penalty for abetting *satī* and jail sentences up to seven years for glorifying it. In December of the same year the Indian Parliament passed an anti-*satī* Bill.

What was most disturbing about the *satī* affair was the support given to the custom by the political leaders of Rajasthan. Those who defended *satī* included leaders belonging to the ruling Congress (I) party and the right wing Bhartiya Janata Party (BJP) and right-of-the-centre Janata Party. The fact that the public performance of *satī* took place 158 years after *satī* was banned officially meant a serious setback for those who struggled for women's rights.

The state administration too did not cover itself with glory in its handling of the affair. The failure of the state administration becomes all the more serious since it is now certain that Rup Kanwar was coerced into self-immolation. Historical evidence suggests that young women were often compelled to perform the outrageous rite. To drive a young woman into the flame and then turn her into a goddess is a terrible mockery of true religion.

The condition of Indian women remains a great paradox. There are the urban women who in fashionable circles speak volubly of women's liberation, while their sisters suffer the most inhuman exploitation and untold disabilities. The first group is far removed from the grim reality of the vast majority of Indian women. Utter deprivation, repulsive superstition, female infanticide, bride-burning and *satī* – all this is a mockery of the rights of the women which the Constitution solemly upholds and proclaims.[15]

The Invisible People of India

The Constitution makes special provisions for assistance to

Scheduled Tribes along with Scheduled Castes. But unlike the Scheduled Castes who are regarded even against their will as part of the Hindu community, the Scheduled Tribes have retained an existence of their own and constitute a distinct group in the Indian population. They have added much to the cultural diversity of the nation.

A distinct identity gave the Scheduled Tribes no immunity from exploitation by the advanced communities. At times they labour under even more disabilities than the Scheduled Castes. Educational levels are lower. Generally they live in areas with poor communication facilities, poor health care and are unable to obtain a fair price for their agricultural produce.

But the tribals enjoy some advantages too. In the eyes of the larger Hindu community, in particular, they have been generally treated with less contempt than the Scheduled Castes. This somewhat advantageous position was due to their cultural identity. In tribal societies women enjoy a comparatively more honourable position than in Scheduled Caste communities. The tribals frequently adopted the less healthy beliefs and practices of the Hindus and the lower classes. Some of these beliefs and practices pertained to women. Early marriage of girls was never a tribal custom. Tribal societies universally observe the rule of marriage of girls after puberty. Early marriage has now become an accepted practice among some tribal communities.

Generally tribal women never suffered from the stigma attached to the menses and parturition. Some tribal women have now adopted the superstition of uncleanness during the menses and child-birth. Proximity of the Hindu communities has cost the tribal women dear.

Though the tribals have never been under any obligation to serve the upper caste communities, they have been reduced to a state of bondage in several parts of the country. This bondage is economic, not social. In this manner, they are as severely oppressed as the Scheduled Castes. One of the ways tribals are enslaved is through bonded labour practices. In return for a loan amounting to more than Rs.300 a man may spend his remaining years in bondage, being obliged to work for his creditor for a mere pittance. As he works, cumulative interest on his loan multiplies, making it virtually impossible for him to repay it. This is the grim existence which thousands of tribals face year after year. If a man so bonded is unable to pay back his loan, he naturally passes on the debt to his son. So it goes on, generation after generation.

There is yet another form of slavery which the state's development agencies inflict on unsuspecting tribals and the Scheduled Castes. These agencies advance loans for which they mortgage their land. Many of those who so obtain a loan are dispossessed to their land and are reduced to a state far worse than before. The heartless system has thrown many illiterate and poor tribals into a condition no less unbearable than bondage. At times it looks as though development agencies have been so designed as to defraud the innocent and ensnare the unwary.[16]

Talk of equality of all citizens will sound sheer gibberish to large sections of tribal population. They do not even manage to secure their basic rights and justice. Equality with other groups in the country must appear to them an unrealisable dream. Yet of all the groups they are culturally the most attuned to the concept of social equality as this is one of the basic principles of many tribal societies.

The growing self-awareness of tribals has found expression in the tribal movements of 1970s and 1980s. Such movements have sprung up among the Santhals of Bihar and West Bengal, the Bhils of Gujarat, the Warlis of Maharashtra and the Bodos of Assam. They have the twin purpose of freeing the tribals from various forms of oppression and bondage and also of bringing about needed changes in tribal societies that would enable them to face the changed times. The Santhals of Bihar have been able to create a greater appreciation of the need of education in the community. Alcoholism, the curse that plagued many tribal groups in India, has also come in for serious criticism. This evil has laid them open to much exploitation in the past by non-tribals. These movements have given the tribals a certain pride in their tribal identity. This is but a survival technique brought into play to prevent their absorption by the more numerous communities.

NOTES

1. The passage is reproduced here from Durga Das Basu's *Introduction to the Constitution of India*, New Delhi, Prentice-Hall of India, 1983, p.20.
2. The word 'socialist' was added to the clause through an amendment to the Constitution in 1976.
3. See Meenakshi Jain, 'Rise of Political Castes in Gujarat', *The Times of India*, (Jaipur ed.), July 22, (1986).
4. *Ibid.*
5. C.S. Sarvanam, (1987) 'Regionalism and Dravida Kazhagam Phenomenon in

Tamil Nadu' in *Social Action*, July-September, p.230 ff.

6. See report, (1986) 'Even the Govt. Goes Against Harijans', *The Indian Express* (New Delhi ed.), August 26.
7. See front-page report, (1988) 'Harijans Attacked in Nathdwara', *The Indian Express* (New Delhi ed.), October 5.
8. For a fuller discussions of equality, see Parmanand Singh, (1985) *Equality, Reservation and Discrimination in India*, New Delhi, Deep Publication, p.17 ff.
9. *Ibid.*, p.23.
10. See Parmananand Singh, 1985, p.101.
11. *Ibid.*, p.47.
12. *The Mandal Commission Report on Backward Classes*, Part I, New Delhi, Govt. of India, 1980, p.58.
13. Arvind N. Das, (1987) 'Caste Killings in Bihar : How These Are Organised', *The Times of India* (Jaipur ed.), June 10.
14. See report, (1986) 'Female Infanticide in Jaisalmer District', *The Times of India* (Jaipur ed.), September 4.
15. For a discussion on the many faces of oppression of women, see Sherna Gandhy, (1988) 'Crimes against Women', *The Illustrated Weekly of India*, July 31 - August 6. p.8 ff.
16. For a fuller treatment of the oppression of tribals, see author's monograph, (1986) *The Bhils of Rajasthan*, New Delhi, The India Social Institute, p.35 ff.

8

CONCLUSIONS

WE HAVE till now briefly followed the course of Indian Social Society. Some periods were marked by clear gains in the search for a social order based on the principle of equality of all groups in the population. There have been frequent setbacks. What does the balance-sheet show?

The first revolt against social elitism was staged by heterodox sects. In their heyday these sects did make an impact. Both Jainism and Buddhism lost much ground in the course of time incorporating some of the insights. If the non-brahmanic sects, the orthodox groups, were able to neutralise much or their impact, the decline of Jainism and Buddhism paved the way for a reinstatement of traditional authority.

After Aśoka's time there was no serious effort by monarchs to mould society on the Buddhist model. The post-Mauryan Buddhist kings had little leisure to devote to social reconstruction. At the end of Harṣa's reign orthodoxy was already on the come-back trail. Soon there would be some help from Śaṅkara, the great champion of orthodoxy.

The reversion to the old model continued to gain momentum after the collapse of the Buddhist social order which depended heavily on royal patronage. Now there was no authority to enforce it.

The *bhakti* movement at first gave signs of a burgeoning new social order based on brotherhood. The adherents of *bhakti* did not abandon the *varṇa* model of society. Within that model, they were prepared to grant some semblance of equality to the lower classes. They conceded that the path of *bhakti* was within the reach of even the lowest. This in itself was a notable departure from the old practice although Śaṅakra, a *bhakta* himself, denied the path of true knowledge to all except the twice-born.

The *bhakti* movement gradually reverted to the rapidly casteist practices and, ultimately, it gained notoriety for extreme casteism. The movement was thus a failure.

Yet the *bhakti* stream could boast of some genuine gains. There would never have been a vernacular literature worth its name but for the *bhakti* schools throughout India. This literature was of immense value to the masses as a source of education and guidance. But that was not its greatest achievement.

The *bhakti* stream produced a breed of men and women, charismatic individuals of all classes, filled with great power, saintliness and humanity, who posed a challenge to the forces of oppression, preached a gospel of brotherhood, unity and equality of all humans. These men and women very nearly approached the power, courage and commitment of the Old Testament Prophets. They are the finest flower of *bhakti*. Some of them would always be remembered for their contribution to the quest for dignity, freedom and equality.

India's relations with the British have proved to be fateful. In some ways, they have been traumatic. In this period the Indians emerged from their shell into which they had been driven by excessive fear of defilement by other nations and cultures. The gains have been incalculable.

Of the three most oppressed groups, whose fortunes we have followed, the śūdras alone have succeeded in altering their social positions. The change was brought by an interplay of many factors. It was the economic opportunities the śūdras grabbed that proved decisive. Some śūdra groups are today counted among the upper castes. These are : the Patels of Gujarat, the Kammas and Reddis of Andhra Pradesh, the Veḷḷālas and Uḍayārs of Tamil Nadu and the Nāirs of Kerala. They are the landed castes of their respective regions. The rise of the Kāyasthas, once numbered among the śūdras, has no parallel. But there can be no doubt that it was on their economic strength that the Kāyasthas succeeded in claiming a higher caste ranking.

The artisan castes have not succeeded in bettering their social position. In recent years, however, there has been a move towards abandoning the ancestral occupation. There is no caste whose members are not engaged in trade in some form or other. An improved self-image has been the saving point of such communities as the Naḍars of Tamil Nadu and the Vokkaligas of Karnataka.

In spite of numerous laws enacted in favour of women during the 20th century, they have remained a sorely oppressed group in the population. New forms of oppression are making their appearance.

Such forms are bride-burning and pre-natal sex determination. The latter is being effectively used to eliminate girls. The older forms of discrimination are still flourishing in traditional communities.

It is often asserted that education will liberate Indian women. But the terrible fate that awaits many educated urban women disproves this theory. It is actually the Indian male who needs badly some education. Unless he is thoroughly re-educated, there can be no liberation for Indian women. The sufferings that are heaped upon widows, the crimes committed in the name of *satī*, infanticide – all stem from the male value system.

Like women, the Scheduled Castes continue to suffer severe social disabilities. The law has not put an end to the grievous discriminations against them. In former times it was the upper caste Hindus who rode upon their backs. Today new communities are moving upward and these have an opportunity to lord it over others. Among the few individuals of the Scheduled Caste communities who make good, there are some who are not averse to exploiting their less fortunate brethren.

The post-Independence era has witnessed some gruesome killings and savagery perpetrated upon the former untouchables. At the bottom of these killings was the self-assertion of the Scheduled Caste communities and their demand for justice.

The claim that the *varṇa*-based society of yore was a society where peace, happiness and prosperity reigned is founded on doubtful historical evidence. Constant repetition has made it seem a historical fact. The *varṇa* theory, as we know it, contained the very seeds of disharmony and tension. Social immobility and conformity were promoted. Some groups were forever condemned to an existence without power, without influence, learning and hope for betterment.

The *Dharmaśāstras*, invoking divine authority had an even more deleterious influence on the people's mind. They not only glorified the *varṇa* order, but made the observance of untouchability a religious obligation. Discrimination, exploitation and oppression never looked more respectable than in the *dharmaśāstras*. But for them, untouchability could never have been enforced so vigorously. It could not have become the terror that it came to be.

The conflicts between communities in contemporary India are but the natural consequence of the cultivation of caste. The supportive system behind caste has crumbled. The priesthood and monarchy formed the supportive system. Deprived of the aid of these institutions, caste has lost its sting. There is no power to enforce it. The Indian people have paid dearly for the institution of caste. They will continue to experience conflict and discord, until the monster is completely destroyed.

Few civilisations have so demoralised their work-force as has the Indian civilisation. Its woefully shabby treatment to its working classes was based on its own work ethic. All physical labour was regarded as demeaning and undignified. But the great irony was, those who despised physical labour were not disinclined to live on other men's labour.

The deepest yearning of the human heart for dignity and equality has found expression in the Constitution. It is but a beginning. The vision charted out there has yet to be realised.

EPILOGUE

THE STORY of the struggles for social equality has taken us across several millennia. It is a moving tale – a tale of triumphs and reverses, of many moments of pride and despair. In the course of the story we were privileged to meet many men and women who dared to dream great dreams.

Yet it is an unfinished tale. The final pages remain to be written. It is not likely that people of our generation will ever hear of the realisation of the dream of equality, nor perhaps will the people of the generation that follows us.

Talk of social equality must have sounded in certain periods of Indian history like asking for the impossible. But now, thanks to the courage and vision of many individuals who possessed compassion and humanity, the goal seems clearly attainable.

No society that permits discrimination against certain of its members can ever hope to enjoy peace and harmony. Indian society appears to have an in-built system of disharmony and discord. To win peace and harmony, it must do away with all forms of oppression. Discrimination is oppression. Rendering justice to all is the only true path to peace and harmony.

SELECTIVE BIBLIOGRAPHY

Banerjee, Nikunj Vihari, *The Spirit of Indian Philosophy*, New Delhi, Arnold Heinemann Publishers Pvt. Ltd., (1977).

Bapat, P.V. (Gen. Ed.), *2500 years of Buddhism*, New Delhi, Government of India, (1956).

Basham. L. (Ed.), *A Cultural History of India*, Oxford, Clarendon Press, (1975).

Bhagowalia, Urmila, *Vaiṣṇavism and Society in Northern India: 700-1200*, New Delhi, Intellectual Publishing House, (1980).

Chandrasekhar, S., *Dimensions of Socio-Political Change in Mysore*, New Delhi, Ashish Publications, (1985).

Collected Works of Mahatma Gandhi, I - XXX, New Delhi, Govt. of India, 1958 onward.

Cultural Heritage of India The, I - IV, edited by Haridas Bhattacharyya, Calcutta, Ramakrishna Institute, 1958(I), 1962(II), 1953 (III) & 1956 (IV).

Dasgupta, S.N. (Gen. Ed.), *A History of Sanskrit Literature : Classical Period*, Calcutta, University of Calcutta, (1962).

Deleury, G.P., *The Cult of Vithoba*, Poona, Deccan College Post-graduate and Research Institute, (1960).

Depressed Classes: A Chronological Documentation, Kurseong, St. Mary's College, (1931-37).

Dhar, Somnath, *Kalhana*, New Delhi, Sahitya Akademi, (1978).

Dubois, Abbe, *Hindu Manners, Customs and Ceremonies*, translated by Henry Beauchamp, Oxford, Clarendon Press, (1943).

Dutta, Manmath Nath, (tr.), *Dharam Shastra: Hindu Religious Code*, I - VI, New Delhi, Cosmos Publications, (1978).

Farquhar, J.N., *The Outlines of the Religious Literature of India*, Delhi, Motilal Banarsidass, (1967A).

Farquhar, J.N., *Modern Religious Movements in India*, Delhi, Oriental Publisher and Book-Seller, (1967B).

Ficher, Louis, *Life of Mahatma Gandhi*, New York, Collier Books, (1962).

Fuchs, Stephen, *Rebellious Prophets:* A study of Messianic Movements in Indian Religions, Bombay, Asia Publishing House, (1962).

Gandhi, M.K., *My Religion*, compiled by Bharatan Kumarappa, Ahmedabad, Navajivan Publishing House, (1958).

Gazetteer of India, The, II, edited by P.N. Chopra, New Delhi, Govt. of India, (1973).

Ghose, Binoy, *Iswar Chandra Vidyasagar*, New Delhi, Govt. of India, (1965).

Ghurye, G.S., *Caste and Race in India*, Bombay, Popular Prakashan, (1969).

Gibbs, M.E., *Anglican Churches in India: 1600 - 1970*, Delhi, SPCK, (1972).

Heyerdahl, Thor, '"Tigris" Sails into the Past', *National Geographic*, September, (1978).

Hume, R.E., (tr.), *Thirteen Principal Upanishads*, Madras, Oxford University Press, (1965).

Jagirdar, P.J., *Mahadeo Govind Ranade*, New Delhi, Govt. of India, (1971).

Jog, N.G., *Lokmanya Bal Gangadhar Tilak*, New Delhi, Govt. of India, (1965).

Karve, D.G. & Ambedkar, D.V. (Ed.), *Speeches and Writings of Gopal Krishna Gokhale*, Bombay, Asia Publishing House, (1966).

Keith, A.B., *A History of Sanskrit Literature*, London, Oxford University Press, (1961).

Kosambi, D.D., *The Culture and Civilization of Ancient India in Historical Perspective*, New Delhi, Vikas Publishing House, (1970).

Kuber, W.N., *B.R. Ambedkar*, New Delhi, Govt. of India, (1965).

M'Crindle, J.W., *Ancient India as Described in Classical Literature*, Westminster, Archibald Constable & Co., (1901).

McCrindle, J.W., (tr.), *Ancient India as Described by Megasthenes and Arrian*, Calcutta, Thacker, Spink & Co., (1877).

Mahabharata of Vyasa, The, translated by P. Lal, New Delhi, Vikas Publishing House, (1980).

Mahadevan, T.K.P., *Ten Saints of India*, Bombay, Bharatiya Vidya Bhawan, (1971).

Maharajan, S.; *Tiruvalluvar*, Makers of India Literature Series, New Delhi, Sahitya Akademi, (1982).

Mandal Commission Report on Backward Classes, The, Part I & II, New Delhi, Govt. of India, (1980).

Masani, Minoo, *Bliss was it in That Dawn*, New Delhi, Arnold Heinemann, (1977).

Mees, G.H., *Dharma and Society*, Delhi, Seema Publication, (1980).

Mookerji, Radha Kumud, *Hindu Civilization*, Bombay, Bharatiya Vidya Bhawan, (1977).

Nemade, B., *Tukaram*, New Delhi, Sahitya Akademi, (1980).

Pant, A.D. & Gupta, Shiv K. (Ed.), *Multi-Ethnicity and National Integration*, New Delhi, Vohra Publishers and Books-sellers India, (1985).

Phadke, Y.D., *V.K. Chiploonkar*, New Delhi, National Book Trust India, (1983).

Piggot, Stuart, *Pre-Historic India*, Harmondsworth, Pelican Books.

Pritchard, James B., (Ed.), (1958) *The Ancient Near East*, An *Anthology of Texts and Pictures*, Princeton, Princeton University Press, (1951).

Radhakrishnan, *Indian Philosophy*, II, New York, Macmillan Co., (1962).

Rajagopalachari, C., *The Mahabharata*, Bombay, Bharatiya Vidya Bhawan, (1971).

Ramakrishna, V., *Social Reform in Andhra*, New Delhi, Vikas Publishing Co., (1983).

Roerich, George, (tr.), *Biography of Dharmaswamin*, Patna, K.P. Jayaswal Research Institute, (1959).

Sachau, Edward C. (tr.), *Alberuni's India*, London, Regan Paul, Trench, Trubner & Co., (1910).

Sanjana, J.S., *Caste and Outcaste*, Bombay, Thacker & Co., (1946).

Sastri, Nilakanta, *A History of South India*, Madras, Oxford University Press, (1981).

Selected Works of Mahatma Gandhi, The, I-VI, edited by Shriman Narayan, Ahmedabad, Navajivan Publishing House, (1969).

Selections From the Sacred Writings of the Sikhs, translated by Trilochan Singh & Others, London, George Allen & Unwin, (1965).

Sen, P.K., *Keshub Chunder Sen*, Calcutta, Centenary Committee, (1938).

Shamasastri, (tr.), *Kauṭilya's Arthaśāstra*, Mysore, Mysore Printing and Publishing House, (1967).

Sharma, Ram Sharan, *Śudras in Ancient India*, Delhi, Motilal Banarsidas, (1980A).

Sharma, Ram Sharan, *Indian Feudalism*, New Delhi, Macmillan India Ltd., (1980B).

Singh, Parmanand, *Equality, Reservation and Discrimination in India*, New Delhi, Deep Publishing, (1985).

Speer, Percival, *A History of India*, Harmondsworth, Penguin Books, (1981).

Srinivas, M.N., *Caste in Modern India and Other Essays*, Bombay, Asia Publishing House, (1962).

Thapar, Romila, *Ancient Indian Social History*, New Delhi, Orient Longman, (1978).

Thapar, Romila, *Aśoka and the Decline of the Mauryas*, Delhi Oxford University Press, (1978).

Tendulkar, G.G., *Mahatma*, I-VI, New Delhi, Govt. of India, (1961).

Tiwari, Parasnath, (1980) *Kabir*, New Delhi, Sahitya Akademi.

Toynbee, Arnold, (tr.), *Greek Historical Thought*, New Delhi, New American Library, (1968).

Veeramuni, K., *The History of the Struggle for Social and Communal Justice*, Madras, Madras Dravida Kazhagam Publications, (1981).

Winternitz, M., *A History of Indian Literature*, I, Calcutta, University of Calcutta, (1962).

Woolley, Leonard, *Ur of the Chaldees*, Harmondsworth, Pelican Books, (1938).

INDEX